Government of *All* the People

ARMINLEAR

Armin Lear Press
825 Wildlife
Estes Park, CO 80517

Government of *All* the People

A Contrarian Shows You How to Effect Constructive Changes in our Democracy

Robert L. Saloschin
"The Wizard of F.O.I.A."

and

Maryann Karinch

ARMINLEAR

Government of *All* the People

Copyright © 2015, 2020 by Robert L. Saloschin

For further information, contact:

ARMINLEAR

Armin Lear Press
825 Wildlife
Estes Park, CO 80517

ISBN: 978-1-7321678-8-9

To Neita

Table of Contents

PART TWO – APPROACHES TO SOLUTIONS

Chapter 6:

Chapter 7:

Chapter 8:

Chapter 9:

Chapter 10:
Ten Guidelines for Responsible Citizenship

PART THREE – MAJOR NATIONAL PROBLEMS
WITII SOLUTIONS

Chapter 11:

PART FOUR: HOW YOU CAN HELP

APPENDICES

Manuals by Citizens for Quality Civilization (CQC)

Table of Contents

Introduction: Meet the Contrarian and What He Offers You

For many years, I read *Forbes* magazine and had a particular interest in a column called "The Contrarian." It explored the advantages of bucking conventional wisdom in investing. My first foray into contrarian investing helped me turn $500 into more than $8,000 in a few years. More than that, the contrarian approach to investing seemed consistent with the way I viewed opportunities and problems in other areas of life.

This book is evidence of how change for the better in America has been rooted in contrarian thinking. It also describes how contrarian thinking can shift policies and leadership in the United States to create a much brighter future for the nation. Both the evidence and the description often rely on stories from my very lucky life. I've often been in the right place at the right time to make a difference in policies that affect your life today—wherever you happen to live in the United States. It is a life of growing up in New York City, serving our nation during war and in Washington, DC, and continuing to affect public policy after retirement from the Justice Department, where my last-known moniker was "The Wizard of FOIA," alluding to a central role I had in implomonting the Freedom of Information Act.

As a corollary, my life provides proof that there is no good reason to accept without questioning opinions or judgments that are generally accepted, commonly deemed correct, widely believed, or traditionally embraced. Of course, those are easy things to do; they save time and effort, but tend to cause people to overlook risks and opportunities.

There are two kinds of contrarians—successful and unsuccessful. What they have in common is they question conventional wisdom. What they don't have in common is that the successful contrarian questions out of analysis, not habit.

The successful contrarians use critical thinking, or often just plain old-fashioned good judgment, in deciding whether, and when, and how far, to go along with conventional wisdom. For that reason, I define a successful contrarian as a person who often considers acting differently from other people, but may or may not do so depending upon the circumstances. The other kind simply wants to be different; these contrarians abhor herd behavior even though they may have no clue why they feel that way.

Anyone can be the kind of contrarian who is simply negative about what other people accept. But to be a successful contrarian requires three things:

1. A willingness to think for yourself and act accordingly, even though following a herd mentality is easier.
2. A willingness to think ahead, to consider how long present trends may last and what may happen then
3. A willingness to look at the past for such guidance as experience may provide.

When I was in high school (1932-36), smoking cigarettes was not considered dangerous. The conventional wisdom was that if you were an athlete, cigarettes might "cut your wind," but that was about all. A few oldsters called cigarettes "coffin nails," but most people paid little attention until the Surgeon General's report many years later. During WW II, I smoked a pack of Camels a day. Later, a doctor I trusted said, "Stop. Now." Suddenly, prevailing opinion about smoking didn't make as much sense. Quitting wasn't easy, but continuing my 20-year habit would have been nothing more than a foolish indulgence.

In 1948, I was chatting with a friend about the coming election between Truman and Dewey. All the polls were showing Dewey far ahead, and my friend said it looked like a sure thing. I said I wasn't sure. He said, "I'll put up $10 on Dewey if you'll put up a dollar on Truman."

After the election, he handed me the $10 and asked, "How did you know?"

"I read the polls."

He protested: "But the polls showed Dewey was a shoo-in!"

I said there were also polls on the issues and they showed majorities for Truman's position on those issues.

I owe you a little explanation. I said to be a successful contrarian, you must use either critical thinking or good judgment. Critical thinking is ideal, but often is not practicable, because of the difficulty and time involved in collection and evaluating enough information. So we often turn to good judgment.

The phrase "good judgment" used to irritate me when I was learning how to fly in 1942; I heard that pilots ought to use it, but I didn't know exactly what it meant. Now I have an idea of what it means, as well as and how it applies to flying and many other things. And if you agree with my definition, then it's easy to see why children, and even many young adults, can't possibly have it: Good judgment is knowledge plus skill plus experience plus temperament.

We can accurately describe and measure knowledge, skill and experience, but I'm not sure how accurately we can describe and measure temperament. Yet consider how important it is, and how some aspects of it are fairly clear. For example, a venturesome, eager-beaver temperament is easily distinguished from a steadier, somewhat reflective one. The former make better fighter pilots; the latter are better suited to bombers, patrol planes and transports. These differences of temperament are frequently age-related. And their practical effect is modified by the individual's culture and by self-control.

To sum up, contrarians throughout history have often led to progress and averted disasters. Galileo was persecuted for correcting the conventional, but false, astronomy of his time. Churchill was a political outcast for years for trying to give timely warning about the rising threat of Fascist aggression. Billy Mitchell was court-martialed in the 1920's for trying to awaken the Army and Navy to the growing importance of air power. The early advocates of automobiles, which suffered from frequent breakdowns, commonly inspired comments like "Get a horse!"

For centuries, the field of statecraft was dominated by monarchists, against whom the adoption of the United States Constitution, with its large dose of democracy, was highly contrarian. And within democracies, giving women the right to vote was a contrarian idea until it became accepted. In the field of economics, conventional wisdom for generations relied on the self-correcting nature of free

markets and on the policy of "caveat emptor" (let the buyer beware). But after many examples of harm to investors
and consumers, plus three years of catastrophic decline
in reliance on free markets (1929-33) a large number of
contrarian ideas such as bank deposit insurance, truth
in securities laws, controls against child labor and other
abuses became generally accepted.

Are contrarians essential to the progress of civilization? They certainly make progress a lot easier than
waiting for a total debacle and then, perhaps, doing what
even the most hidebound people may finally realize is
necessary.

In addition to the well-known people named above,
there are many less famous examples of persons—inside
and outside of established institutions—who tried (and
sometimes succeeded) in pointing to dangers or missed
opportunities in groups that suffered from closed cultures
and tunnel vision. I am one of them—someone from the
ranks of civil service who was determined to use my good
luck and ideas to solve problems efficiently.

It would make me very happy if, after you read this
book, you challenge conventional wisdom judiciously. You
will no doubt be an even more interesting person than you
are right now, you will surely increase you ability to contribute to solving problems, and you will probably make
some enemies among the naysayers and lazy thinkers. In
short, you will be positioned to improve the quality of life
in your family, your work group, your community, your
country, and possibly even the rest of the world.

Have you ever complained about America? By that,
I mean have you ever been so annoyed by some aspect of
life in the United States that you can't help but talk about

it? It could be a sweeping issue such as public school education or immigration, or it could be a specific irritation like the price of gas or salaries for Wall Street barons. Those specific issues suggest much bigger ones, of course, so your focus on them means that, on some level, you care about the state of the nation.

If you have ever complained about America, then welcome to this contrarian world of mine. My friends, family, and colleagues are bright people who, like you, occasionally gripe about the state of affairs in the United States, but we wouldn't want to live anywhere else. It is people like you I have had the pleasure of exchanging ideas with for decades.

To set the stage for the material in the upcoming chapters, I'm going to put words in your mouth in the form of questions—questions that I've heard a lot from concerned citizens. I think this Q&A will give you a good sense of what's to come in the book.

Q.   I'm concerned about our country's future. But there are serious differences of opinion about what are our most important problems and their causes. First of all, what do you think are the big problems?

A.   Here are some, in no particular order: unemployment, recession, bankruptcies, foreclosures, fraud, ignorance, fear, accidents, instability, excessive debt, many kinds of neglect, family malfunctions, incompetence both in individuals and organizations, environmental degradation, resource depletion (why have codfish and oysters become so expensive?), crime, drugs, terrorism, injustice, corruption, waste, confusion, irresponsibility.

Some troubles, like ignorance, may also be a cause of other troubles. Some troubles are widespread, even in high places. Some have always been around, to varying degrees.

Q.   Can you identify the basic cause, or causes, of these troubles?

A.   First, let me deal with human nature as a cause. It is often a powerful contributing factor in these troubles, even a motivating factor. But the troubles would not be very serious except for a failure of the controls on trouble-making behavior. These controls are either by self-discipline or by various social disciplines, including law, markets, and elections. Bear in mind that although we can't change human nature we can change behavior to a considerable extent. So to be practical, to find the curable causes of our troubles, we should look at weaknesses in our controls on behavior.

Q.   Doesn't "controls on behavior" conflict with our treasured American rights of personal liberty?

A.   That depends on what kinds of behavior and what kinds of controls you're talking about. Destructive behavior that's uncontrolled can lead to anarchy.

Q.   Can you identify the basic cause, or causes, of the weaknesses in our controls on troublesome behavior?

A   My approach is partly based on anthropology. I think the most basic cause of our troubles is the uneven rates of change in the various parts of our culture. This disrupts the culture patterns, including law, that affect and control behavior. Those patterns evolved in villages and tribes to discourage antisocial behavior, but they have not always adapted well to modern conditions.

To restate this in the simplest way, technology changes much faster than social controls. Thus, nuclear technology can fall into the hands of terrorists, rogue nations, inept custodians, and so on. Another example: the technologies of disease control may lead to population increases that the earth's resources may be unable to sustain. A third: automotive and communication technologies merge into the growing hazard of teenagers and adults using cell phones and text-messaging while driving.

Q.   We're talking about world problems, not just national ones—isn't that right?

A.   Some of these troubles, and certainly the basic cause we've just identified, are not just national, they are largely global. Some troubles may require some kind of international cooperation. But our chief instrument for trying to deal with global problems is our own national government.

Q.   If new technology creates problems that the old controls can't handle, why not just develop new controls?

A.   We often do, but sometimes it's not easy. For example, if someone develops a very enticing, addictive, and profitable recreational drug, such as cigarettes, that has dangerous long-term health effects or other risks, controls may be slow in becoming effective.

Q.   Most technological innovations offer clear benefits. When cars and planes came along, their problems were met by licensing, regulation, and so on. Isn't that progress?

A.   Yes, but that's not the whole story. There are two additional important causes of troubles to consider, in addition to the uneven rates of change in various parts of the overall culture.

One that may sound surprising is success, both the prolonged kind and the quick kind. Those who enjoy a great deal of success for too long tend to become "dumb and happy." This leads to carelessness and incompetence. This may have been a factor in the decline of the Roman and other empires and of General Motors, for example. And for half a century after WW II, the United States was the world's most successful nation. As to quick success, it can lead to problems such as exuberance and poor judgment.

The second factor, which is associated with the rapid growth of technologies, is specialization that has not been adequately related to things outside of the specialty. This increases the danger that specialists may fall into a closed culture, with groupthink, and be blind-sided. That's not a minor risk in our complex and volatile world. Examples include Detroit's auto industry, some people entrenched in Wall Street, and those government leaders who became bogged down in ventures such as the Vietnam War.

In addition to the risk that specialists may develop a closed culture, top executives may lack understanding of problems facing their specialists, impairing morale and effective management.

Q.   So let's tentatively agree that our troubles have these three basic causes: the uneven rates of change within our culture, prolonged or quick success, and unlinked specialization. How do we deal with them?

A.   It isn't easy, but it isn't hopeless either. Man is a pretty adaptable animal. Here are three preliminary steps in coping with problems:

First, get the significant facts. If they are unknown or in dispute, at least keep track of the questions about them and such evidence as may be available.

Second, keep in mind the three fundamental realities: the world of nature and the two components of human behavior. Behavior is a mixture of human nature, which can't be changed, and culture (that is, learned and shared practices and attitudes) which can be changed, although changing it can be tricky. (For example it's usually easier to introduce technology into some nations than to introduce culture elements such as respect for dissent or gender equality.) Chapter 1 discusses these three fundamentals.

Third, achieve and maintain perspective, largely by considering other times and other places. This includes past disasters that may be instructive, plus the range of practices in other groups and other nations. History, viewed analytically, is a tremendous data-bank of experience. Looking at what competing cultures do is just common sense.

Q.   Are you seriously urging that every responsible citizen should become an expert on our problems and their causes by doing what you just suggested?

A.   I'm not suggesting that we become "experts" in the usual sense. I'm suggesting that, in a practical, commonsense way, we can join with other citizens who are thoughtful, reasonably well-informed, and concerned about our future. Parts One and Two of this book discuss how to do this.

Q.   You said history is a resource for understanding today's problems. Can you illustrate?

A.   History is experience. Analyzing mishaps is how aviation progressed from a risky activity to a very safe one. I'll give you two famous illustrations, the decline and fall of the Roman Empire and the Great Depression.

Edward Gibbon did a detailed and classic study of Rome's deterioration in his *History of the Decline and Fall of the Roman Empire*. A condensation published in 1979 lists a dozen causes of Rome's decline, including "a widening gap between rich and poor" and the "suppression of the middle classes while the rich pursued a life of luxury and avoided the responsibilities of government.[1]" Others have suggested Rome's decline was due to getting lead into their water supply.

Thomas Cahill has a complementary perspective on the fall of Rome in *How the Irish Saved Civilization*. As the title suggests, it's mostly about how Irish monasteries preserved the classical learning of ancient Greece and Rome. But the book has an incisive chapter on two reasons why Rome fell. One was that Rome's long-established liberal immigration policy, which had greatly strengthened Rome, began to have the opposite effect. The other was the deterioration of Rome's tax policy, with the rich paying less and less, while the tax collectors bore down more heavily on the poor.

Rome was not the only empire that suffered from the reluctance of influential groups to pay taxes. The

French Revolution, which led to France's reign of terror and its Napoleonic wars, arose because France's otherwise powerful monarchy couldn't collect taxes to pay for its military and other expenses from any of the three wealthy groups of that time: the aristocracy, the Church, and to a lesser extent, the rising merchant class.

The Great Depression had several causes. Recently supporters of free trade have called attention to the Smoot-Hawley Tariff of 1930, which raised U.S. tariffs on over 20,000 imported goods to record levels. It worsened the Depression. But the Depression's most important cause, which had been building up for years, is that productivity had outstripped purchasing power, first in the nation's then large agricultural sector and later in the rest of the economy. The effect of insufficient purchasing power was delayed by the spread of installment buying, but finally resulted in unsold inventories and layoffs. This was aggravated by some crazy credit practices. On the one hand, speculation was stimulated because stocks could be bought with only ten percent down. On the other hand, perfectly creditworthy homeowners had great difficulty in renewing the short-term mortgages then prevalent whenever money became tight.

Q.   Are you implying today's economic weakness has similar causes?
A.   To a fair extent, yes, especially as regards purchasing power in relation to productivity. The recent, well-publicized efforts to "restore confidence" by "unfreezing credit" will work only to the extent that potential borrowers are creditworthy. Creditworthiness may be based on several factors, but like purchasing power itself, it usu-

ally depends chiefly on income that is both sufficient and sustainable.

Q.   What caused purchasing power to fall behind productivity this time?

A.   Middle-class incomes stagnated while productivity increased. Previously well-paying jobs were outsourced to countries with much cheaper labor. This applies not only to manufacturing, but also to some professional and business services. Tax changes that were made some decades after WW II shifted wealth increasingly to the very rich, who invest in various ways, some of which stimulate productivity. The nation's ability to buy what's produced did not keep pace. This breakdown developed gradually during decades of "trickle-down" economics. It was postponed for a long time by more credit cards, home equity loans, and so on, but finally it arrived.

Q.   Are you saying our problem is imports, or the tax laws?

A.   To some extent both imports and tax laws are involved. Some imports, partly depending on prices, quality, and other factors, are beneficial, while others are not. High levels of personal wealth, as a motivation and reward for providing real benefits, may be helpful or may be excessive. What we should work toward on these complex and important subjects is a better balance: one with "all things considered," including both short and long term economic sustainability.

Q.   You agree that one of our main troubles is excess debt. Can't we reduce it by inflation, which makes it eas-

ier for debtors to repay creditors? Wouldn't this work for
all debtors, including the U.S. government, with its ever-
increasing trillions of debt?

A.   Yes, but we have to be careful. The less valuable
money becomes, the easier it is to pay off creditors. However, history shows that excessive inflation (over about
three percent per year) can be extremely destructive.
When inflation gets too high people start to rush to buy
before things get even more expensive, which causes still
more inflation. In Germany a runaway inflation in 1923
wiped out the savings of the middle class, contributing
to a sense of desperation that helped pave the way for
Hitler. Inflation weakens the ability of governments and
businesses to sell bonds to finance necessary or desirable
projects. Inflation also discourages individual savings,
and savings are both an element of security and a foundation for investments.

Q.   What is your position on imports as a problem?

A.   Briefly, to consider all aspects of the subject. I'll
give you two examples, both well-known: cars and Wal-
Mart.

My first car was a used Model A Ford which my
family bought for $25. During my college years (1936 –
40) it ran fine, despite using lots of dirty motor oil at three
cents a quart— oil that had been drained out of other
cars. (I still dream about "Where did I park that car?")
After our marriage in 1949, we also bought only American cars for decades. Today people recognize that Detroit
got bogged down making gas-guzzlers. But people forget
how murderously unsafe Detroit's cars were before Ralph
Nader, Congress, and maybe some product-liability law-

yers cracked down. I still have maintenance records on a new 1967 Ford which had repeated brake, steering and other failures. And as outrageous as it may seem, the automatic transmission fluid became mixed with the engine coolant. In addition, when we pulled the front door closed, the handle broke off in our hands. We also experienced a potentially lethal defect in a new 1957 Chevrolet. So in recent decades all our cars have been from Japanese or German companies, perhaps largely made in the U.S. Our son-in-law recently got 280,000 miles out of his Honda with only routine maintenance.

What this boils down to is that Detroit's Big Three lived for decades of success in a closed culture, and what was outside that culture finally caught up with them. The tragedy is that the leadership of the United Auto Workers, which represented their employees, also did nothing to reverse the obvious drift of Americans toward buying foreign cars that better met their needs.

Wal-Mart is not such a clear case.

The plus side of Wal-Mart is obvious: lower prices and greater convenience for consumers. Lower prices are especially helpful to the less affluent, particularly during hard times.

On convenience, Wal-Mart carries forward the postwar phenomenon of supermarkets into even broader categories of products. The advent of supermarkets, together with refrigerators and freezers, helped emancipate housewives from frequent shopping at separate green-grocers, bakeries, and butcher shops, allowing more time for careers. Perhaps Wal-Mart increases this liberating effect. But Wal-Mart's negatives are serious. On a recent trip to Childress, Texas, I went into a big, new Wal-Mart.

I bought a well-made folding recliner at a low price. Like much of Wal-Mart's merchandise, it was made in a low-wage foreign country.

But these bargains have quite a downside. A few blocks from Wal-Mart was the Childress business district, now deserted streets and boarded-up stores. What happened to the families of those small businessmen? How does this affect the community? And what has happened around the U.S. to manufacturers of the products which Wal-Mart now buys from abroad? Is it realistic to consider benefits to consumers without also considering the detriment to producers and breadwinners?

The damage may be more than economic. There are family, child-rearing and civic values—planning, responsibility, and keeping a balance between competition and cooperation—often associated with the independent work, decision-making and incomes that go with small businesses, family farms, and stable academic, governmental and professional careers.

These middle-class conditions and values, which are closely linked to the responsible exercise of freedom, may be part of what makes a successful democracy. While this is not to say that a culture of broad responsibility cannot be developed among employees of a large corporation, it is probably less likely.

Keeping the benefits of institutions like Wal-Mart, while ending their detriments, is a real and important challenge.

Q.   You've clarified some of your views on imports. Now please explain why success—lots of it, or for a long time—is a cause of trouble for a family, a corporation, an industry, or a nation.

A.   For many years, the risks of family success was recognized by the phrase "shirtsleeves to shirtsleeves in three generations," meaning that the first generation works hard to build a fortune, the second generation enjoys the success and the fortune plateaus, and the third generation consumes what's left of the fortune, taking the family back to nothing.

Prolonged success tends to breed overconfidence, carelessness, even incompetence. It also tends to engender development of closed cultures, which are usually pleasant, but which give less attention to things that don't seem to be an immediate threat or opportunity. The development of closed cultures is probably encouraged by the spread of occupational specialization, which is often rewarded by success.

Persons in a successful closed culture tend to accumulate wealth, which is often passed on to their children. In time this inheritance helps create a kind of caste system, somewhat like those in traditional European societies, although with less rigidity. Thomas Jefferson described this as an "artificial aristocracy," based on birth and wealth, which he contrasted with a "natural" aristocracy based on talent and virtue.

Persons in a closed culture (whether or not upscale) tend to develop a sense of belonging. This helps develop comfort, esprit-de-corps, loyalty and possibly even efficiency. But it also tends to develop an "us – them" attitude, a defensive "turf" attitude, or an excessive reliance on stereotypes in dealing with outsiders. Hence the recurrent hostility between "elitists" and "populists." Such attitudes are perhaps reflected in the old saying "birds of a feather flock together."

To have various groups living in their own closed cultures is not helpful in dealing with complex national or global troubles. The problem is illustrated by the incredulous reaction of film critic Pauline Kael to Richard Nixon's victory in the 1972 presidential election: "I live in a rather special world. I only know one person who voted for Nixon. Where they are I don't know. They're outside my ken." Even if we prefer to continue living as a big or small fish in a particular pond, we should be more aware of what's happening in the other ponds, especially since the ponds are likely to become, or already are, connected with each other.

Q.   How serious a problem is the antipathy developed in closed cultures?

A.   Here's an example. When Franklin Delano Roosevelt took office in March 1933, almost all Americans were badly scared, and for good reason. Roosevelt's actions ended the desperation, but also ruffled some feathers, especially among the wealthy, some of whom called him a "traitor to his class." This antipathy, which has been passed down to later generations, has led to endless efforts for revenge. Efforts have been made to rewrite history; universities have been encouraged to favor particular ideologies; government agencies set up to protect investors or workers (for example, the Securities and Exchange Commission and National Labor Relations Board) have been weakened; government itself has been portrayed as evil by leaders who characterize the government as the problem, not the solution[2]; and tax cuts for the rich have produced serious deficits, which were quietly welcomed in order to "starve the beast," that is, reduce the size of our government.

Q. Are you being fair?

A. I admit that it's hard to blame people who follow what their forebears told them, particularly when every now and then something pops up that reinforces their attitudes. Worthwhile government programs sometimes suffer from unnecessary bedevilment caused by one-size-fits-all, a lack of common sense, or other weaknesses. But my general comments about closed cultures merit attention.

Q. Can you summarize what problems the New Deal did not solve?

A. Shakespeare's Macbeth said, "We have scotched the snake, not killed it." That summarizes the U.S. economic and political history from the 1929 crash to today. The New Deal stopped Wall Street's shenanigans, but in time Wall Street developed new shenanigans. That also applies to other aspects of our economy, such as the recurrent tendency of productivity to exceed purchasing power.

Q. So what do we do?

A. Save capitalism from itself, by a better linkage of profit to service and stability.

Q. Where do you start?

A. Organizations that undermine capitalism through corruption. They are symbolized by such physical locations as Wall Street (finance) Madison Avenue (advertising), and K Street (lobbying).

Q.   What are the most critical, basic problems that we need to recognize?

A.   Changing the culture of our future movers and shakers.

Q.   Who are they? What do they need to do?

A.   Both of your questions are illuminated in a 2009 op-ed by Elliot Gersen, the American Secretary of the Rhodes Trust and a leader in the Aspen Institute. ("From Oxford to Wall Street" *Washington Post* 11/21/09) Until about 1980, Americans with Rhodes Scholarships at Oxford chose careers in universities, writing, medicine, scientific research, law, the military, and public service. But since that time, many Rhodes scholars have chosen increasingly lucrative careers in business and finance. Similar shifts probably have occurred in other long-recognized indicia of trained brains, such as Phi Beta Kappa, law review editorships at leading law schools, and so on.

Q.   What caused this reallocation of brain power?

A.   As a preliminary, don't assume that our best brains are always marked by well-known indicia such as Rhodes Scholarships, and Ivy League universities. Many are not. For example, history has recognized Harry Truman as a smart and successful president even though he never went to college. But as to the misallocation, the most obvious cause is the extremely high compensation packages in corporate and financial activities.

The second cause is that our colleges and universities as a part of general education (not as trade schools) often fail to present the concept of the good life in clear focus, with specific examples of living well on incomes available in public service, academia, the professions, small business, and so on.

The third cause is insufficient public recognition of worthwhile careers rather than lucrative ones. Adam Smith, best known as the apostle of free enterprise in his book *The Wealth of Nations*, also bemoaned the widespread tendency to admire the rich and powerful more than persons of merit and virtue: The Theory of Moral Sentiments, Part 1, Section 3, Chapter 3. In a somewhat similar vein, President John F. Kennedy, in his 1961 Inaugural Address said, "And so, my fellow Americans: ask not what your country can do for you—ask what you can do for your country." This restoration of better balanced values requires support by individual citizens and by faith, political, media and senior groups.

It should be clear in our culture that citizenship involves responsibilities as well as rights, and the more fortunate the citizen is, the greater are his or her responsibilities. The Bible expresses a similar thought: "From those to whom much is given, much is expected." (Luke 12:48)

Our future as a nation depends on, among other things, a sense of cohesion. Glorification of the extremely wealthy few over the many who provide necessary and useful service weakens the ability of our democracy to cope with problems and trends that need attention, and tends to erode national cohesion.

Prologue: How Three Great Men Shaped the Contents of this Book

Although I spotlight three men who helped shape my ideas, I also owe a great deal to many other wonderful people, many of whom are noted individually in the Acknowledgments. Of course, some of these influencers are people I've never met, but who helped build the civilization on which my activities were based.

The three men in the spotlight are Bobby Kennedy, who was the Attorney General of the United States; Bill Rehnquist, who later became the Chief Justice of our nation; and Ralph Linton, whose name few people recognize, but who contributed greatly to making the result of World War II better than the results of World War I. In addition, his work continues to contribute to our understanding of economic phenomena, terrorism, and other aspects of human behavior.

Ralph Linton

At the end of World War I, some of the victors imposed a harsh peace on the people in some defeated nations; that created much resentment that contributed to World War II. But at the end of World War II, we succeeded in effectively changing Germany and Japan from aggressive autocracies into peaceful democracies.

The great difference was largely due to one man: Ralph Linton. (Of course, it was also due to someone in or near the White House who decided to involve Linton in the treatment of defeated populations.)

I was fortunate in having Linton as a professor in college before the war. I had completed a course in economics that did not fully explain economic events like the Great Depression. I then took Linton's course in cultural anthropology, which helped to close the gap.

Linton was president of the American Anthropological Association, and the author of our textbook, *The Study of Man*. Our class also had a second textbook, Our Primitive Contemporaries, which described the way of life (that is, the culture, or attitudes and practices) of eighteen isolated tribes.

It's well known that early in World War II, Albert Einstein sent a letter to President Franklin D. Roosevelt on the risk that our enemies might develop an atomic bomb. In response, the President started the Manhattan Project, which did develop that bomb. In a similarly preemptive move, to avert mistakes made in World War I and in other wars, our government set up a school of military government headed by Linton to train experts in dealing effectively with defeated populations. (These two wise actions underscore the importance of the leaders of large organizations being open to inputs that may have serious effects on the organization's future.)

As luck would have it, I encountered some graduates of Linton's school during the war in the Pacific. I was in the Navy as a navigator in Patrol Bombing Squadron Nineteen, which operated fifteen large flying boats, each with a crew of three officers and eight sailors. Our squadron had been based in Eniwetok, but we were moved to Saipan, which had just been taken from the Japanese after a lot of fighting. The reason we were moved to Saipan was because it was not too far from Iwo Jima, the Navy's next goal. The Navy wanted us at Iwo Jima because our powerful radar could search the entire ocean between Iwo and Japan for possible enemy interference with our invasion of Iwo.

Unfortunately, Iwo did not have any harbor to base our big seaplanes. So it was decided to base us near the invasion beach, with a big seaplane tender (a naval vessel designed to support a squadron of flying boats) planting fifteen anchored buoys where we could park our planes. The seaplane tender also met our other needs, such as JATO (jet-assisted take off) rockets for extra power for taking off in rough ocean conditions, where our engines alone wouldn't be adequate.

To help pass the time in Saipan before we went to Iwo, I was able to borrow a jeep for some sightseeing. I drove away from the military area into open country. A few miles later, I saw a small building with a big sign "Off Limits to All U.S. Military Personnel." This aroused my curiosity and I opened the door, seeing a few men inside. They explained it was an internment camp for enemy civilians of all ages, some from Japan and some from the local island.

We started chatting about various things and I happened to mention Linton. Their jaws dropped and one said, "You studied under Linton? Disregard that sign—you're free to go in all you want." They all had been trained in Linton's school, and they weren't going to wait to the end of the war to start re-acculturating this defeated population.

Linton even affected my own conduct on Saipan. Once I was scheduled to spend the night, together with three sailors, on one of our planes moored in Saipan's harbor. As soon as the boat dropped off the four of us at the plane, one of the sailors excitedly said, "Look at what I've got—a souvenir to mail to my girlfriend."

He then opened a small box containing the somewhat dried ear of a dead enemy soldier. This kind of thing was not hard to find; out tents were just a short walk from a wooded hillside containing several fortified enemy caves, which the Marines had captured, partly with flame throwers.

I did not want to hurt the sailor's feelings, but I felt I should say something. I suggested that he write his girlfriend to keep his gift confidential, at least until the war was over. Humiliation, even from afar, was still negative behavior that went against the nature of what Linton was teaching.

There's one more thing about Linton that's important. When I was commissioned as a Naval Reserve ensign in August or September of 1941, I said goodbye to various people, including some at Columbia. Linton, whom I believe may have served in World War I, gave me a bit of practical advice: He said, "Be aware of the importance of your outfit." He was referred to the relatively small unit in which you are serving directly. Linton added that I might find myself in an outfit unlike any group in my past experience, except possibly my family.

How right he was. My immediate boss in the Bureau of Aeronautics treated me like an uncle treating his nephew, helping me in learning how to be a better pilot. And when I joined a new squadron that entered the Pacific theater, we developed friendships that continued after the war with annual reunions until many of us had died.

It makes me wonder whether the culture of "outfit" might help improve some civilian organizations.

Bobby Kennedy

Bobby worked hard at creating a spirit of real teamwork among the hundreds of career lawyers in the Justice Department, most of whom had never met an Attorney General. He tried to meet them all, with much success.

One day I arrived at work a few minutes late and in need of a shave. As I entered my office, my secretary said, "The Attorney General is waiting for you in his limousine at the Attorney General's entrance."

I dashed down and joined him in the back seat. As we drove to Capitol Hill, he said, "We're testifying before the Senate Foreign Relations Committee on the Administration's proposed communication satellite legislation." This was part of the Cold War, but it also involved the future of our big communications companies.

All went smoothly that morning and Bobby never showed any sign of impatience or irritation at having to wait for me to join him.

Some time later I received an offer in my home mail to charter a family-size cabin cruiser in Florida and bring it to Maryland at a ridiculously low price, provided I completed the trip in the first half of June. The offer was from a company that chartered these boats in Chesapeake Bay in the summer and Florida in the winter, but had trouble twice a year in moving its fleet north or south.

I felt this would be a great family adventure with my wife and two young daughters. But I had some assignments in which the Attorney General was interested, and I hesitated to take eleven days' leave at that time.

Finally, I decided to mention this to Bobby. He was actually enthusiastic, and he even suggested it might be better to allow two weeks instead of eleven days for the trip. But I said I'd be back in eleven days and I was.

Bobby's success in establishing a friendly and informal atmosphere at Justice paid off. A big event in the civil rights era was the Freedom Rider crisis. These riders wanted to travel by bus from Washington, D.C. to New Orleans without racial discrimination. They were attacked by mobs at bus stops and the local authorities wouldn't protect them, so they turned to the Justice Department. None of the ways that Justice might help would work; these approaches are covered in Chapter 3, as is the solution that I came up with. The point here is that we solved a very serious problem immediately because Bobby engendered a collegial atmosphere that allowed me to speak up and contribute what I suspected about the Interstate Commerce Commission's powers and duties.

Bill Rehnquist

President Richard Nixon had appointed William Rehnquist as head of the Justice Department's Office of Legal Counsel (OLC) in 1969. Our office, which included more than a dozen career lawyers like me, provided advice to presidents and cabinet-level officials on a wide variety of subjects. During both Republican and Democratic administration, it was common to appoint a law professor as head of OLC. Bill was not, but he was valedictorian of his Stanford Law School class, in addition to having earned a Master's degree in government from Harvard.

One day he called me into his office and said, "Bob, there's one subject on which I'd like to depart from standard OLC practice." The practice was that, when a new piece of work arrived in our office, it would be assigned to whichever lawyer was least burdened by existing assignments. He said he expected that the recently enacted Freedom of Information Act (FOIA) was likely to develop into a subject of major importance. Therefore, he wanted any questions on FOIA that came to OLC to be assigned to me. His concern was that at least one of our lawyers develop in-depth expertise on FOIA.

I was pleased by this because when FOIA was enacted, I had thought it was a somewhat unusual event. Yet for a year or so, Bill's decision did not take up most of my time. I was even able to go to Europe for two weeks in late 1970 as a member of the U.S. Diplomatic Delegation to a conference that hoped to develop international agreement on a treaty to extradite airline hijackers. (In those days hijackers were not suicidal, like those in the 9-11 terrorist attack. They were Americans who wanted to go to Cuba and Soviet citizens who wanted to leave the Soviet Union.) Amazingly, despite the Cold War, we cooperated with the Soviet delegation and achieved the desired treaty.

When I returned to the United States, FOIA work began to increase as more people outside of the legal community recognized the important opportunities that FOIA represented.

An early example involved the Veteran's Administration (VA), which provided hearing aids to veterans who had wartime hearing damage. The VA had purchased various brands to test for which would be best for the veterans. Consumers Union wanted the records of those tests to publish the information for the public and asked the

VA for them under FOIA. The VA said "no." Consumers Union sued under FOIA and the VA was defended by an office in the Justice Department's Civil Division, which argued that several parts of FOIA justified the VA's denial of access. The court rejected all these arguments and ordered the VA to release the test records.

To me, the defense of the VA tended to damage both the public and other federal agencies. The public was entitled to information generated at the taxpayers' expense, and not justifiably withheld. And some federal agencies might later be burdened by a precedent which tended to narrow the law's exemptions from compulsory disclosure.

I decided to go to Bill with these problems and my suggestion for a cure. I proposed creating a Freedom of Information Committee to screen final denials of FOIA requests by federal departments and agencies before the Justice Department would defend the denials in court. Bill checked with the head of the Department's Civil Division, Bill Ruckelshaus, which handled these court cases, and he agreed.

The new Freedom of Information Committee consisted of two Civil Division lawyers and three OLC lawyers, including me as chairman. A notice was sent to all departments and agencies describing the new procedure.

For a few years, this new procedure worked rather well. Meetings were easily arranged by phone, usually with two people from the agency planning to deny access, and meetings usually took less than two hours. We always gave the agency our opinion at the end of the meeting, based on the law, the facts, and related policies. Our opinion, given orally, simply said, "Your final denial is okay," "Your final denial is not okay," or "Your final denial is doubtful." A later survey showed that agencies almost always followed our "okay" or "not okay," and they often released the records in a doubtful case.

We also reminded agencies that they could make a discretionary release of exempt records unless some other law prohibited such release. And sometimes, I avoided an unnecessary meeting, as when Ralph Nader wanted Agriculture Department records of the percentage of fat in various brands of hot dogs, which the Department bought randomly at supermarkets and tested for fat. I told them on the phone a denial would not be defended.

By the mid-1970s, the public's use of FOIA increased to the point where we couldn't hold meetings on all final denials, and we began to shift our efforts to mass guidance using seminars and newsletters. This growth had several causes: Ralph Nader's success, a spreading realization of FOIA's value for attorneys, academics and writers, and, of course, the growing public concern about government secrecy stimulated by the Vietnam War and by the Watergate scandal.

A brief overview of FOIA is in order so that's it's clear why the Justice Department's allocation of human resources to its implementation was well worth it. FOIA helps keep citizens informed, the necessity of which in a democracy is a fundamental message of this book. But FOIA has some negatives. For example, there was a popular craze in the 1970s of asking the Federal Bureau of Investigation (FBI)) for records about the requesters. The huge volume of these requests forced the FBI to shift more than 300 of its employees to working on these requests. Other government agencies sometimes have had to delay important projects because personnel had to be diverted to responding to FOIA requests, which the law requires must receive prompt attention.

Another important note is this: FOIA helps show how our laws are administered, but FOIA doesn't apply to Congress. That means FOIA is of little or no value in revealing how our laws are made. Sometimes important changes in our laws are made with little or no Congressional or public discussion. This can happen when there is no emergency, and this aspect of our government merits some attention. In Chapter 5, a discussion of immigration legislation that passed during the Lyndon Johnson Administration provides a stark example of what I'm talking about here.

I have to thank Bill Rehnquist for anticipating the growth of FOIA and putting me into it. This expanded my awareness of the variety of our government's involvements in the ever-increasing complexity of our world, both in our own country and abroad.

I realize that Bill was quite conservative on some subjects, as shown by his dissent from the Supreme Court's 7 to 2 decision recognizing a federal right to abortion in Roe v. Wade. Nevertheless, Bill was also a very intelligent and decent man. I recall that in his OLC days he had to decide whether an agency head could fire an employee for objectionable public statements. Although the answer would usually be "yes" in the private sector, Bill concluded that the agency head could not discipline the employee for exercising his free speech rights unless his expression interfered with the agency's mission.

Summarizing their value to my thinking, each of these three men embodied wisdom about human behavior. Each saw the practical value of government policies and action that empowered individuals. Each had his eye on the essential processes that make democracies work.

Throughout the rest of this book, it should be abundantly clear how important these considerations are in effecting constructive changes in our democracy.

PART ONE—OUR

PROBLEMS AND THEIR CAUSES

Our Nation's Problems and Their Three Basic Roots

1

"Problems" refers to all conditions and trends that affect, or may affect, our lives negatively. In rare cases, a problem may seem to affect only one person, however, problems are shared, directly or indirectly, by all of us and our descendants. Problems are the things we should worry about in American society. We may not agree on the solutions at the moment, but most of us (at least those reading this book) are rational beings who agree on some of the problems.

I expect that you go along with my idea that agreeing on at least some of the problems is a start toward agreeing on the solutions.

All of our problems arise from a cause, or a combination of causes, rooted within one or more of three great categories of reality. These categories are:
- Mother Nature,
- Human Nature, and
- Human Cultures.

Mother Nature as a Root of Problems

By "nature" we mean the environment, including its resources. There is a great deal of literature on soil, seas, atmosphere, plants, animals, and other parts of nature. But what follows is a summary designed to focus your attention on the fact that Mother Nature, once regarded as bountiful, is becoming stingy.

The Earth is our home, and its resources are essential for our lives and fundamental to our wealth.

Unfortunately, the earth's resources are not un-limited, and some of them are being rapidly used up. I hope you are not one of those people who think that our children who are alive now or those born in the first decades of the Twenty-first Century can move to the moon or another planet. That alternative is too feeble for serious consideration.

Among the chief resources of the earth that are facing serious depletion are the resources for food, energy, and good places to live. These resources can be extended by exploration, technology, and conservation, but they can't be extended indefinitely.

Up to now, due chiefly to three historic developments, humans have prospered greatly and increased greatly in numbers. The development of agriculture as a replacement for hunting and gathering increased the reliable food supply. Discovering the causes and cures of infectious diseases promoted longevity through the reproductive years. And the third development has been modern technology, especially in transportation and communication. These advances have led to the wide dissemination of knowledge and products, so that more and more people can thrive.

But the signs of diminishing resources are quite clear. As to food, some formerly great sources of valuable proteins and other nutrients have become scarce and costly.

No summary of the causes of problems that are based in nature's limited resources can avoid a brief reference to the issue of global warming. Whether or not we will suffer man-made global warming due to putting excessive carbon dioxide into the atmosphere, the pressure on the earth's limited resources will remain a serious problem. Global warming would aggravate the problem by flooding low-lying land where many people live and produce food. Carbon dioxide, which is produced by combustion but also exhaled by animals, is consumed by green plants. Therefore reversing the destruction of the world's forests in many places, such as the Amazon River watershed, would seem to be a wise precaution.

Finally, no summary of nature and its limited resources would be complete without noting that an ever-increasing world population would put increasing pressure on the world's resources. Even ancient societies and primitive tribes recognized that they needed to keep their numbers within the capacity of locally available resources, and they did so in various ways, some of which we would disapprove of.

Today the problem of world population growth pressing on limited resources may be eased because many advanced nations have reduced their birth rates, and some developing nations are also doing this. But the pressure on the earth's limited resources may be aggravated by the so-called revolution of rising expectations. This means that people around the world will no longer accept a minimal or subsistence standard of living while others enjoy much better standards.

If overpopulation is neglected too long, it also could lead to abrupt reversals of national policies, resulting in low birth rates and aging populations, generating increased social needs in excess of productivity.

Human Nature as a Root of Problems

I use "human nature" in its common, everyday sense. As

in the case of the environment and its resources, there are huge amounts of literature on this, including various schools of psychology and psychiatry. However I will provide just a summary of why the causes of our problems sometimes are rooted, in whole or part, in human nature.

Human nature can be defined as the built-in tendencies of human beings to act and feel the way they do. It has three main aspects: tendencies that are common to almost all persons, tendencies which vary considerably from person to person, and the fact that both of these kinds of tendencies usually cannot be changed, although their manifestation in actual behavior can often be changed by cultural or other external influences.

Tendencies shared by almost all include the drive for self-preservation (despite some impulses toward suicide), and the drives to satisfy needs for food, sex, sleep, activity, variety, security, pleasure and self-esteem.

The tendencies that vary considerably among persons may include a restless desire for distinction; a strong desire to be undisturbed by changes; a drive to dominate other persons; empathy for plants, animals, or other people; appreciation for works of art; and varying degrees of comfort when dealing with things (for example, higher in mechanics or engineers) or in dealing with people (for example, higher in politicians or nurses) or in dealing with ideas (for example, higher in lawyers or analytic historians).

One of the best clues to why the causes of our problems often are found in human nature comes from Winston Churchill. He let the cat out of the bag in the first volume of his famous history, The Second World War. Buried in the middle of a paragraph on page 182 are the following words: "...very silly people, of whom there are extremely large numbers in every country..."

Putting aside the fact that experienced politicians like Churchill usually refrain from derogatory public statements about the people whose votes they seek, let's carefully note that Churchill did not call the people stupid, he said "silly." And high levels of silliness can be manifested at all levels of intelligence.

Silliness generally arises from some aspect of human nature that diverts our attention or distorts our judgment regarding situations that call for certain actions. The Great Depression could have been avoided by timely attention to lagging purchasing power and excessive speculation, but few people were interested in reforms during the booming Twenties. The horrors of World War II, which crushed France and many other nations, could have been avoided with little or no bloodshed if France had blocked Adolf Hitler's moves in the Rhineland and Spain before Hitler was ready for a big war, but pacifism and appeasement blocked action.

Unfortunate effects of human nature are often linked to groupthink, a problem discussed later in this book. Human nature is almost certainly a factor in problems caused by success. Prolonged success, as in the case of ancient Rome or General Motors, tends to induce carelessness. Quick success, as in the case of Hitler and various enterprises, seems to induce exuberance and lapses from good judgment.

Human Cultures as a Root of Problems

There is much confusion about the word "culture." I do not use the word "culture" to refer to some upscale aspect of the life-style of "better" or more fortunate persons or classes. I use "culture" as it is used by cultural anthropologists, and as it has become increasingly accepted, to refer to behavior and the attitudes of various groups whose members have some degree of cohesion. These groups may be a tribe, a nation, a religious denomination, a business corporation or other institution, a profession or other occupation, a family or clan, and so on.

For the sake of clarity the word "culture" is sometimes applied chiefly to groups, such as nations, that include persons of all ages, while the word "subculture" applied to the culture of other or smaller groups, or to some part or aspect of a group's culture.

In today's world, almost all adults participate in the culture of the nation to which they belong, and also participate in the subcultures of various other groups to which they also belong, based on family, occupation, employment, neighborhood, faith or ethnicity, school or sports teams.

Culture includes all behavior and attitudes learned from others: whether we eat with chopsticks or knives and forks or with our fingers, and how we interact with persons who differ in gender or age. Thus it may make sense to speak of the culture or subculture of the Marine Corps, or of Ivy League professors, or Teamsters Union members, or Goldman Sachs.

The causes of problems that are rooted in cultures or subcultures fall into a few general categories. One category is culture elements so incompatible with the rest of the culture that they create problems until they are abandoned or prohibited. Examples in our own history include obtaining labor by owning slaves, settling personal disputes by dueling, achieving pleasure by using opium or its derivatives, and polygamy.

A second category relates to when changes in some parts of a culture create problems in other parts. This is common when technology changes. No license was needed to make a trip on horseback, but making trips by driving a car created a need for licensing, insurance, time payments, and more.

When manufacturing by independent craftsmen was replaced by factories and assembly lines, it caused a whole series of adjustments in markets, in laws, and in family and community life. Some of these adjustments were unpleasant, and some of them are still going on, for instance the ease with which jobs in manufacturing can be transferred to foreign countries with cheaper labor.

It is especially important to note that changes in technology often occur faster than necessary adjustments in other parts of our culture.

The third main category of cultural factors that causes problems centers on clashes between cultures. These clashes are not limited to international relations; they also arise within nations due to migrations or other forms of globalization.

Most culture elements of a technological, financial or military nature are considered for acceptance in almost all nations. But certain culture elements from Western and other advanced democracies such as freedom of expression for unpopular persons and unpopular opinions, gender equality for women in education, jobs and driving cars, separation of church and state, and due process of law to protect individual rights, are often rejected in various parts of the world, sometimes with punitive actions.

And when migrants from those places enter advanced nations, assimilation into the culture of their new nations may be a slow process, generating tension or hostility for both newcomers and for the majority.

A different kind of culture clash, which is difficult to measure, arises from persons who feel that cultures associated with a particular nation are obsolescent or even harmful, and should be replaced by a shift of allegiance or affiliation to the world's entire population. This culture may arise from past abuses or shortcomings by nations, or by involvement in today's activities by multinational corporations or various international non-profits.

It is not clear what problems, or benefits, may arise from clashes with this international culture, but it seems clear that the world's future for quite some time will largely depend on nations and on how they act.

Eight Categories of Our Nation's Many Problems

2

Common sense tells us that if we really want to cope successfully with our problems, we have to be aware of them. Experience shows that problems we don't know of can blind-side us, catching us off-guard and doing more harm than if we were alerted or prepared.

This is why most of us have insurance. It isn't easy to buy adequate insurance against many major problems, however, such as unemployment, lost investments, drawn-out wars, severe inflation or severe deflation, violent and white-collar crime, various kinds of extremism, and many kinds of confusion that demoralize normal activity and waste time and money.

So the first rule in listing the problems that face our country is to try not to miss anything that might prove to be a real problem. But experience shows that despite our effort to be inclusive, we may overlook some problems. Therefore

(a) the list should be kept open for future additions (and possibly deletions of problems that have definitely been solved), and

(b) some problems on the list should be stated in a broad way to cover new problems of the same kind.

Inclusiveness is only one feature of a good list, however. An effort should be made to classify the problems on the list as a way of starting to ascertain their interrelationships, magnitude, and urgency.

The eight classifications I've used are our economy, environment, demographics, global relations, politics,

9

education, cohesion, and values. I want to clarify what I mean by the latter two.

Cohesion is the sense of belonging to our country that must be sufficiently strong in our population to preserve the viability of our nation and its government. When cohesion is weak or absent, the result is usually a "failed state." The problems that erode cohesion may be grounded in (a) disaffection toward our nation or its government for any reason, real or fancied, or (b) identification with some class, group, entity or cause that overrides or replaces the sense of belonging to our country. Democracy pre-supposed adequate cohesion.

"Values" refers to those cultural attitudes that help maintain a successful society. These values, which can be fostered by good education, can be summarized as good will plus good sense. Good sense includes common sense, plus uncommon sense when necessary. Values problems generally arise from complacency or from involvement in some form of excess. Values problems include various forms of extremism, destructive greed, and lack of civic and social responsibility.

Our Economy

- Unemployment and underemployment due to the following reasons:
    - Use of relatively cheap foreign labor.
    - Changes in technology that increase productivity or reduce demand.
    - Insufficient purchasing power for the goods or services being produced.
    - Lack of skills or knowledge needed for the work to be done.

- o Disadvantage of particular categories of workers, such as by geographic location, by age, by industry, by level of education, by ethnicity, by previous criminal or other records, or other factors.
- Excessive debt incurred by individuals and families, by various for-profit groups especially some in financial activities, and by some governments, especially the federal government. This problem leads to several related problems including
  - o bankruptcy,
  - o foreclosures,
  - o weak creditworthiness,
  - o higher interest costs, and
  - o less funds available for necessities, enhancements, and productive investments.
- Serious global challenges to the economy and power of the United States from rapidly growing manufacturing economies in China and other nations
  - o This results in imports which, together with foreign oil, greatly exceed the value of U.S. exports
  - o The difference is made up by loans from foreigners and by selling profitable U.S. properties to foreigners.
- Mismanagement in health care, including delivery, costs, quality control, preventive care, research and education of both providers and consumers.
- Problems of wasted talent, either by failure to adequately educate persons with much potential, or by employment of persons with well developed talents in work not requiring their abilities, or in lucrative

work of a predatory nature, such as granting credit at very high interest rates.

- Problems of waste, confusion and distraction caused by over-emphasis on innovation and the "latest thing," without sufficient regard for the KISS principle ("Keep it simple, stupid!"). We need more stability, simplicity and standardization, especially in areas like consumer electronics.
  - o While progress depends on innovation and competition, rapid changes and lots of choices burdens many consumers and degrades their quality of life.
  - o Indulgence in excessive innovation involves not only some areas of technology, but also some occupational sectors that are overly prone to fads. Almost all highly competitive kinds of business that sell to consumers advertise products that are "new." I did the same thing when I tried to sell my navigation invention called Mapigator in the 1940s; the concept of "new" still seems to grab consumers' attention. The word does not imply better, though, and fads arise out of large numbers of people embracing "new" without caring about "better." Through the decades, we have seen this with diets, fashion, technology, cars, and even education with fads such as "new math."
- Excessive complexity and other problems in our tax systems.
- Problems in transportation policy, as it involves standards of living, energy and environmental con-

cerns, safety, and destabilizing shifts of population to large metropolitan areas.

- o These areas then become burdened with costly expansions of public facilities and services.
- o Concurrently, smaller places with adequate facilities experience a loss of economic opportunities and tax bases.

Our Environment
- Flawed energy policies and practices, including
    - o costly dependence on unstable foreign and domestic energy sources and
    - o various adverse impacts on the environment, which also affect the economy and standards of living.
- Short-sighted policies and practices related to resources, such as deforestation to clear land for industrial agriculture

Our Demographics
- Problems relating to both legal and illegal immigration.
- Inadequate provision for aging national populations, such as already has occurred in Japan and is occurring in the United States and other countries.
    - o These problems need not include general declines in a nation's productive capacity for such basics as food, clothing, shelter and various manufactured products, because modern technology steadily reduces the amount of labor needed in producing these

things. But aging will require adjustments in financing the needs of increased numbers of the elderly.

- o While this may mean more tax revenues to support entitlements, it also would mean more purchasing power to support business-es.

Our Global Relations

- Problems in foreign relations related to coping with a world that's increasingly globalized and interde-pendent,
  - o in which our country is only about 4 percent of the world's population,
  - o in which new military and other technolo-gies may spread quickly, and
  - o in which tensions generated by past wars, colonialism, religious differences, poverty or national ambitions still persist.

Our Politics

- Political parties that have left large numbers of citizens dissatisfied because of unsolved national problems, foreign-relations problems, or confusing/ conflicting positions.

Our Education

- Hit and miss approach to education on all levels, due to multiple deficits in the following:
  - o   parent-teacher cooperation,
  - o curriculums,
  - o the teaching profession,

    o   the role of lifelong education and

    o   motivation for learning.

Our Cohesion

- Legal, legislative and regulatory systems that have become so complex that, as of 2012, twenty-two law firms have grown to more than 1,000 lawyers, providing services that only very wealthy interests can afford.
- A citizenry that was not adequately prepared in schools and colleges for the responsibilities of citizenship in a modern democracy, or which during adulthood has either neglected its responsibilities, or has had to work overtime to make ends meet, or has suffered from inadequate or one-sided information on public policy concerns.
- Irregularities in the criminal justice system that divide the nation due to variances in how different populations are treated by law enforcement systems and the courts.

Our Values

- The need to temper the passions of ideological factions on issues such as abortion, gay rights, capital punishment, gun control, and so on, which require candor expressed with civility, respect for the facts, reasonably broad perspectives, an effort to work out reasonable compromises or even perhaps an "agreement to disagree" or to let time deal with the issue, shifting attention to other pressing problems.

- Commercial and Infotainment systems that have fostered excessive consumerism and celebrity worship, shifting attention, money and skills to the products and personalities being promoted, at the expense of more urgent or valuable investments and activities that need greater recognition and support.
- Proliferation of corruption, including legal but corrupting activities affecting political campaigns, land-use policies, government contracts and grants, and so on in various cultures and subcultures here.

The above list in the eight categories of problems, of course, is both imperfect and incomplete. Modify it as you choose, flagging the items that seem most urgent or important, or that you might have a special interest in. To make that process a little easier, I offer you another listing of problem areas, some of which found their way into multiple categories in the above list, and which overlap in some salient ways:

- Unemployment
- Excessive debt
- Insufficient purchasing power
- Growing inequality
- Excessive waste
- Economic instability
- Pollution
- Depletion of natural resources
- Climate change
- An aging population
- Rapid population increase

- Difficulty assimilating some immigration
- Terrorism
- Adverse national balance of trade
- Difficulty in achieving cooperation on global problems such as spread of nuclear weaponry
- Carelessness in voting and in choosing candidates for elections
- Imbalances and secrecy in financing election campaigns
- Corruption in public services
- Lack of public information about some legislative activities
- Failure to recognize some types of public service, including service outside of assigned job duties
- Failures in developing readiness for education during early childhood
- Weak parental involvement during school and college
- Inadequate curriculums
- Need for further professionalizing of teaching
- Weaknesses in higher education
- Weakness of education in developing responsibility
- Failure of education adequately to utilize outside resources such as documentaries and guest speakers
- Failure of education to stimulate the motivation to learn
- Loss or absence of national cohesion
- Values that tends to weaken our nation by displacing a sense of common goals and civic responsibility with consumerism, celebrity worship, and predatory greed

- Failure to make quality health care available to all our people
- Failure both to control and to fund the rising costs of health care
- Failure to train and supply a sufficient number of primary care doctors and certain other types of care providers
- Failure to deal effectively with modes of lifestyle that increase illnesses, such as obesity and substance abuse
- Weaknesses in our criminal justice systems, giving some classes of people distinct benefits over others in terms of defense and incarceration
- Insufficient transparency in creating laws
- Excessive complexity in tax and other fields of law, leading to a situation in which many people find legal representation unaffordable
- Failure to develop energy policies that assure for the long term adequate, clean and safe supplies at reasonable and stable prices
- Problems in transportation policy in meeting needs and providing improved opportunities for personal travel and for shipment of goods
- Problems in transportation policy that foster wasteful shifts of jobs and population to already congested areas
- Problems in maintaining national security with due regard to foreign relations, global economic trends, and military personnel
- Problems in balancing the roles of parent and worker in child-rearing and family viability

- Impairment of free expression in academic, governmental and other organizations by disciplining or firing persons who expressions are deemed to run counter to standards
- Playbook problems, that is, problems in advocating or administering worthwhile policies and programs that alienate people and meet resistance or fail because of lack of common sense, extremism, failure to communicate, and so on
- Wasteful allocation of national talent
- Failure to deliver basic civics education to the future electorate and instead, emphasizing only subjects that seem directly tied to jobs, plus failure to teach meaningful history, including important developments and their causes and effects
- Need to address financial services to focus them more clearly and effectively on service in the key areas of banking, insurance, and investing
- Need to monitor and control relationships between government agencies and businesses in order to minimize undue influence, corruption, and waste.
- Problems relating to both legal and illegal immigration
- Problems stemming from ideological passions on issues such as abortion, gay rights, capital punishment, and gun control.
- Ineffective workplace management in large organizations where top executives do not understand difficulties that lower-level specialists must cope with, or where specialists do not understand matters outside their specialty.

Unsolvable Problems—Are There Any?

3

There is an important benefit in understanding the difference between an uncontrollable world and an indeterminate one. The fact that something has not happened does not mean it cannot happen; it only means that the way to make it happen is as yet unknown. We might never try to cure a disease if we believed that it was incurable or uncontrollable. The effort would be pointless. Most diseases medical science has conquered were at one time thought to be uncontrollable when they were really just indeterminate, and that change in attitude has made all the difference.

Psychologist/Author Ellen J. Langer,
Harvard University
Counterclockwise (p.24)

Maybe some problems are unsolvable, at least at a particular time and in prevailing conditions. But problems that seem insolvable often are solved, given time, effort, changing circumstances, or some open-minded consideration.

In a report from New Delhi, India ("A Risky Fatalism in India," *Washington Post*, January 16, 2011) David Ignatius discussed the long-standing tensions between prosperous India and unstable Pakistan, both of them nuclear powers. He quoted a prominent Indian who said, "You have to recognize that some problems can't be solved."

For several centuries England and France had bad relations, including several wars. That changed in 1871, due to the creation of Germany as a united and powerful nation. England and France became allies. At the same time a new era of bad feeling arose between France and Germany, which invaded France three times, in 1870-71, 1914 and 1940. Yet today France and Germany cooperate as peaceful members of the European Union.

Another example: Polio (infantile paralysis) was considered the worst public health epidemic in the United States after World War II and had become a growing menace since the mid-Nineteenth Century. It killed or crippled many people, with no cure or means of prevention. Then the polio vaccine developed by Jonas Salk was introduced in 1955 and polio no longer threatened American children.

Another example: for many years banks were subject to "runs", causing them to fail, with depositors losing their money. But in the 1930s the creation of federal insurance of bank deposits ended that problem.

Another example of a problem that seemed insolvable at the time was a dramatic episode in the civil rights era: the Freedom Rider crisis of 1961.

During the Kennedy years, civil rights activists called Freedom Riders staged tests of a Supreme Court decision (Boynton v. Virginia, 1960) stating that racial segregation in public transportation was illegal. Regardless of that decision, places all over the South continued to onforco Jim Crow laws, which were state and local laws dictating segregation practices. They covered where blacks and whites were to sit on the bus and at bus stations, and required they use separate rest rooms and separate lunch counters.

The Freedom Riders bought tickets for trips into Southern states from Greyhound and Trailways, which handled most interstate bus trips. The first Freedom Rides originated from Washington, DC on May 4, 1961. Men wore coats and ties; women wore dresses. This non-violent protest and those that followed stirred up the anger of white segregationists who turned the Freedom Rides into bloody events at terminals and on buses.

The Kennedy Administration, and especially Attorney General Robert Kennedy, saw this as a huge embarrassment, among other things, and wanted an immediate way to sedate the violence. They concluded quickly that they wouldn't get action from Congress, because a large part of the Democratic membership of Congress was Southern Democrats who wouldn't buck the will of their constituents.

The other avenue was to go to court and get an order to either stop the demonstrations or stop the Jim Crow practices—the latter being preferable. But they felt that would take a year due to appeals and this was an immediate problem with people getting hurt.

Using the U.S. military was also impracticable for both legal and operational reasons.

Then I remembered something I had read about ten years earlier. When I first went to the Civil Aeronautics Board in 1952, I had to read the laws under which the CAB operated, enacted in 1938. I recalled reading a section, which in very general and sweeping language, prohibited airlines from any form of discrimination or preferences with lots of synonyms. I had a hunch. My hunch was this had been copied from earlier laws regulating other modes of interstate transportation—railroads, trucks, and buses.

I decided to speak up about my hunch and Bobby Kennedy welcomed the impromptu display of expertise: I said that you may find the same provision, word for word, when Congress decided to cover interstate buses. It took less than five minutes to look it up and see it was true.

That indicated a way out.

I said, "We can file a petition with the ICC under that section of the law relating to interstate buses to order the bus lines to stop discrimination in their buses and terminals."

By the end of the day the petition had been filed. The ICC was shocked. Despite their experiences with discrimination that took the form of uneven services or financial inequalities, they had never had anything to do with racial problems before.

The FBI was ordered to go into bus terminals and take pictures of the "white" and "colored" signs at rest rooms and waiting rooms, and every other area that might have been affected by the Jim Crow laws, to collect evidence of discrimination. Evidence in hand, on November 1, 1961, the ICC ordered the bus companies to stop the Jim Crow practices, and that ended the problem.

Emerging Problems Facing Our Nation

4

These problems differ from most of those cited in earlier chapters because they probably require some major shifts in our national perspective in order to address them with some success. Unlike something such as emergency response services, which arguably doesn't require a sense of cohesion to address effectively, these problems will not go away unless a majority of people in this democracy support, or at least accept, proposed solutions with solid promise.

1. **Austerity**. We must make successful adjustments to the mounting pressures for austerity. Ever since World War II, many Americans have been living beyond their means, and some other nations have followed us in this. But we are now a debtor nation. Our federal, state and local governments, and many of our people, are deeply in debt. So are some European nations, and they have started to raise taxes and cut spending, leading to protests and violence. We will face more expenses to update our aging transportation infrastructure and to support our aging population and its health care. We also face increasing and costly pressures relating to energy, water supplies and arable land. In order to avoid the worst kinds of austerity and perhaps its disruptive public reactions, we will have to reduce waste, increase efficiency, and cut back on excessive consumerism.

2. **Global Competition.** China and some other nations have taken over U.S. leadership in many

fields of manufacturing, chiefly by reason of their abundant, relatively cheap and increasingly skillful labor, and by their nationalistic trade policies. Our trade policies, in contrast, have supported globalized free trade. The result has been a serious excess of our imports over our exports, leading to more debt and to the sale of U.S. assets, such as profitable toll roads, to foreign investment. Until people in countries like China become rich enough to buy what they produce or perhaps we produce, and until the United States becomes more competitive, we may have to adopt a variety of measures, some perhaps temporary, to restore our competitive vigor and to achieve a better balance in responding to globalization.

3. **Problems of the Elderly and Young Adults.** Growing populations of elderly people are occurring in all advanced nations and in some developing nations also. As of this writing, China is considering elimination of its one-child-only policy, which has contributed to a burgeoning elderly population in that country since implementation of it in 1978. A large elderly population not only creates economic burdens that will require some economic adjustments, but it also creates important opportunities for improving critically important aspects of American life, especially in education. (Some years ago, the public school that my grandchildren attended invited me to talk to the second and fourth grade classes. I spoke to the fourth grade about WW II and to the second grade on what makes an airplane fly, and both classes showed strong interest.)

Part of the reason we aren't implementing such opportunities is related to "cohort separation." In many cultures in the past, family life brought children, parents and older relatives together. Today in many of those same cultures, the young run around with the young, those in mid-career mix with their peers, and the elderly chiefly interact with their own age group. This cultural shift warrants attention as to its causes, its benefits and detriments, and possible adjustments. Cohort separation has an equally negative effect on young adults who do not receive the full benefit of mentoring, among other educational and career advantages that interaction with older people can yield.

Ironically, in the face of cohort separation, we will have the physical proximity of many young adults to their parents because they can't afford to live on their own. Either their post-graduation jobs don't provide enough income to allow them to be self-sufficient, or they can't find a job at all. The result is a shocking rise in the number of young adults returning home:

A Pew Research report earlier this year showed that the share of Americans living in multi-generational households is at its highest since the 1950s. Young adults ages 25 to 34 are most likely to return to the nest. Almost 22% of young adults were living at home in 2010, up from 16% in 2000 and rising the most since the re-

cession that began in 2007 and technically ended in 2009.
(Source: *USA Today,* October 16, 2012)

4. **Cultural Tensions.** The spread of information of many kinds to almost all the world's population continues to cause changes in customary patterns of behavior and belief, especially in fields such as economics and technology. But it has also caused sharp conflicts between modern cultures and some traditional religious and political attitudes. Modern secular values such as respect for science, freedom of expression, separation of church and state, gender equality, and governments elected by majority vote are often rejected or grudgingly watered down in many nations, and sometimes have even generated terrorism.

These cultural conflicts are both international and internal. International conflicts call for the skillful conduct of foreign relations and of national security. The importance of this is obvious in a world with terrorism and nuclear proliferation. Internal conflicts may be equally difficult, however. In advanced nations, some migrants from traditionally rigid cultures have difficulty in accepting the values of modern cultures. And in a highly pluralistic society like the United States, some religious groups with deep traditional roots reject modern culture and the values of a large part of our citizenry.

These internal conflicts may be reflected in changing ideas of what's meant by "ordinary American." According to Kathleen Park writing in the *Washington Post* (June 13, 2012), it used to mean "people who go to work every day, marry and raise families, pay their bills and taxes, serve their communities and country, and respect the difference between God and Caesar." Now, at least in some political circles, she says it means "an under-educated, overweight bloke who holds smarty-pants elites in contempt. And, you can be sure, vice versa." To the extent this may be accurate, it erodes national cohesion, as discussed in a later chapter.

History suggests that the remedies for these conflicts probably require several things, including time and better education, a subject also discussed in a later chapter.

5. **Loss of Trust in Government and Other Institutions.** In the course of a book review in the Washington Post of May 6, 2012, Robert G. Kaiser, who for many years has covered national politics, notes an important long-range trend shown by opinion polls: In 1964, before our deep involvement in Vietnam, 77 percent of Americans trusted our government to do the right thing most of the time. Ten years later, after Vietnam and Watergate, this percentage dropped to 36 percent, and Kaiser says polls show it has now dropped to less than 20 percent. He adds that several generations of Americans have grown up "reflexively" distrusting their government.

A healthy democracy certainly does not call for a citizenry with a blind trust in government. But neither can it function well if the citizenry has an indiscriminate distrust of government. The same is true of other major institutions in fields like finance, education, and other areas of public concern. Excessive trust leads to carelessness and corruption; insufficient trust leads to demoralization and lethargy.

Correcting the harm caused by excessive trust or excessive distrust of government or of other major institutions requires two things: first, making such changes as may be needed to justify a more sensible level of trust, and second, ongoing civic education so that the citizenry can keep up to date on how much trust is justified.

Ongoing civic education is especially important when there are vigorous campaigns either to glorify or to badmouth government. Glorification campaigns have typically been conducted by totalitarian autocracies, and may sometimes be used for public relations by other institutions. Negative campaigns may be used in democracies by political parties that are either in or out of power, by groups that oppose certain government policies, or by persons with deep-seated and long nurtured resentments, such as some wealthy families who felt that Franklin Roosevelt was "a traitor to his class" and who have passed their feelings about government on to later generations.

Loss of confidence in other large institutions—large Wall Street players, some large labor unions, large religious organizations, and some parts of higher education—has also become more apparent, due to some combination of their shortcomings and their weaker image.

Putting the Eight Categories of Problems in Context

5

In Chapter 2, I listed what are arguably the eight major categories of problems in the United States. Having now considered so-called unsolvable problems, I hope you have a context for a richer understanding of the eight categories of problems. This chapter's relatively in-depth look helps pave the way to Part II, which discusses approaches to solutions.

Before delving into the problems, let's take another look at how they break down into subcategories, all of which are discussed here:

Economic Problems: Purchasing Power, Regulation and De-regulation

Environmental Problems: Pollution, Pathogens, Availability of Resources, Climate Change

Demographics: Our Aging Population, Problems Related to Immigration

Global Relations: China, Venezuela, etc.

Politics: The Party System

Education: Teacher Competence, Curriculum, Integrity, Funding

Cohesion: The Double-Edge Sword of Diversity, Citizenship

Values: Extremism, Corruption

Economic Problems

As the leaders of the former Soviet Union and of China finally realized, capitalism is the most productive economic system ever developed. And trade across national borders can often greatly improve the economics of the nations that participate in it.

Yet capitalism and globalized trade have also demonstrated at least three serious problems. These are (1) instability: repeated boom-and-bust cycles resulting in serious recessions and depressions with lots of unemployment; (2) excessive debt, which burdens many young people, families, businesses, and levels of governments; and (3) growing inequality that leaves major parts of populations either in poverty or in financial stagnation, weakening the funding needed for higher education, for retirement, and for sufficient purchasing power to maintain prosperity. Bloomberg Business Week launched a series of articles called "The Wealth Debate" after the Occupy Wall Street movement sparked protests around the world. In them, several top economists have pointed out that excessive inequality is not just a moral or social welfare issue, it also damages the economy.

All three problems have affected our country. All of them can be better understood when economics is bolstered by economic history and by the interplay between economics and other factors, including politics, demographics, technology, environment, law including its administration, and various aspects of foreign relations. Unfortunately, many schools and colleges leave large numbers of citizens and even some political leaders pretty much in the dark on these subjects.

An interesting clue to our present problems is offered by Phil Angelides, who was chairman of the Financial Crisis Inquiry Commission, which reported on the cause of the crash in 2008. Writing in the *Washington Post* of June 30, 2011 he says, "The financial sector's share of corporate profits climbed from 15% in 1980 to 33% by the early 2000s, while financial-sector debt soared from $3 trillion in 1978 to $35 trillion by 2007." In other words, the best way to get rich in our country was no longer to produce better values in tangible products and in various services used by the public, but to go into Wall Street and play the games, old and new, largely using borrowed money. This strongly suggests that some parts of the financial sector of our economy have a persistent tendency to go far beyond the economy's legitimate needs for financial services.

The financial sector of our economy is really three different sectors, although in recent years a large company can operate legally in all three. These sectors are (1) conventional banking, including checking and savings accounts, credit cards, home mortgages and short-term small business loans; (2) liability and casualty insurance; and (3) financial services relating to investments, both to raise long term capital for businesses and governments by fostering the creation of stocks and bonds and to provide investors with markets where stocks and bonds can be bought and sold.

This third sector has been quite lucrative and the cause of much trouble, including the 1929 crash and the crisis of 2008. Sometimes the problem has been developing flawed financial products, and sometimes the problem has been foolish speculation, manipulation, or other dubious practices.

A very important economic problem is the persistent tendency of productivity to grow faster than purchasing power. This was a major cause of the Great Depression of the 1930s and is a major cause of the post-2008 sluggish economy.

It's elementary economics that purchasing power is the desire plus the ability to buy what's offered for sale. Modern marketing can stimulate desire, but ability to buy depends on either wealth (that is, net worth, meaning assets minus liabilities) or income or credit, or some combination of these three.

When the ability to buy depends on wealth, the ability will ultimately fail unless wealth is replenished; besides, many consumers have little wealth. Credit can provide purchasing power for various periods of time but it ultimately depends on either wealth or income.

Since purchasing power directly or indirectly depends on income, purchasing power will not be adequate in the long run to buy what's produced unless income is sufficient and sustainable. A basic cause of the Great Depression of the 1930s was the steep decline of farm incomes during the 1920s.

Today a basic cause of our sluggish economy is the continuing diversion of manufacturing incomes to low-wage foreign workers. While in both the Great Depression and in today's sluggish economy there have been several additional causes, weak purchasing power is probably the cause of greatest importance.

The same point, with somewhat different wording, appears in "Debt Isn't Our Biggest Issue" by Bill Gross, founder of Pimco, an investment management firm (*Washington Post,* August 12, 2011): "But while our debt crisis is real and threatens to grow to Frankenstein proportions in future years, debt is not the disease—it is a symptom. Lack of aggregate demand and investment is the disease." And of course aggregate demand depends on purchasing power.

Illustrating this problem is the reality of multi-national corporations shipping American jobs overseas. It is a particularly vexing problem when a company like General Electric moves the headquarters of its X-ray business from Waukesha, Wisconsin to China at the same period of time when GE's chief executive is serving as the President's "jobs czar," as was CEO Jeffrey R. Immelt in Barack Obama's administration.

A contributing problem in our sluggish economy may be a shortage of certain specialized skills, despite our high level of unemployment. Geoff Colvin, senior editor at large with *Fortune*, wrote about the rise of top-notch engineering talent in China in a July 29, 2010 article. In terms of numbers of graduates in engineering, America is behind China, yet that alone is only part of the cause for alarm. He also notes the composition of the graduating classes. An estimated 10,000 Chinese students earned a Ph.D. in engineering in 2009. The spring 2010 graduating classes in the United States had about 8,000 Ph.D. engineers, but an estimated two-thirds of them are not even U.S. citizens, so where they will take their expertise after graduation is uncertain. American companies will locate where they can get the talent they need to do a job at an affordable price. If they don't find capable and affordable engineers in the United States, they will go elsewhere.

No review of our economic problems can overlook long-standing disagreements about the effects of governmental regulations on businesses. The most frequent assertion, often used in politics, is that such regulations are a burden on business which prevents businesses from being fully productive, which would also create more jobs.

Actually, the problem is not that simple. It's true that some regulations burden the profitability and productivity of some businesses. Some of those regulations were designed to reduce dangers to the health or safety of employees or consumers and thus lower the costs of medical care and disability. Perhaps those objectives could be achieved with less red tape.

Many regulations, however, have been and still are favored by certain kinds of businesses, with the concurrence of governments and the general public. Examples include some kinds of businesses that require large investments of capital, such as railroads, and some kinds of utility services. Such businesses and their investors seek regulation that provides some degree of protection from vigorous competition, and have often received it.

A dramatic example of this occurred in 1938, when Congress decided that a handful of struggling airlines needed some regulatory protection from cut-throat competition in order to attract the investment and talent required for developing the great future potential of air transportation. Forty years later, with greatly expanded airlines, Congress decided to end that protection. One result has been lower fares on heavily travelled routes. Other results have included many airline bankruptcies, deep pay cuts for pilots and other employees, greatly reduced and poorer service to small and medium-sized cities, slower and poorer services due to increased reliance on very large "hub" airports, curtailment of amenities plus the need to try to assure that all seats are sold on all flights, and serious concerns over long-term increases in fuel costs. An indirect result has been to shift businesses, jobs and population to large, better served cities, increasing traffic congestion and possibly taxes. For a detailed report on today's airlines, including the possible future impact of financial pressures on safety, see *Attention All Passengers* (HarperCollins, 2012) by William J. McGee.

Of course, regulations that block or reduce competition can easily be abused, when they are used by existing businesses for their own benefit, while depriving the public of greater choices and lower prices. Resolving such issues should be based on a detailed examination of the particular kind of business in question and of the full range of the public's interests in it.

Environmental Problems

By environment we mean our home, the planet earth, which includes the land, the oceans, what's under the land and oceans, the atmosphere, and the space above the atmosphere that's useful for satellites which provide communications, navigation, and other uses.

Environmental problems can be grouped into four main categories: pollution, pathogens, the depletion of natural resources, and the effects of climate change.

Pollution problems are caused by substances which create health hazards in the air we breathe, the water and food we consume, or in the plants or animals we rely on. These substances can be created in various ways: by producing exhaust from burning certain fuels under certain conditions; by various industrial activities; by products that contain ingredients which have unintended harmful side-effects; and by lack of sanitation.

Pathogens include things found in nature, some living and some not, which cause diseases. Included are many kinds of bacteria, other micro-organisms, viruses,

elements such as arsenic, and highly radioactive substances. There is reason to believe that some pathogens,
when exposed to modern medications such as antibiotics,
may be able to evolve into varieties that are resistant to
such medications.

Depletion of natural resources was noted in Chapter 2 as a basic reality that causes various problems. As
stated in that chapter, Mother Nature, once regarded as
bountiful, is beginning to be stingy.

Depletion of resources is creating problems in at
least three important areas: food, energy, and good places
to live.

Codfish, supplying both sides of the Atlantic for
centuries, as well as once prolific oysters, are now scarce.
Caviar from sturgeon, an affordable luxury when I was
a boy, has increased to roughly $2,000 per pound. To put
this into perspective, that means the teaspoon of caviar
you put on a cracker for an appetizer is worth about $20.
Aquaculture will replace some wild seafood resources, yet
to what extent and at what costs are unclear.

Major food supplies depend on agriculture, and on
animals raised on agricultural products. This depends on
the amount of arable land and on adequate supplies of
water. Arable land is being converted to urban and suburban development, and supplies of good water, also needed
for cities and various industries, are under pressure in
many places, including those dependent on underground
aquifers that are hard to replenish.

We've had plenty of early warning on these matters: almost a century ago we had a national disaster
called the Dust Bowl, a warning about the importance of
arable land that's adequately watered. Triggered by se-

vere drought, the Dust Bowl became a devastating phenomenon because of decades of farming without crop rotation or measures to prevent wind erosion.

As to energy, the limitations of resources are already evident. The British Petroleum oil spill in the Gulf of Mexico highlights the costs and risks of extracting oil from wells a mile below the surface of the ocean. The costs of mining for coal and minerals may be controllable and bearable and necessary up to a point, but the long-run picture seems obvious. Renewable sources of energy will become more necessary and more practicable, but it is unclear at what costs. Running cars partly on fuel produced from corn caused an increase in the price of corn, leading to food riots in some nations. Air transportation in particular, which requires lots of affordable fuel with a high energy-to-weight ratio, is already under financial pressure, and it faces an even more problematic future.

As to good places to live, the desirable requirements seem to be a good climate, good opportunities to earn a living, good recreational opportunities, and freedom from violence, crime, and other negatives. These requirements are not well satisfied in large parts of the world. As a result, desirable residential real estate soon becomes scarce and expensive. Some other areas may become attractive in the future, but it seems unlikely that many people will move to places without the desirable factors noted above. Instead, the current trend is to move into already congested urban areas.

Climate change produces the problem of rising sea levels, due to the melting of ice in polar and Antarctic areas. This may inundate low-lying areas that are heavily populated and produced much food. To meet the needs of the world's increasing population, attention is being given to converting major forested areas (in the Amazon River watershed and in sub-Saharan Africa) to farming to produce food. But it is well known that trees remove carbon dioxide from the air, and thus cutting down huge areas of forest may aggravate climate change.

Demographics

Our demographics present problems related to both age and size. The problems include an increasingly aging population with increasing needs for health care and pensions; a total population growing more rapidly than the populations of other advanced nations, due chiefly to immigration; and some immigrants having difficulty in assimilating to our values of tolerance.

Our Aging Population

I briefly referenced issues related to the aging population in Chapter 4, which is focused on emerging problems that are likely to intensify over the next couple of decades. These issues of aging also deserve a close look as an existing problem.

The United States, as well as other advanced nations, is experiencing a growing surge in the percentage of its population who are elderly. This is due to increased longevity, which in turn is due to modern medical care and other improvements in standards of living. In some nations and among some socioeconomic classes, the preponderance of the elderly may be intensified by low birth rates.

Most of our elderly no longer engage in productive work, if "productive" is defined by contributions to the Gross Domestic Product. In addition, they require more medical care, which is generally costly because it's ongoing and often addresses serious conditions such as heart disease and bone deterioration. Many also require maintenance care because the simple act of bathing isn't so simple anymore. This creates the growing problem of how to pay for the kinds of care our elderly citizens require. To give some perspective on the magnitude of the problem, roughly 13 percent of the population of the United States belongs to the American Association of Retired Persons (AARP).

This is a double problem: a problem for government in trying to help the elderly, and a problem for many of the elderly themselves, and sometimes also for their children, due to a lack of sufficient retirement income or assets to meet their needs.

Retirement incomes in the United States have three main sources: Social Security, employer-provided pensions, and a retired person's own assets. The second of these has been seriously weakened since the latter part of the Twentieth Century as many employers have dropped "defined benefit" pension plans and substituted "defined contribution" plans, which contribute money to a fund usually invested in stocks, but with no assurance as to the amount of a pension. In addition, if an employer becomes unable to make payments toward retirements, the government's Pension Benefit Guarantee Corporation provides only partial restoration of the retiree's loss. It is thus obvious that future retirements may be less secure and less adequate, especially if Medicare's help in meeting rising health care costs is curtailed in order to reduce the growth of federal debt.

In short, the current population of retirement age and elderly people may have thought it was coming to old age with proper preparation for sustenance and care throughout life, but many of them are caught by surprise over changes in economic realities and public policies and their well-being is now one of our nation's problems.

Problems Related to Immigration

Let's not jump to conclusions here about "good" or "bad" immigrants. Part of the reason we have immigration problems is because we have a history of being asleep at the wheel when it comes to immigration legislation.

Healthcare reform, economic stimulus package, the federal budget—they have all sparked complaints about Congress passing laws that are a thousand pages long without time for legislators and the public to learn what is being enacted. But the lack of legislative and public attention to what gets into law is not a new problem.

The Immigration Law that aggravates so many citizens today passed without public hearings or debate.

From 1958 until 1981 I was a career lawyer in the Justice Department. During most of this period I was in the Office of Legal Counsel (OLC). OLC is sometimes regarded as a "shadow Supreme Court," because federal courts have always refused to give advisory opinions, even if needed by presidents or heads of agencies; OLC performs the Attorney General's function of providing this guidance. OLC also interprets laws that apply to all agencies to avoid multiple and inconsistent interpretations by agencies.

Early in 1965, Norbert Schlei, the then head of OLC, told me to draft a Presidential message transmitting a proposed revision of our immigration laws to Congress. The only guidance I had was that President Lyndon Johnson, during his 1964 election campaign against Barry Goldwater, had told voters of Italian and Greek descent that the immigration laws discriminated against immigrants from those countries and that he planned to change those laws.

Schlei revised the draft and sent it to someone in the White House where that someone revised it further.

Based on White House interest in the subject— which was part of a long list of legislative actions the president wanted to have addressed in the first 100 days of his Administration—I expected a lot of work on immigration changes, similar to the amount of work I had a few years earlier when the Kennedy administration proposed legislation on communication satellites. But no additional tasks arose. We were told the delay was due to a subcommittee chairman in the House of Representatives. Still, since I had expected more work, I improved on my background on immigration with the help of a senior official in the (then) Immigration and Naturalization Service.

Suddenly, we learned that the new law had passed Congress. I received a telegram from the White House inviting me to President Johnson's signing ceremony on Ellis Island in New York harbor. The President arrived by helicopter, signed the legislation in front of more than 100 invitees, and took off.

Immediately after the ceremony, I learned about some features of the new law. It abolished the previous law, which had contained the national origins quota system. That system had sought to keep future immigration similar to past immigration as regards the proportions from the various countries. Instead every country in the world, large or small, was given an annual quota of 20,000, and there were other provisions that led to a large increase of Hispanic immigration. The quota of 20,000, when multiplied by the number of countries in the Middle East and other nations with largely Islamic populations, may account for the increasing number of Muslims in our country today.

Let's take a look at how the law probably got through Congress. I say "probably" because the exact nature of the back-door deal-making reflects a collection of secrets held by the people involved.

President Johnson was at the height of his power in early 1965. He was well aware of the importance of the first hundred days of earlier presidents; and as a former Senate Majority Leader he was very effective on the telephone when dealing with key legislators.

The President's rather stormy political career in Texas may have given him a motive to increase Hispanic immigration. He had run for the Senate and believed with some justice that the election had been stolen from him. He ran again and apparently decided that two could play in that kind of politics. He won his second Senate race by a narrow margin with the help of local political leaders in South Texas, which had a considerably Hispanic population. Could this have had some bearing on how the new law turned out?

Let me add that I have much respect for President Johnson's service to our country in matters like Medicare, Medicaid and civil rights. I leave to the judgment of others his record on immigration.

When I returned to Washington, I learned that this major law, which was passed without public knowledge of its contents and without legislative and public debate, presents two special problems facing our country. The first is the lack of transparency in how major changes in our laws are achieved or blocked. This is at least as important in a democracy as the Freedom of Information Act, which illuminates how our laws are administered, not how they are made.

The second special problem is immigration policy, as to both legal and illegal immigrants. This highly emotional subject has not had a balanced and comprehensive public review for a long time. A perfect solution is almost impossible. Therefore the problem calls for a compromise, in which our country's interests are well served, but in as humane a manner as practicable.

Global Relations

Our global relations present problems in several respects, chiefly in combating terrorism; correcting our serious trade imbalance, which has increased our unemployment and our national debt; and in establishing effective international cooperation on a broad range of global problems affecting health, the environment, and peace.

I want to focus on just two countries as indicative of how our global relations policies affect nearly every aspect of our lives in the United States, and how chinks in those policies signal extreme problems. The two countries are China and Venezuela.

China

Judging by their actions and policies in the last few decades, the leaders of China have hit upon an impressive formula that is rapidly increasing China's economic power and thus its military and diplomatic power. China is also a big creditor of the debts of the United States.

With more than four times the population of the United States, including lots of well-educated people, China's recent dramatic expansion has been made possible by smart leadership and relatively little dissent. Meanwhile, the United States, while still the world's only superpower in a military sense, is falling behind economically. In addition, our citizenry increasingly suffers from divisive anger aimed at Washington, DC, Wall Street, "elitists," "populists," and various other targets (depending on the day).

China's leadership formula rests on two main supports. First is a deep-seated nationalism. This is grounded in China's very long history as a successful civilized nation, and is intensified by resentment of China's more recent severe degradation by various colonial powers, chiefly Europeans and Japan, and fortunately to a much lesser extent by the United States.

The second support of the Chinese leadership's formula appears to be a shrewd reading of modern history, both economic and political. Like the leaders of the former Soviet Union, the leaders of China correctly recognized, along with most of the rest of the world, that a command economy is far less productive than a capitalistic economy. They also seem to have recognized that an autocratic government is more successful when headed by an oligarchy rather than by a single dictator.

The Chinese apparently question the notion that World War II proved the superiority of democratic nations (England and the United States) over dictatorships

(Germany, Italy, and Japan). In this view, the democracies were dangerously slow in responding to the growing menace of their enemies, and the democracies might well have lost the war if it had not been for serious strategic errors by Germany and Japan (Germany's attack on Russia before finishing its war on England; Japan's attack on Pearl Harbor, causing an immediate U.S. mobilization, instead of first absorbing the resources of French, Dutch, and English colonies to strengthen its war machine).

The Chinese may have concluded that if Germany had been led by a small oligarchy instead of a single leader, the mistake of its premature attack on Russia would have been less likely. Such a conclusion might be bolstered by reference to the errors of Napoleon and other one-man rulers, possibly including some past Chinese rulers.

This discussion is not meant to imply that China is planning a big war, although the Chinese almost certainly intend to make sure that no other nation, like Japan in the 1930's, can attack China without serious retaliation. In addition, China may assert control over some islands and resource-rich ocean areas near its coast. But the main point of this discussion is that China intends, through economic growth, to become in many respects the world's largest economy in the Twenty-first Century, like the British Empire in the Nineteenth Century and the United States in the Twentieth Century.

Venezuela and Other Problem Areas

The 2012 re-election of the now-deceased Hugo Chavez in Venezuela signaled a serious threat related to the United States related to economic influence and terrorism. The threat continues to emanate from South America, where Chavez had convinced several countries to follow his lead and where his legacy lives on. In his book, *Latin America in the Post-Chavez Era*, South American expert Dr. Luis Fleischman focuses on the implication of Chavez' continuing power for U.S. foreign relations. He opens with this:

> For more than a decade, Latin America has been facing a significant political phenomenon. New regimes have emerged in Venezuela, Bolivia, Ecuador and Nicaragua and all see themselves as being revolutionary . . .
>
> These new governments claim to reject capitalism and try to replace it with a "Socialism of the Twenty-first Century". They repudiate economic globalization to support economic nationalism. They speak about regional economic and political unity and condemn imperialism and U.S influence in the continent. Ironically, there is nothing contemporary about the models they worship: They have glorified and revived the half- century old, failed and moribund Communist Cuban revolution and its eternal dictator Fidel Castro more than a decade after the fall of the Berlin wall[1].

A very condensed statement of the foreign relations problem is that Venezuela has allied itself with Iran and other hotbeds of terrorism, as well as the thinking such as that dominating Cuba and now Russia under Vladimir Putin. With his considerable economic clout coming from Venezuela's oil reserves, Hugo Chavez was able to afford to "buy friends" in the form of other South American countries, and to import military expertise from places like Iran—all with the intent of reducing the so-called imperialistic power of the United States worldwide. (Chavez and Putin grew so close that Putin even gave Chavez a puppy in September 2012.)

If asked what the greatest foreign relations challenge we face is, many citizens would cite challenges related to the Middle East. In fact, in a post-presidential election story[2], CNN contributors targeted four of the top ten problems as coming out of the Middle East. In considering China and Venezuela, however, we can see that the global economic and political agendas of these two powerful nations represent some of the most profound threats to our future. Some of those threats are intertwined with those coming from the Middle East.

Politics

Here's a very important problem: Too many Americans are turned off by politics. There are several reasons for this, and it's quite understandable, but it's also quite dangerous. History is littered with the collapse of empires, and with wars and other disasters that could have been avoided by better politics. If our country is to be a successful democracy with peace, prosperity and freedom in our complex modern world, politics is unavoidable.

The only way to get rid of politics is to put our nation under an autocratic government, like a monarchy that rules by divine right, or a dictatorship like Adolf Hitler's Germany or Joseph Stalin's Soviet Union. So the real problem is to make politics work better for our country.

The founders of our nation were a bit hesitant about political parties, fearing the dangers of dividing the country into "factions." But parties emerged when the Constitution was submitted to the states for ratification. Those favoring ratification were called Federalists, those opposed were the Anti-Federalists. They lost but they made an important contribution by encouraging assurances that a Bill of Rights would be added to the new Constitution.

We have developed a two-party system, but one which is open to a third party—or even a fourth or fifth—if enough citizens want one. Our system arguably works better than democracies with lots of parties. But all successful democracies require that the parties (a) offer a real choice, and (b) are willing to compromise when appropriate or necessary. A compromise is not always a formal agreement, because the party in power sometimes adjusts its position on an issue to accommodate some concerns of the opposition.

U.S. history shows only a few departures from the above, usually in emergencies. These include Lincoln's response to secession and the attack on Fort Sumter; Franklin Roosevelt's response to the economic breakdown and the near collapse of banking in March 1933, and the responses to the 1941 Japanese attack on Pearl Harbor and to the September 2001 terrorist attack on New York and the Pentagon.

The problems of American politics can be summarized under two main headings: first, there's a need to recognize that there's blame enough for all, and second, there's also a need to recognize and to support those who help make democracy work better. They include some politicians, some career civil servants, some journalists, some educators, some historians and other scholars, and some other citizens.

Starting with blame for all, let's begin with citizens who shirk their civic responsibility, which at a minimum is to vote after considering the pros and cons of the issues and the qualifications and records of the candidates. Civic responsibility should also include two important perspectives: a time perspective that covers both historic experiences and current trends affecting our future, plus a place perspective, covering how our problems are handled in other places.

Of course, it's only fair to admit that some of the blame put on citizens who fail to do these things might better be shifted to educators who don't prepare citizens to understand how our economic, governmental, international and other systems work. But educators might respond that schools are ultimately controlled by the public, so the public should be blamed. Yet education doesn't stop after schooling, so let's blame the news media, some of which fail to provide large parts of our population with adequate news and analysis, or which provide one-sided, ideological content. Journalism might then respond that in a free country it's the citizen's responsibility to choose media that support intelligent, responsible voting.

The commonest target in this blame game, of course, is politicians. They might broadly be defined as persons who spend a fair amount of their time in the machinery of party politics, local, state or national, at the precinct or higher levels. This might include some people who arrange political campaign financing, sometimes in connection with lobbying activities.

"Politicians" also should include many persons who were candidates for elective office on party slates, and some persons who hold or have held appointive government positions that are not in a civil service or other nonpartisan status. (At the federal level, some important subcabinet appointments which are made politically, for example in the Justice Department, are typically given to professional persons with little or no political activity background).

Perhaps the blame most often leveled at politicians is about corruption. Both parties have suffered from this, at all levels of government. Corruption in local governments frequently involves land use decisions such as zoning, the location of public projects, and so on. Corruption at all levels can occur in appointments, in contracting, and in influencing laws and regulations, or influencing how they are interpreted or administered.

Corruption seems to be more common in some places than in others. Illinois Governor Blagojevich is the fourth Illinois governor to be convicted of felonies since 1973. This should make citizens wonder how candidates for elective office are chosen in various places. At the same time citizens might also wonder whether qualified persons would be willing to be nominated.

Blaming politicians for conduct that may seem corrupt is not confined to criminal conduct. Blame is also leveled against politicians who are believed to be unduly influenced by large campaign contributions arranged by lobbyists for wealthy interests, to the detriment of the general public. Further discussion of corruption problems occurs later in this chapter.

No discussion of the blame leveled against politicians can overlook their gerrymandering of congressional districts (and possibly of some local or state legislative districts). This occurs every ten years as part of the re-districting to adjust for population shifts after each decennial census. Both parties have been guilty of it. Its motive is to give the state's dominant party more and/or safer seats in the legislature, with perhaps some consolation for the weaker party, which may lose seats but at least ends up with safer ones.

This undercuts the idea of a democracy and weakens the influence of independent-minded voters.

The discussions of how to fix redistricting and other politically-related problems occurs in Part III.

Education

As a nation, our approach to education has problems related to objectives, management, professionalism of teachers, and so much more. And they occur at every level, from preschool to continuing education for professionals and other adults. Education should support economic competitiveness, effective citizenship, and personal satisfaction.

The ongoing and accelerating development of technology in most fields—medicine, warfare, computers, economic production, communication—offers most of us a higher material standard of living, but at the price of a world of daunting complexity. To cope effectively with the many choices and problems of today and tomorrow, and for society to identify and manage successfully the benefits and risks in major areas of policy and subcultures, individuals will require a very high quality of education.

Lacking high quality education, society may be increasingly dominated by the few, and these few may have inadequate competence and values. Their leadership will thus be questionable, yet the rest of society will be poorly equipped to question them. History suggests that a contributing cause for the decline and collapse of some empires and nations may have been the weakness of their education systems, compounded by the incompetence of their leaders. More recent examples are the incompetence of both leaders and citizens in the great Western democracies in the 1920s and 1930s that led to the Great Depression and World War II.

American education has many important strengths, but since the focus here is on problems, let's look at the obstacles to quality. Here is a checklist, not meant to suggest order of importance, but simply a guide for use in evaluating the quality of education in a particular class, school, school system, or larger educational entity.

- Insufficient competence or insufficient authority in teachers or in principals, even to maintain discipline. Incompetence can often be alleviated by proper training. An insufficiency of authority that impedes quality work may be due to legal, administrative, political, or bureaucratic causes.
- Insufficient emphasis on student writing, especially in classes that are too large.
- Cheating. Cheating may be aggravated by "teaching to the test" in preparing for standardized tests.
- Excessive use, or poor quality, of audio-visual materials.
- Automatic promotions and mainstreaming of children who disrupt classes or require teachers to di-

vert excessive attention away from the rest of the class.

- Student intimidation, including bullying, coupled with a lack of effective student government.
- The need of public schools for some alternative to selective admission and retention that is available to private schools.
- Negative outside influences on children, including excessive or improper TV, violence-focused video games, antisocial subcultures of "success," and gangs.
- Bad textbooks, that is, poor quality, dumbed-down, or not enough for each student
- Inadequate funding. Salaries are the biggest part of most school budgets, followed by technology, especially computers, which tend to be structured to deliver information rather than help to engender critical thinking.
- Mis-allocation of funding, especially to excessive headquarters bureaucracies and to overemphasized spectator sports.
- Substandard administration, including administration that interferes with quality teaching.
- Loss or absence of a required core curriculum that covers all of the basic parts of a quality education, including the development of critical thinking.
- The educational philosophy or attitude that children should be taught only the things that they like to learn.
- The presence of "turf" attitudes by some of the players in education, to the extent it may interfere with cooperation and progress toward quality education.

- Failure to provide timely, adequate analysis, service, and funding to meet the needs of children with learning differences and physical challenges.
- Failure to identify and correct the causes of lagging academic performance by certain populations, including inadequate educational services, insufficient home support, negative peer pressure by students who discourage academic effort by their classmates, and social and cultural factors that delay effective assimilation.
- Failure to recognize and to prepare adequately the increasing percentage of students who will need post-secondary education to cope with an increasingly competitive world.
- Failure to measure adequately the high school dropout rate, reportedly 30 percent as a national average[3], and failure to determine its causes and take actions to reduce the rate.

This list is not complete, of course; there are other possible obstacles to quality education, including community attitudes that do not reflect an understanding of, or appreciation for, quality education. That said, there is some good news and there are valuable lessons to be learned from certain communities showing significant decreases in dropout rates. For example, the dropout rate for Hispanics was cut nearly in half during the first ten years of the Twenty-first Century.

Cohesion

Erosion of our national cohesion is not a new problem, but it is a very important one, and there are some new kinds of erosion to consider.

Group cohesion is generally vital to group survival. Every organized human group, such as a family, a work, faith, recreation, political, or other group, including a tribe, a nation, a federation, and so on, depends on maintaining the cohesion of its members. This means that the members have a sense of belonging to the group and are willing to continue to belong. (The word "belonging" is more or less similar to loyalty or allegiance.)

When the United States declared its independence in 1776, part of our population continued its allegiance to England and some of them moved to the Bahamas. When our draft Constitution was submitted to the states for ratification in 1787, there was vigorous opposition on the ground that the proposed federal government would fall into the hands of an elite oligarchy. This concern later motivated supporters of President Jackson. When our southern states seceded in 1861, Robert E. Lee, a graduate of the U.S. Military Academy at West Point, felt a stronger cohesion to his native state of Virginia than to the United States. During the Great Depression and the New Deal, some opponents of President Roosevelt called him "a traitor to his class." More recently the promotion of diversity and multiculturalism may have overshadowed common and unifying values. At the same time the idea of a world of independent nations has been challenged as an obsolete and destructive culture of nationalism, and as an impediment to solving global economic, environmental and other problems.

One of the oldest kinds of erosion of national cohesion is the presence in a nation of a class perceived as having unwarranted superiority. Jefferson described this as an "artificial aristocracy" based on inherited family wealth. In Europe this kind of elitism led to violent revolutions. Jefferson favored what he called a "natural aristocracy" based on talent and virtue.

Today we have largely shifted to what Jefferson had in mind, which we call a meritocracy. But for various reasons many Americans are not happy with it, and the reaction against it has led to a revival of populism. While it should seem obvious that every nation in today's complex world needs its own meritocracy, it is necessary to briefly recognize some of the reasons a democracy like ours may reject its meritocrats. First, they sometimes make big mistakes, like getting us deeply involved in the Vietnam War, and deregulating certain financial enterprises. Second, they are often inclined to ignore the experience and views of persons with less prestigious positions but with substantial backgrounds in the subject at hand. Third, they often employ their meritocratic credentials obtained from Ivy League or similar institutions in the pursuit of personal financial gain in Wall Street or Madison Avenue rather than working for the interests of our nation. Fourth, even when they address national needs they do so with the group-think of privileged groups. Fifth, when they devise and administer necessary or desirable public programs, they do so with a rigidity that citizens often experience as a "one-size-fits-all" lack of common sense, causing frustration and wasted time. Sixth, meritocrats seldom establish and maintain effective channels for ongoing exchanges of information, questions and ideas with other meritocrats and with individual citizens and civic groups.

The populism generated in reaction to meritocrats is sometimes stimulated and exploited for political rea-

sons by special interest groups acting in their own interests. This might be called fake populism and may lead
to further frustration and to possible further erosion of
national cohesion.

There are many other tensions that may erode national cohesion. Within academia some professors may
look down on teachers colleges and may regard the clergy
as not very bright. Some prestigious legal and academic
groups have long had negative attitudes toward military
professionals. And of course there are widespread antipathies based on ethnicity, race, religion, national origin,
gender, sexual orientation, occupation, life-styles, and
even age. Some of these antipathies may be increased by
large influxes of immigrants. And those who believe that
"government is the problem" may have downgraded the
reputation, morale, and recruiting of various public services.

The founders' motto for preventing diversity from
becoming divisive was "E Pluribus Unum" (From many,
one). Our increasing neglect of meaningfully teaching history and civics in our schools may have further weakened
our national cohesion.

World experience also throws some light on both
the forces that maintain national cohesion and the forces that erode it. Most successful nations have a common
territory, common language and a common history, with
a common government and often common or compatible
religious cultures. The success of ancient Rome was enhanced by liberal immigration and by granting autonomy
to conquered areas, but Rome declined when taxation was
shifted from the rich to the poor and when immigration
became more a matter of benefits than of bonding.

In recent centuries the long histories of France, Spain and the United Kingdom (England, Scotland, Wales and northern Ireland), plus the consolidations of Italy and Germany in the nineteenth century, may be contrasted with places where nations seem to struggle for sufficient internal support, such as the Balkans, Iraq, and the Soviet Union before it broke up into separate nations.

Bearing in mind the many functions that governments in successful nations provide for their populations—protection from foreign and internal assaults, relief from natural disasters and man-made misfortunes, support for education, research, transportation and environmental protection, the rule of law, and so on—common sense would seem to call for alertness to all developments that may further erode national cohesion.

It should also be clear that national cohesion is not incompatible with necessary international cooperation on global problems. Indeed, effective international cooperation is probably less likely to the extent it may have to depend on weak or unstable nations.

At its core, national cohesion is inextricably linked to shared emotions as much as, or more than, shared opinions about critical issues. As a prime example, a shared sense of pride in being an American has led to powerful cohesion. It can supersede a vast number of differences of opinion over issues; on a good day, our Congress demonstrates that. Another example is how the nation (at least temporarily) has come together in times of crisis such as the attacks of September 11, 2001, and the devastation caused by hurricanes Katrina and Sandy. The most profound example in our collective memory, however, was World War II.

With these various examples of working together in mind, consider the problem of national cohesion in the light of what we have deemed are standards of citizenship, that is, what criteria one must meet in order to even be considered an American.

Toward the end of President Lyndon Johnson's Administration, I got an assignment that was quite fascinating: scrutiny of the seven ways that Congress had said a person would lose U.S. citizenship and drafting the Attorney General's opinion on how valid these seven ways still were in light of a recent Supreme Court case.

Beys Afroyim was a Polish-born American citizen, naturalized in 1926, who went to Israel and voted in an election there in 1951. Nine years later, when he tried to renew his American passport, the State Department refused and declared that voting in a foreign election constituted a renunciation of his U.S. citizenship.

He sued, and the case of Afroyim v. Rusk made it all the way to Supreme Court in 1967. (Dean Rusk was listed as the defendant in his role as Secretary of State.) The Supreme Court decided in Afroyim's favor, which set the legal precedent that a U.S. citizen cannot be deprived of American citizenship involuntarily.

This created great confusion in two places: the State Department's Bureau of Consular Affairs, which issues and revokes passports, and the Immigration and Naturalization Service (INS). The question was whether or not the each of the seven provisions was still valid in light of the Supreme Court's determination that citizenship could not be taken away without a person's consent.

I reviewed the provisions to prepare an opinion for the Attorney General to send to the State Department and the INS. I had to analyze myriad kinds of conduct and determine in each case whether it was ambiguous or clearly indicated that the person now regarded himself as part of another nation.

The angles of the issue could incite debates of all kinds. Voting in a foreign election could mean voting for a prime minister, or voting in a local election affecting schools. If you had your kids in that foreign school, the issue would be important to your family, but not indicate an interest in renouncing your citizenship. So I went through the list and gave pros and cons about them with that kind of legal dichotomy in mind.

I sent my draft opinion to Attorney General Ramsey Clark, who was set to leave office in a couple of days. He called a meeting about the document with me and my immediate boss. We proceeded to the Attorney General's private office, which has a nice fireplace.

He told us he had read the opinion that had been prepared for his signature. He was disturbed by it. He hesitated to sign it. He said, in deciding which provisions are still viable and which are not, that the Supreme Court opinion sums up the critical issue in this way: whether or not the person's action shows a transfer of allegiance.

Clark then said something like, "Aren't we giving too much value to allegiance to a given nation? What about people who feel an allegiance to the world? To all humanity?"

My boss and I kept our mouths shut. We had done a whole year of work on this and got a response that spun the whole discussion into some other philosophical universe. I thought, "Clark is on the federal payroll and he's acting like he's Prime Minister of the Globe."

My boss, who was rather sensitive, said to the Attorney General, "We really shouldn't dump this problem on your successor because it's a very time-consuming issue. Also, State and INS have been waiting anxiously for a year for an opinion and they don't know what to do with cases like this until they get it." And then he proposed revising the wording to lay less stress on allegiance.

So, he took it home and brought it back the next day, which was about a day before the Attorney General's term of office was to end. He deleted the word "allegiance" and put in another word that he dreamed up. Something intended to mean the same thing.

Clark signed it.

Ramsey Clark's history since he left the government could have been suggested by this incident. He has worked hard for his reputation as some kind of advanced humanitarian activist. For one, he served as a defense attorney for Saddam Hussein, the former dictator of Iraq. To put it politely, he was some strain of advanced thinker.

This question of allegiance is still very much alive with issues of dual citizenship constantly creeping into the national conversation.

Each nation decides for itself what constitutes citizenship, so the United States can't decide who is a citizen of France or South Korea, for example, but it can certainly decide who abides by its own criteria for citizenship.

I read a letter to the *Washington Post* in which a woman openly described herself as a citizen of both the United States and the United Kingdom. From an American perspective, that's hard to understand. When you become a naturalized citizen, you foreswear allegiance to other governments. Yet each nation has the power to decide who one of its citizens is.

> **Text of the Oath of Allegiance**
>
> I hereby declare, on oath, that I absolutely and entirely renounce and abjure all allegiance and fidelity to any foreign prince, potentate, state, or sovereignty, of whom or which I have heretofore been a subject or citizen; that I will support and defend the Constitution and the laws of the United States of America against all enemies, foreign and domestic; that I will bear true faith and allegiance to the same; that I will bear arms on behalf of the United States when required by law; that I will perform work of national importance under civilian direction when required by law; and that I take this obligation freely, without any mental reservation or purpose of evasion, so help me God.

The ideological discussion of whether or not independent nation-states are a good thing has engendered a lot of serious conversation among intellectuals, and you find it discussed as a practical matter among people in multi-national corporations who have their feet on the soil of many countries doing business.

From both my professional and personal point of view, I think that the nation-state is a good invention, just like the family is a good invention. Just because some families are lousy or dysfunctional doesn't mean families should be abolished.

While some nations have been, or still are, excessively nationalistic or dysfunctional, that doesn't mean that nation states should be on the way out. A world of good nation-states can provide democracy, human rights, security, and experimental laboratories that may point the way to progress for other nations. In order to provide the most significant benefits, national cohesion is required.

And our national cohesion does not conflict with our cooperating and perhaps sometimes helping other nationals in appropriate situations.

In the detailed discussions of solutions to problems in Part Three, there is no discrete focus on solving the problem of diminished national cohesion. The reason is this: Cohesion comes out of shared ideals, values, goals, experiences, and even shared enemies. When a nation embodies as much diversity as the United States does, it may not be possible to nurture the kind of cohesion that a more homogeneous population could achieve. This reality does not diminish the importance of the problem; it simply makes the solution elusive. That said, I have devoted Part Two to some key characteristics of our population to suggest steps toward ways we might pull together as a nation a bit more.

Values

As I noted in Chapter 2, "values" refers to cultural attitudes that help maintain a successful society and can be summarized as good will plus good sense. Two key forms of values problems in our society are extremism and corruption.

Extremism

I define extremism in a typical way as the quality or state of being extreme. It is a unique problem because extremism is applauded when large numbers of people agree with the logic or morality of the extreme behavior or point of view. It might also be condemned and incite a violent response if enough people fear and/or abhor the expression of extremism.

Three clichés shape the discussion of extremism in this chapter, which illustrates how we have at times cheered, and at times denounced, extremism.

- Might makes right.
- Birds of a feather flock together.
- More is better.

Before exploring manifestations of extremism that have been problematic in American society, consider this: Those who adopt an extreme point of view often find themselves sounding a great deal like those who espouse the opposite point of view.

Might makes right.

Throughout American history, we have had numerous examples of extremism in which the cliché "might makes right" comes to life. In other words, people with an extreme point of view prevailed because they were more powerful. Prohibition is one example. The temperance movement had the might of a great number of women in the citizenry as well as men who joined with them with a passionate commitment to elevate morality in society. During the thirteen years the United States had Prohibition, many came to agree with famed journalist H.L. Mencken who wrote: "There is not less drunkenness in the Republic, but more. There is not less crime, but more. There is not less insanity, but more. The cost of government is not smaller, but vastly greater. Respect for law has not increased, but diminished."

On the federal level, a might-makes-right mentality may take hold whenever the same party occupies the White House and holds the majority of seats in the houses of Congress. An analogous situation occurs on the state and local levels as well when there is prolonged and over-whelming party dominance.

During the New Deal years when I was in college (1936-40), the young lawyers who were known as Felix Frankfurter's "happy hot dogs" had impressed me. Frank-furter was a Harvard Law professor (and later Supreme Court Justice) who sent these young lawyers to Washing-ton, DC to play an important role in crafting New Deal policies. I would say that my respect for lawyers like that, as well as for President Roosevelt himself, influenced my decision to go to law school and my interest in affecting politics in my hometown of New York City.

Roosevelt did not like the big Democratic machine in New York City known as Tammany Hall, which was corrupt as well as powerful, and he tried to break it. Orig-inally, Tammany Hall was an actual place on East 14th Street, where the Tammany Society built its strength and reputation by helping immigrants get their citizenship, find jobs and housing, and gain political clout in the mid-19th century. All these people could then vote for Tamma-ny candidates, so the Hall's influence grew to enormous proportions.

Roosevelt did not immediately succeed in breaking Tammany Hall's lock on Democratic politics in New York, but he did get some important assistance in the form of Fiorello LaGuardia. LaGuardia was a very popular, three-term mayor of New York, but a bit unusual in that he was a Republican supporter of the New Deal and associated closely with an anti-Tammany group that supported Roo-sevelt's bid for re-election to the Presidency in 1936.

The effort to clean up the Democratic Party in New York continued for many years after World War II, with the battles occurring on a precinct-by-precinct basis. I got linked in with anti-Tammany volunteers during that time.

Just before the election of 1948, in October and November, I would stand after dark on cold street corners somewhere on upper Broadway and take a little two-step folding wooden ladder—my "soapbox"—with an American flag and a photograph of the person running for office. There was practically no one on the street standing still. They were scurrying to stores and to their homes. And I would start talking. The trick was to see if, under those frigid circumstances, I could build up a crowd. It gave me an experience that a person doesn't normally get in the ordinary range of public speaking.

I spoke without any outline or script. What I said contained two themes: the contrast between the insurgents who were trying to take the organization away from Tammany Hall (in terms of their character, honesty, and qualifications), and how this might benefit the people in that neighborhood through improved services, lower taxes, and so on.

I tried to engage in dialogue with passersby so they would stop. It's a standard trick for trying to build up a crowd. I probably would not have confronted them about an issue like, "What do you think about your taxes?" It might have been, "Where did you get that beautiful jacket?" The point is to be cordial and inviting, or at least interesting.

I was talking at the top of my lungs, but I couldn't keep that up very long—maybe fifteen minutes—because I had no public address system.

In addition to making the speeches on the folding ladder, I met the opposition head on. The pro-Tammany Hall people had panel trucks and a microphone, so the speaker was high above the crowd and able to command a lot of attention. I went to one of those meetings and heckled the speaker, poking holes in his pitch. That gave me a large audience without having to get a truck or wear out my voice.

When the election was over, the speechifying stopped, but the leaders of Tammany Hall geared up their efforts in other ways to defend themselves against the rebels they saw as trying to take over the leadership of the Democratic Party. Carmine DeSapio, who turned out to be the last leader of Tammany Hall, decided he wanted to get some young lawyers who worked for prestigious firms on his side. I attended a luncheon meeting where he spoke to about ten of us.

DeSapio didn't impress any of us very much. He was wearing dark sunglasses, even though the luncheon was indoors, but it was more than that. What he said offended people, or at least didn't engage them. He described the volunteer work he was offering, but said nothing about the more fundamental questions of public policy—not city policy, state, national, or foreign—which are the reasons that people with a civic consciousness would get involved in politics. We were well-educated, idealistic people and by not even mentioning policy, DeSapio lost everyone in the room. We weren't yet deeply into the financial rat race in our law firms and he missed a chance to keep our eyes trained on making a difference.

He failed, possibly because he was so young himself at the time. When De Sapio took over as head of Tammany Hall in 1949, at 41, he was the youngest boss in the history of the Hall. Thanks largely to the efforts of Eleanor Roosevelt, Tammany Hall collapsed completely in 1961—after exercising influence over New York politics for 150 years. She spent years marshalling the forces against DeSapio because she blamed him for derailing her son Franklin D. Roosevelt, Jr.'s political ambitions. It's a good illustration of how "might makes right" only until someone or something mightier comes along.

Birds of a feather flock together.

Much of reality television reflects a form of extremism engendered by what many people deem entertaining and/or that makes them feel good. This is the shallow end of the pool in terms of groupthink, much like a widespread and disproportional appreciation for a certain type of physical beauty. On the deep end, it could be a point of view about a social issue, such as amnesty for illegal immigrants, which great numbers of people embrace even though a great number also see that as an extreme position.

Regardless of what these large numbers of people agree on, sharing an extreme thought as a "value" of our democracy is potentially destructive. Hence, I see some groupthink as major problem that can be a cornerstone of extreme behavior. This affects both the leaders and the membership of many groups.

Groupthink means going along with what others think or say instead of thinking for yourself. The old saying "birds of a feather flock together" may help to illuminate groupthink. Groupthink is partly inevitable, but we need to recognize it and at times question it. Groupthink may be either established ideas or innovative ones.

When should we question groupthink? The easy answer is when things seem to be going wrong. A smarter answer, perhaps, is before things seem to be going wrong.

Like all nations we always have had a fair amount of groupthink, and we will always have some of it. It's a lot easier than thinking for yourself, and it's often safer, at least in the short run. It's reflected in popular sayings such as "go along to get along" and "don't make waves." Another example, "forty million Frenchmen can't be wrong." Oh, yeah? What about when they built the Maginot Line, the barrier built after World War I between France and Germany meant to keep the Germans out? Even those who know little about World War II know that it took Germany little more than a month to conquer France.

When our country was founded in the late 1700s, the prevailing groupthink in the Western world was that a nation consisted of several established classes: royalty, nobility, yeomanry, bourgeoisie, and peasantry or serfs. Our Declaration of Independence was a highly contrarian rejection of that prevailing groupthink. Our founders thought for themselves and sometimes disagreed with each other, but believed in trying to compromise their differences in the interest of progress.

Our history includes several big disasters caused in part by policies that involved groupthink. The Civil War was caused in part by the groupthink of extremists such as those who attacked Fort Sumter and John Brown who attacked Harpers Ferry. The Great Depression was caused in part by the groupthink of the 1920's of easy come, easy go, which merged into anything goes. Anything goes also seems to be a kind of groupthink that affects Wall Street from time to time. Persistent kinds of groupthink become part of the culture of various groups. The rise of aggressors that led to World War II was facilitated by the groupthink in the democracies of isolationism, pacifism and appeasement. The aggression itself was largely based on official groupthink fostered by the Nazis, Mussolini, and the Japanese militarists.

Recent history shows the persistence of groupthink regardless of which political party is in power. We got badly bogged down in Vietnam under the Democrats because, naturally enough, the situation was viewed in the context of the Cold War. Yet a more careful analysis of Vietnam would have noted that nationalism and anti-colonialism were at least as strong motivations as communism. In our second war with Iraq the administration assumed that by getting rid of the brutal dictator Saddam Hussein we would be greeted as liberators and our job would be completed. This assumed that the population of Iraq would act like the populations of France, Norway, and others when we freed them from Hitler's armies, disregarding important differences in the history and culture of these nations. Also disregarded was our own history of botched occupations after the Civil and Spanish-American wars, contrasted with our successful occupations of Germany and Japan after World War II.

Now for an alert about three pitfalls that relate to groupthinks. First, if those who belong to an institution, such as a business or government agency, a professional, religious or political organization, and so on sometimes disagree among themselves, that demonstrates that the institution is open-minded and free of groupthink. Not necessarily. Although a division within an institution may reflect or stimulate individual thinking, it may simply mean that the institution is divided on one issue among many, or is divided into two kinds of groupthink. It does not prove that the persons in the institution are thinking independently on all matters affecting the institution.

The second pitfall: If you or I agree with what others are saying and writing, aren't we engaging in groupthink? Again, not necessarily. If we subject what others say or write to our critical consideration and then agree, with or without some reservations, we're not guilty of groupthink.

The third pitfall: groupthink is wrong. Again, not necessarily. Both history and common experience have many examples of correct groupthink. However, these examples may have followed incorrect groupthink, with the transition based on individual thinking, sometimes stimulated by unhappy developments.

Perhaps a useful way for citizens to limit the damage from misleading groupthink is to form the habit of trying to evaluate what they read on a scale between advocacy at one end and, at the other end, factual reporting and challenges to prevailing assumptions.

We have oodles of advocacy in our newspapers, editorials, letters, op-eds, commentary, plus material in magazines, books, websites, talk radio, TV, sermons, blogs, speeches, and more. Sometimes advocacy is mixed with factual reporting or challenges to prevailing assumptions. And there's usually nothing wrong with advocacy, if it's not deceptive, if it deals with something that merits attention, and if it's subjected to competing viewpoints. In fact, advocacy is necessary for progress in our democracy, in our economy and in the rest of our culture, and it's protected by the First Amendment. Today advocacy in all its forms is one of America's dominating industries, our great MAPPAC (our Marketing – Advertising – Public Relations – Punditry and Advocacy Complex).

But advocacy is not enough. Reading or listening to most pieces of advocacy may produce agreement, disagreement, confusion or boredom, but it seldom stimulates much thinking.

A recent article is a striking exception to the general run of advocacy communications. In a sense it is advocacy against advocacy, or more precisely against the common practice of accepting or rejecting advocacy by the careless method of groupthink. Instead it insists on individual thinking, at least by those who may participate in some kind of leadership.

This article was a lecture to the class of plebes (freshman cadets) at the US Military Academy at West Point. The lecture was printed as a 12-page lead article in spring 2010 issue of the American Scholar, with the title of "Solitude and Leadership." The author, William Deresiewicz, is an essayist and critic who had spent ten years teaching at Yale University, and had written an earlier article on the "The Disadvantages of an Elite Education."

The long and short of "Solitude and Leadership" is that the student in West Point and other leading colleges are supposedly being trained to assume leadership roles, either in the Army or in other institutions, but that real leaders are not those who play the game of career advancement to get ahead, but those who think for themselves about how the organization they work for should function. The article cites the real leadership of Gen. David Petraeus, who turned around the operations of our Army, which had been bogged down in Iraq. Despite the word "solitude" in the title, the article does not say that independent thinking must be done alone, and in fact it describes how discussion with another person may improve individual thinking.

The article severely criticizes many widespread practices by persons in large organizations in business, government, academia, and so on, particularly behavior that wastes time on what are often just fads and distractions. For example, it says, "Multitasking is not only not thinking, it impairs your ability to think. Thinking means concentrating on one thing long enough to develop an idea about it."

History contains many examples of disasters such as wars and depressions that are caused in part by groupthink. In retrospect, it's quite clear that World Wars I and II, the Great Depression, and even the Civil War were unnecessary. (Great Britain ended slavery without a war.)

The success of democracy partly depends on the compromise of conflicting positions. A bad case of groupthink can obstruct the development of acceptable compromises and the development of useful new ideas.

More is better.

The section on our nation's economic problems examines this cliché (or to some, a mantra) in terms of the effects of extreme consumerism and extreme capitalistic impulses on our economic stability. In this chapter, I want to focus on a complex example of "more is better" in terms of our fundamental rights as citizens.

National cohesion, which is a topic explored earlier in this chapter, can suffer a near-fatal blow when the people of a nation feel that they receive different treatment legally based on who they are. While "Equal Justice

Under Law" are the noble words engraved on the U.S. Supreme Court's building in Washington, D.C., every knowledgeable citizen knows they represent an ideal more than a reality. Why? A piece of the answer is how the cliché "more is better" operates within the legal community.

My long and varied experience as a lawyer may help shed more light on this. My decision in 1939 to go to law school had been inspired by the young lawyers in Washington who devised improvements in many fields that are still serving our country. But World War II interrupted my years in law school, and when I graduated in 1947 Washington seemed to be stalled, so I took a job in a big Wall Street law firm. After Harry Truman's surprise defeat of Thomas Dewey in 1948, Washington seemed more inviting and, newly married in December 1949, I took a job in the new slum clearance program. I then spent six years with the Civil Aeronautics Board, mostly on the expansion of our country's airlines. Finally I moved to the Justice Department's Office of Legal Counsel (a decidedly newsworthy operation in the early Twenty-first Century for its opinions about torture related to terrorists), which handled an incredible variety of legal and practical problems, some of them arising from major historical developments like the Cold War and the Civil Rights era. After concentrating on problems under the Freedom of Information Act from all over the government, I was appointed Director of the Office of Information Law and Policy. When I finally retired from government I divided my time between an excellent law firm near our home in Bethesda, Maryland, consulting for an American Bar Association Committee, and launching a civic group focused on national policy concerns. In short, without trying to sound noble, I did what I thought a lawyer should do: apply my knowledge of the law and experience for the benefit of fellow citizens.

The law and the work of lawyers today has become so complex it's hard to describe briefly, but here are two efforts: First, law is a means of social control which involves penalties prescribed by governments. Second, law is a large subculture consisting of many sub-subcultures, such as criminal law, contract law, tort law, litigation, counseling, negotiations, lobbying, advocacy, adjudication in various tribunals with varying jurisdictions and procedures, legislation and rule-making, plus various kinds of international law, tax law, military law, real estate law, domestic relations, and many other specialties.

How does law affect the average citizen? In many ways, some of which we are rarely aware of.

The good news is that American law is a blessing that protects the personal rights and opportunities of everyone, because of our longstanding structure of a Constitution with its Bill of Rights, plus statutory, judicial and regulatory law that can only be changed through procedures that are at least potentially under the control of the citizenry. Those who have lived under autocracies will tell you that American law, despite its frustrations, is far better than living under tyrants.

The bad news is symbolized by an old saying, "Ignorance of the law is no excuse." Today, however, ignorance of much of the law is inevitable. Lawyers themselves often turn to specialists, and sometimes the specialists have to report that the law itself is unclear.

Partly as a result of this growing complexity, which can have important financial and other effects on individuals, small businesses, communities, regions, and so on, there are now huge law firms, containing more than a thousand, or even more than 2,000 lawyers.

These large firms can offer more complete services to their clients, typically large corporations, than could a smaller firm, partly by operating in several nations, and partly by more completely fortifying a client's goals, by an intense analysis of known concerns ("the devil is in the details") and by a comprehensive review of the client's peripherals, to minimize the risk that the client may unexpectedly be blind-sided.

These kinds of in-depth legal services can be quite expensive, perhaps beyond the means of most clients. Therein lies the problem of the more-is-better type of extremism.

Bear in mind that when a person needs a doctor, the doctor's fees are usually paid either by health insurance or some public program like Medicare or Medicaid. Not so as to most lawyers' fees. Although lawyers will often be willing to sue for damages in personal injury cases on a contingency fee basis, and the government may pay for lawyers for criminal defendants, most legal work is charged to the client, and when the client cannot or will not pay for it the work isn't done, unless lawyers will do it on a "pro bono" or charitable basis. And since a great deal of legal work is billed on a per-hour basis, clients may not know in advance how large the bill might be. As a result, large corporations and very rich individuals may receive legal services of a quantity and quality seldom provided to others.

These cost considerations do not affect only average citizens and small businesses. They also affect government prosecutors and regulatory agencies, all of which must operate within their budgets. For the cost of prosecuting the murder charge against a well-healed and well-lawyered defendant like O.J. Simpson, a Heisman Trophy winner and National Football League star, the prosecutor's office probably could have brought cases against several run-of-the-mill defendants.

If the possible defendants are large corporations and their top officials, prosecutors or regulatory agencies think twice before starting a big battle. They did so effectively in the case of Enron, but did not bring criminal charges against the big tobacco companies, which had marketed cigarettes known to be addictive and causes of lethal diseases like lung cancer. When I commented to a friend who was also a lawyer on this failure to prosecute the tobacco companies, he gave me the probable answer, saying, "They have too much money."

Corruption

No discussion of America's problems can avoid the topic of corruption in the political and governmental arenas, since politicians are located between us citizens and the nation's policies, together with the way policies are administered. Corruption in the legal arena merits attention as well. Lawyers and judges have a professional responsibility to honor the nation's policies at the same time they have a responsibility to try to change them when policies conflict with laws.

It's important to look at the definition of political arena in the broadest sense, since anyone from a city council member to the President of the United States operates there.

Corruption, as the word is usually understood in the United States, is a worldwide phenomenon, but it is not considered wrong in all locations. One of my co-author Maryann's associates, who had been with the Central Intelligence Agency as a clandestine officer for more than two decades, noted that agents would commonly be briefed on the standard corruption practices in other countries so they could be sure to get their phone service installed and their utilities turned on. In short, in many countries it has long been accepted as the normal or principal method of compensating government personnel. This did not stop Congress from passing the Foreign Corrupt Practices Act, making it a crime for American business people to make payments to foreign officials that their business competitors from other countries were free to make. This is very much in the news as I write this, with the CEO of the Las Vegas Sands Corporation accused of violating the Act in his payments to a Macau (China) lawyer who represented his firm's interests in this booming gambling capital in the People's Republic of China.

But the United States itself has had a long history of accepting certain kinds of behavior that arguably should be considered corrupt. This is not just a matter of corrupt big-city machines such as once flourished in New York, Chicago, and other cities. It has long been a factor at the federal level as well. During George Washington's first term as president, there was a small after-dinner meeting in New York called by Secretary of State Thomas Jefferson and attended by Secretary of Treasury Alexander Hamilton, and Vice President John Adams. As Jefferson recorded the conversation, Hamilton said that a government free of corruption would be "impracticable." (The

Life and Selected Writings of Thomas Jefferson, Random House, 1944, pp 126-127.) Jefferson went on to say that Hamilton's views did not reflect on his personal character, but only on his political philosophy.

Fast forward to today, looking at the cultural picture, and briefly at how our culture is reflected in our laws.

It would probably be safe to say that most Americans see nothing wrong in making small political contributions, and in fact this is often considered a laudable exercise of civic responsibility in our democracy. Large contributions, however, are often seen as an effort to buy influence, perhaps for the benefit of wealthy interests. And in-between sizes of contributions may be seen as a kind of insurance to assure access to those in power, but not undue influence.

As to the law, the regulation of campaign contributions has a long and complex history, including a controversial U.S. Supreme Court decision in 2010 that corporations have a right to free speech that includes a right to make campaign contributions.

This subject is too complex to discuss here. But one thing that seems to be basic in the law of corruption is whether there was a "quid pro quo." In other words, was there an agreement that, in return for money or something else of value the recipient will behave in a certain way in his governmental activity?

If such an agreement can be proved, it is usually considered bribery and both parties to the agreement may go to jail. But sometimes no agreement can be proved, perhaps because there was no actual agreement, except a reasonable expectation by both parties that favors by one would lead to favors by the other. Is that corruption in fact if not in law? Or is it just human nature, indeed laudable courtesy, to be nice to those who have been nice to you?

To give a simple categorical yes or no answer to this question doesn't work. What helps is to consider the conflicts of interest in the person who accepts money or other benefits, such as switching from a job in a regulatory agency to a job with higher pay in a company subject to that agency's regulation. Bluntly put, does the hope or chance for a nice corporate job impair the duty of the agency official or employee to protect the investing, consuming, or traveling public?

In today's world, almost every adult in an advanced nation is subject to potential conflicts of interest. The most common kind of conflict is allocating time and attention between family and occupation. Other claims on one's support may come from faith groups, neighborhood groups, political groups, the nation, trans-national interests, professional affiliations, old friends, and others.

With this reality as a background, governmental corruption can properly be seen as subordinating the interests of the general public, or of one's constituents, or of the part of the public covered by the laws that one has been assigned to administer, in favor of other interests, including one's own interests.

A good model for applying this conflict-of-interest concept to the problem of corruption can be drawn from the traditional professions: the duty of the doctor to the patient, of the lawyer to the client, of the clergyman to the parishioner, of the military officer to the nation, and might we add, of the public official or employee, whether elected or appointed, to the citizenry.

Perhaps the best way to think of corruption is that it is a breach of trust, knowingly engaged in by a government person, contrary to that person's duty to the general public, or to a sector of the public as prescribed by law, which subordinates the interests of that public to some narrower interest and to the person's own financial interests. With this concept in mind both individuals and institutions may perform better.

Would Jefferson and Hamilton agree with this clarification of corruption? Probably Jefferson would, but I'm not sure about Hamilton. Maybe Hamilton would rationalize a government official accepting benefits from some business interest by reasoning that if the business is good for the public, accepting the benefits will serve the public and, thus, is okay.

The two greatest safeguards against corruption, over and beyond laws against bribery, would seem to be transparency for dubious activities and respect for conflict-of-interest standards. It's particularly important that the actual source of large donations be public information.

PART TWO – APPROACHES TO SOLUTIONS

General Observations

6

Solutions from Changes in Human Culture
Solutions from Improved Enculturation
Solutions from Risk-Taking
Solutions: Fix It or Scrap It?
Unintended Consequences of Solutions

It's silly to expect a good solution to any problem if we don't understand the nature of the problem. As I noted in Chapter 1, our collective problems are rooted in Mother Nature, human nature and human culture. That is, the environment and its resources, our characteristics as human beings, and all learned and shared kinds of human behavior and attitudes.

Even though Mother Nature has some capacity to repair or to adapt to some adverse developments, that capacity offers little hope for solving most of the problems spotlighted in Part One.

Similarly, changing human nature in itself is not a source of solutions because human nature cannot be changed. It's true that the practical impact of human nature on behavior can be changed in various ways, including an effective involvement of what Abraham Lincoln called "the better angels of our nature." But such involvements must be formulated and applied from within human cultures.

Solutions from Changes in Human Culture

Most solutions to our problems, therefore, must be found within human cultures. These solutions may sometimes include technological changes. But bear in mind that the development and utilization of technologies is itself a cultural phenomenon. It's true that individual inventors may play an important role in such changes. However, their contributions partly depend on prior developments, and the acceptance and uses of their inventions clearly depend on prevailing cultures.

Solving problems by offering a new and better element in some culture or subculture doesn't necessarily succeed. Some new culture elements are contagious and spread easily; others do not. The invention of the safety pin was contagious; the concept of separation of church and state has been far less contagious. Sometimes a single event moves an element from one side to the other. For example, for generations, our population has resisted widespread gun-control measures and rooted their argument in Second Amendment rights. The anti-gun lobby did not have a contagious solution to the problem of gun-related violence. After the December 2012 massacre of school children and teachers at the Sandy Hook Elementary School, however, it was the opposing side, represented vocally by the National Rifle Association that seemed to have a less contagious idea (that is, placing armed guards at all schools). Instead, ideas such as controlling military-type guns or taking additional measures to deny guns to those diagnosed with a mental illness attracted additional attention.

We can summarize this preliminary general discussion of solutions in a practical, useful way:

1. We can solve most of our problems if we apply enough of two things, both of which can be found

in our culture: good will and good sense. Here's the rub: Both differ from person to person to some extent. This is where groupthink—described as a problem in Part One—actually may have a positive component, in true yin/yang fashion. In other words, some parts of groupthink may be essential to a successful culture.

2. If we agree that good will consists of applying the Golden Rule, otherwise known as the ethic of reciprocity, then solutions to our problems will be shaped by the pressure to "do unto others..." Of course, we have to make appropriate adjustments for preferences that may differ from our own, and for the careful application of "tough love" in order to deter clearly harmful conduct.

3. Good sense consists of common sense plus uncommon sense. Common sense can generally be found from experience, both the everyday kinds and the kinds that can be extracted from a careful examination of history, or from the experiences of people in other places. Uncommon sense may be more difficult, because, in addition to risking the irritation or opposition of some people, uncommon sense requires (a) the ferreting-out of all assumptions, (b) critical thinking, sometimes called the scientific method, which includes the collection of facts by observation or experiment, and (c) the rigorous application of open-minded deliberative skills.

Solutions from Improved Enculturation

The 2013 violence at the Boston Marathon and at Connecticut's Sandy Hook Elementary School in 2012, plus other mass killings in recent years, call for expanding our awareness about the importance of enculturation. Most of these events have been placed into either of two policy categories: gun control or protection from terrorism. That's valid to some extent, but attention should also be given to something that almost all of these tragedies have in common, namely, that almost without exception they all were committed by young adult males who were inadequately enculturated.

American anthropologist Conrad Phillip Kottak explains in his book *Window on Humanity:*

> Enculturation is the process where the culture that is currently established teaches an individual the accepted norms and values of the culture or society where the individual lives. The individual can become an accepted member and fulfill the needed functions and roles of the group. Most importantly the individual knows and establishes a context of boundaries and accepted behavior that dictates what is acceptable and not acceptable within the framework of that society. It teaches the individual their role within society as well as what is accepted behavior within that society and lifestyle

Traditionally, young males were enculturated by their families, schools, and faith and recreational groups. Today, however, the mix of enculturating inputs includes violent commercial entertainment, a great variety of online materials that generate attractions and repulsions of many kinds, and a globalized influx of many cultures and subcultures, some of which resist assimilation in modern democracies.

At the same time, the enculturating power of families and schools has weakened. Many families now have only one parent, or have two parents, both of whom work full time. Schools and colleges face many pressures that narrow their goals to training for jobs, neglecting subjects that help develop healthy civic and social perspectives.

How do we address these problems? Obviously, our schools and immigration policies need attention. Schools and colleges should emphasize that both personal and national success require enculturation that meets three requirements: (1) self control, (2) basic interpersonal skills, and (3) responsibility to those who serve us or need us. Immigration should include evaluation of persons seeking entry and adequate education for citizenship. And, of course, our families and entertainment sectors need heightened awareness of the need for society to address the challenge of under-enculturated young men (and women). If we don't, the impacts on our way of life, including our safety and personal freedoms, are profoundly negative, as we have seen.

Solutions from Risk-Taking

Although it's wise to be careful about important things, history also shows us that taking serious risks is sometimes justified or even necessary to avoid even greater misfortunes. Examples: Abraham Lincoln's recognition that the attack on Fort Sumter required an armed response in order to avoid the dissolution of the United States, and Franklin Roosevelt's decision to give fifty de-

stroyers to England to help that nation survive Hitler's
power. A similar example on a personal level is to un-
dergo the risks of surgery in order to combat—or in the
case of women with the BRCA genes, to avert—a serious
illness.

Solutions: Fix It or Scrap It?

One form of extremism occurs when any part of a
nation's culture isn't working well, so the trend is to drop
it rather than fix it. Sometimes dropping it is the right
solution, as in the cases of dueling and slavery. But experience shows that dropping a troublesome subculture is
sometimes a poor idea. Here are three examples:

- The early years of the industrial revolution (the
  early 1800's in England, and the late 1800's in the
  United States) were very harsh on a large part of
  the population. One response to this was communism, which finally was adopted in Russia, China,
  and several other nations. Now, decades later, communism has been abandoned almost everywhere
  because of its poor productivity, although the name
  "Communist" has been kept in China to describe a
  capitalist economy with an autocratic government.
  But most capitalistic nations have dealt with its
  harshness by a series of reforms.
- A second example is our consuming culture, which
  has included alcoholic beverages. Alcohol abuse
  was especially severe in the late 19th and early 20th
  centuries, partly due to extreme working conditions
  from which many sought relief in a bottle. After
  some limited attempts to reduce excessive drink-

ing, our nation adopted the Prohibition Amendment to the Constitution. After slightly more than ten years, it became clear that Prohibition was doing more harm than good and it was repealed. (This failure could easily have been foreseen, because a majority of adult Americans used alcohol, and most of those users consumed it in moderation with pleasure and little or no adverse effects.)

- The third possible example, which is still somewhat unclear, is abolishing capital punishment. It has been abolished in many European nations and in a number of states in the United States. There are good arguments against capital punishment, some of which are well-supported by its history, especially when administered to a defendant who did not receive a fully adequate legal defense, or when race prejudice was a factor in the result. Nevertheless, public opinion polls in both Europe and the United States show that a large part of the public has misgivings about the total abolition of capital punishment. This sentiment may parallel several actions of the Supreme Court, which ruled against capital punishment but soon reversed that ruling, and overturned other previous rulings on capital punishment. Between 1879 and 2009, the Supreme Court made 43 rulings on the issue of capital punishment and three of them overturned others. One example is a 2005 ruling that overturned a 1989 ruling stating that the Eighth Amendment does not prohibit the death penalty for crimes committed at age sixteen or seventeen.

The past and present defects of capital punishment would seem to be remediable.

First, traditional modes of administering it, such as hanging, the electric chair, a firing squad, or use of a series of three injections, are not necessary. Use of a general anesthetic would make the prolongation of a blood donation procedure totally painless.

Second, considering the vast amounts of money spent on some kinds of litigation, paying for a fully adequate defense in a capital case is clearly the right thing to do. And to make even more certain that justice is done, both federal and state pardon offices could be expanded and assigned to make a careful and thorough review of capital cases for possible commutation or pardon.

Third, we perhaps should ask ourselves: What do we mean by a "human being" in referring to a person on trial in a capital case? To make this point clear, supposed that Adolph Hitler had been captured before he committed suicide. Was he a human being? Yes, in the biological sense of the term. But in terms of his behavior, and character, perhaps he would be better described as an inhuman being. If he had been a defendant in the Nuremburg trials after World War II, would those who are totally opposed to capital punishment oppose it in his case?

Fourth, we should consider death in the light of all aspects of our civilization. In many cases death is a tragedy. In some cases, however, it is a release from severe unhappiness. Unfortunately, our culture includes activities that kill many innocent people. Such deaths are many times more numerous than those resulting from sentences for crimes.

Opponents of the death penalty might also weigh their priorities against other governmental policies that cause death. Under traditional military law, failing asleep on watch duty in war time is a capital offense, and an enemy who is captured while not wearing the enemy uniform is deemed a spy and may be shot. Much more common are governmental failures to provide adequate and timely life-saving services, such as ambulances and emergency food, shelter, and medical care, including preventative care. In addition, government programs to reduce lethal hazards in many kinds of activities could be improved to reduce tragic deaths. The number of innocent people killed by drunk or reckless driving far outnumbers the number executed after conviction of murder in a civilian court.

This calls to mind so many gray-area "solutions" to problems, such as former New York Mayor Michael Bloomberg's initiative to outlaw super-sized soft drinks as a way of countering obesity and related health issues in his city. In the harsh light of science, not just public opinion, is this a real solution, or the way to sidestep a problem?

The impulse to scrap rather than to fix some part of our culture sometimes even extends to such basic institutions as the family and the sovereign nation-state. It is perfectly clear that some families and some nations are seriously dysfunctional and do serious harm. The difficulties of curing their shortcomings lead some to favor their abolition. The case against families is made by some libertarians who reject the constraints and responsibilities required for family success. The case against the nation-state is based on the history of excessive nationalism and on the difficulty of obtaining enough national cooperation to solve global problems. But anyone who reflects on the many vital roles of families and nations in maintaining civilization will hesitate to join those who would scrap either of these institutions.

Here is another general observation about possible solutions to problems: Part of a solution is whether and how the solution might be put into effect. Even a solution that's great in theory falls short if the implementation misses the mark. As a corollary, when it does, the unintended consequences of the solution have the potential to be worse than the original problem.

Consideration of a possible solution should therefore include its possible unintended side effects. For example, parking in post-World War II New York City was tight, but it got much worse due to a well-intentioned decision by Mayor Robert F. Wagner, Jr. The mayor decided to improve street cleaning by prohibiting curb parking on one side of the street on Mondays, Wednesdays, and Fridays, making that side easier to clean, and prohibiting it to the other side on Tuesdays, Thursdays and Saturdays for the same reason. This drove the residents crazy. As more families acquired cars, they wanted free and convenient parking. With the GI Bill of Rights that made it financially easier for middle-class people to buy homes, the city's street cleaning program made the suburbs look like the only reasonable place to be. In addition, the mass movement of middle-class families to the suburbs was an important factor in the tragic deterioration of the city's once-excellent public schools.

A more contemporary example is anti-redlining measures, which are designed to counter long-standing practices of denying, or even charging low-income people more for, certain financial and other services. Among them are laws such as the Home Mortgage Disclosure Act (HMDA) of 1975 and Community Reinvestment Act, a 1977 law. Essentially, they aren't bad laws, but not every part of them stood the test of a good "solution" to the problem of redlining. One outcome was government pressure on banks to offer sub-prime mortgages to people with only marginal capability to repay the loan. To some degree, non-payment of those sub-prime mortgages contributed to the financial implosion in 2007-2008 that led to widespread unemployment, loss of investment income by individuals and organizations, and a massive number of foreclosures.

The lesson: a solution to one problem may create an unexpected problem, and even when the failed solution is abandoned, as in the repeal of Prohibition, the 18th Amendment to the Constitution, it may take a long time to find a better solution to the original problem and to find solutions for the unexpected problems created by the failed solutions.

Avoiding unintended consequences may be one of those areas where human common sense may be supplemented effectively by technology. Computer-generated models used to calculate outcomes have a potential to be a valuable tool. Input your solution, add a few variables, and see if the computer and your common sense match in terms of the consequences of the so-called solution!

Eight Upgrades to Secure Our Nation's Future

7

With the United States' development of nuclear weapons in 1945, the nation became the world's superpower. By many measures, we've also been the richest nation on earth. In many respects that's still true. However, we are only 4 percent of the world's population. And we live in a rapidly changing world. Today we are a debtor nation, and much of the world is growing in wealth, potential power and aspirations. What to do?

We live in a complex and dangerous world. History reveals many great and small nations that have collapsed or suffered greatly. To avoid such misfortunes, we need to upgrade eight things: our understanding of what's happening, and the seven major subcultures on which our behavior, both personal and public, largely depends. Here's a short summary of these needs.

Stronger Situational Awareness

Both leaders and citizens need a more accurate and comprehensive perception of our current situation, and especially of significant trends. This perception must be broadened both time-wise (past, present, future) and subject-wise (environmental resources, demographics, technology, subcultures, and the potentials of groups identified by nationality, socioeconomic class, ethnicity including religion, occupation, generational cohorts, and so on). These subjects warrant attention in other nations and in various parts of our own nation.

Many citizens are aware of the decline and fall of ancient Rome, and the more recent successful transformation of the worldwide British Empire into today's smaller United Kingdom. Such perceptions can be enhanced by, for instance, the best seller *Collapse: How Societies Choose to Fail or Succeed* (Penguin Books, 2005) by Jared Diamond. It describes what happened to several ancient and modern societies affected by threats to their futures. For readers without enough time to read its 500-plus pages, much of the book's benefit can be found in its detailed Table of Contents and in its Part Four: Practical Lessons.

Adjustments in Seven Major Subcultures

(capitalism, religion, law, democracy, technology, enter-tainment and education).

Capitalism

Traditional free-market capitalism has two great virtues and three weaknesses that need attention. Compared to feudalism, mercantilism, or a Soviet-style command economy, capitalism is very productive, providing greatly improved standards of living. Its other great virtue is to harmonize well with important aspects of individual freedom, both through entrepreneurship and by reducing the rigidity of earlier class boundaries based on inherited family status and wealth.

The three weaknesses of capitalism that need attention are its insufficient stability, sustainability, and equity (meaning fairness).

a) Instability: Centuries of boom and bust including the Great Depression and the recent downturn, made clear the problem of instability with its resulting waste and suffering, sometimes leading to totalitarian governments and wars. Greater stability is needed not only in markets for goods and services, but also in the areas of banking, insurance, and investment, together described as "financial services."

The problem of instability has led to much recent discussion about the causes of the Great Depression. There is much to learn from the analysis and points of view for a twenty-first century nation at risk of recurring economic downturns. Here are the different causes that different factions emphasize or cite:

- abuses in financial services;
- higher tariffs adopted in 1930;
- the government's long delay in taking actions effective enough to stop the worsening situation;
- easy credit to buy stocks on 10 percent margins, along with inadequate credit for home mortgages, which required frequent renewals when credit might unavailable,
- the monopoly pricing power in a few industries.
-

All of these causes were involved, but most discussions pay little attention to one of the most important causes of the Great Depression and of similar downturns: the failure of purchasing power to keep pace with productivity, resulting in cutbacks and layoffs, which further reduced purchasing power, a vicious cycle.

One important aspect of this insufficiency was in the then large farming sector, which had borrowed to buy more equipment and land to expand production, but was then faced with crippling declines in crop prices.

After World War II, purchasing power revived and prosperity returned based on incomes accumulated during the war, and the GI Bill of Rights, the Marshall Plan, the Interstate Highway Program, and the strength of labor unions, all of which increased demand for American products. The effect of insufficient purchasing power can be delayed by some kinds of credit, such as the "time payments" in the 1920's and today's credit cards, and so on. But the damage can't be postponed indefinitely, although inflation may make it easier to pay off debts.

b) Sustainability: The simplistic glorification of economic "growth" in a planet of finite resources, with the destruction or depletion of forests, ocean fisheries, arable land, potable water, and underground supplies of fossil fuels and metals, in the face of global increases in populations with their rising expectations, makes this weakness increasingly urgent.

c) Equity: The history of monopolies and of predatory financial players, plus past industrial involvement in child labor, unsafe work places, and employee losses of jobs and pensions, together with avoidable losses to small businesses, consumers and investors, combine to indicate the need for greater equity. The harshness of early industrial capitalism in

Europe between 1750 and 1850 led to communism which took over several nations, and fostered a fascist reaction that led to World War II.

The conclusion: We need to preserve capitalism's productivity and its contributions to freedom, while upgrading its stability, sustainability and equity.

Religion

Organized religions have long provided support for several widespread human needs and desires, such as the need for a sense of belonging, hopes for future salvation, guidance on some aspects of behavior, support for the viability of families, and answers to some difficult questions. They have also given many in society various enjoyable experiences such as beautiful music and memorable art and architecture. But for more than a century organized religions have been under increasing stress, especially in advanced European nations and among more educated groups, partly because of the traditional and continuing religious involvement in some cherished factual assertions that have been challenged by the growth and prestige of scientific knowledge. One reaction to this stress has been "intelligent design," which accepts evolution rather than a literal reading of the book of Genesis as fact, but ascribes it to divine guidance. In a somewhat similar vein, doubts about traditional theological facts might be assuaged by suggesting belief adhered to as working hypotheses or as personal policies.

An obvious practical remedy might be for religions to shift attention to important subjects where science, as such, does not speak. Although scientists are also citizens and, as such, often express vigorous policy opinions, science itself is only concerned with facts – what is, was, and might be, not what should be. Science itself is neither moral nor immoral, it is amoral, and focuses only on determining facts.

But what should be done about facts that involve questions of values, of good and evil, where religion can offer constructive contributions? Religion may be helpful to many people, who may no longer care about traditional theological assertions but who are concerned about policies and practices affecting the quality of life of themselves and of many others, including the less fortunate and future generations. For example, the Golden Rule, which ostensibly involves religion more than science (although immunologists have documented the effect of positive human interaction on the immune system), and which is recognized in some form by most denominations, might be emphasized more effectively. If the rule is applied with imagination, vigor and common sense, it can help advance the culture of enlightened social and civic responsibility. Of course, religious efforts to combat major evils should be tempered by good judgment. Fighting the evils of alcoholism by advocating Prohibition proved to be a failure; opposing war by the peace movement of the 1930's led to the appeasement of aggressors and a very bloody World War II. In general, real progress in worthy causes is more likely if passion is tempered by pragmatism.

Law

Like other professions, law has become increasingly specialized, complicated and expensive, even to the point of undermining our ideal of "equal justice under law." These trends undermine the five basic functions of law in an advanced society:

1. Providing enough certainty to support the launching and operation of useful private and public projects,
2. Reinforcing deterrence of antisocial acts or omissions that undermine health, safety or general well-being,
3. Supporting fair and efficient resolution of various disputes,
4. Offering methods (procedures and institutions) to achieve agreed-upon goals, and
5. Affording protections for individual rights, particularly for weak or unpopular persons and ideas.

Over the years there have been some important improvements in how these basic functions of law are performed, but more improvements are needed. Today, the practice of law in work like litigation, counseling, negotiation, lobbying, and so on is generally fairly strong for those clients who can afford prevailing fees, but generally much weaker for persons and institutions that can't.

This disparity in affordability takes many forms, for example, the well-funded homicide defense of retired football hero O.J. Simpson, as compared to the limited defense typically available for indigent defendants; the common reluctance of some prosecutors to use their limited resources against powerful economic entities; the development of contingent-fee representation in some kinds of tort litigation; and the limited budgets and questionable effectiveness of various regulatory agencies that were created to protect consumers, investors, smaller businesses and the general public.

The alleviation of this situation will involve some adjustments in both the culture and the compensation patterns of the legal profession. Such adjustments should include re-emphasizing that the law (like the other traditional learned professions of medicine, the clergy, and military leadership, which also were largely based on English and American development) includes important standards of service to society which are not to be overshadowed by the pursuit of personal wealth.

Certainly lawyers, like other learned professionals, should be well compensated. But the United States has a far larger percentage of lawyers in its population than any other advanced nation. Therefore it should be possible for our legal profession to come closer to meeting society's needs than is the case today.

These needs go beyond traditional legal services in the private sector and in law enforcement. They include coping with excessive complexity: the modern expansion of legislation, regulations, codifications and official forms into hundreds or thousands of pages, which few legislators, administrators or lawyers have the time to read. The burden may be even worse for small businesses or the average citizen.

This situation leads to waste, mistakes and higher costs. It also alienates public support for government activities which are well-intended or necessary.

Progress toward reducing the burdens of complexity necessarily involves the legal profession, but turf feelings should not exclude thoughtful non-lawyers from participating in developing improvements. Modern societies are too interrelated to leave important policy matters in the hands of experts and specialists alone.

Democracy

Democracy is a system of government in which a majority of the population is able to choose the government's leaders, and thus can indirectly control the government's policies. Democracy is the opposite of autocracy, which is a government controlled by a powerful monarch, dictator, or a small, self-perpetuating oligarchy.

History seems to indicate that democracies are usually able to deliver better results over time than do autocracies, at least where a nation's population is fairly well educated. The success of democracies may be due to their greater openness and ability to perceive and correct mistakes, plus their respect for the rights of citizens, thus helping to earn and retain their support.

However, history also shows that democracies often neglect or misunderstand serious problems until they are on the brink of disaster: for example, England's adherence in the 1930s to its policy of appeasing Hitler's aggression until it was almost too late; also, the United States' failure to cope with slavery until war resulted, and also the failure of the United States and other democracies to prevent or counteract economic declines until serious damage had occurred.

Such weaknesses of democracy may help explain why China's present leaders, while embracing capitalism, seem to believe their country will be better off with an oligarchy than with democracy.

Cures for democracy's weaknesses are easy to spot but hard to achieve. First, the popular culture, which glorifies star athletes and entertainers, should ease off on the common, indiscriminate badmouthing of "politicians" and "bureaucrats." Some of them are good and some bad, as in other occupations. They often perform, with varying degrees of success, vital and difficult functions for our safety and prosperity. Politicians often must balance conflicting interests and values among their own constituents and with the rest of the nation, while considering their own chances in the next election. Career civil servants try to carry out the sometimes-conflicting objectives of laws and of political leaders, despite some discouraging conditions, unforeseen problems, or inadequate resources.

Secondly, both as students and as voters, we need to take our civic responsibilities much more seriously. Students should know basic civics, including key features of the Constitution. They should also have a sufficient, in-depth grasp of both U.S. and world history to provide some perspective on our major problems (some of which tend to recur), including their causes, attempted remedies, and the results which followed.

One obstacle to this necessary education for citizenship is the fear of school administrators that teaching history in depth will embroil them in controversies. The correct answer is to present all sides and stimulate students' awareness. It would also be helpful to use interesting documentaries about, for example, Jefferson, Franklin, Hamilton, Jackson, the two Roosevelts, Churchill, Truman, Eisenhower, Nixon, and other former presidents and founding fathers (and mothers), as well as about periods such as "Between the Wars" a documentary narrated by Eric Sevareid, using such materials as a basis for both classroom and adult discussions. Such discussions might bring adults into classrooms, or bring students into adult discussions.

Third are problems with democracy's procedures, like re-drawing Congressional district boundaries in ways designed to create "safe" districts for one or both parties, plus procedures for registering or voting that may discourage participation, and questions about political parties' procedures for nominating candidates.

Fourth, upgrading democracy calls for more attention to the financing of election campaigns. The well-known ability of lobbyists for wealthy interests to influence Congress (and also the executive branch), as well as state and local governments, depends largely on their ability to arrange large contributions by their clients and their executives and friends. Money talks, and in an age of information glut money can often drown out the voices of those who are less affluent or less connected. Among suggested remedies are more prompt and complete publicity about large contributions, and more free television time, including more debates between the rival candidates.

Technology

Throughout history, new technologies have been the chief driver of change. Technology brings better standards of living but also difficulties and disruptions.

Major benefits have included methods of food production more reliable than hunting and gathering; helpful uses of fire, the wheel, and metals; new ways to record and transmit information; improved medical procedures; and new sources of power from electricity and fossil fuels for many uses such as better mobility. The detriments include various hardships and problems, some already cured, some still emerging.

Technology is related to science, on which it often relies, but they are not the same. Science pursues knowledge through experiments and observation. Technology pursues improved ways to satisfy various needs and desires, for example, more or better food, clothing, shelter, communication, transportation and protection, plus things like entertainment, reliability, self-esteem, profit, and so on.

In modern times technology has functioned largely through capitalism. However, many advances have come from academic, government, and independent inventors and researchers.

Improvements in technology to better safeguard our nation's future call for attention in most if not all sectors of our national life. Such improvements should seek to enhance the net benefits of technology, that is, the benefits after subtracting or eliminating the detriments. Two useful general guidelines in developing such improvements are as follows:

First, give greater attention to side-effects. For example, chemical and other technologies in food production should be evaluated not only for effects on health and the environment but also for possible side effects on various parts of the economy, on other nations, and on communities, family functionality, and lifestyles of producers, distributors and consumers. Similar evaluations are indicated for transportation, information and other areas of technology.

The second guideline to improve the net benefits of technology is greater attention to the process of innovation, including its speed, which may be too slow or too fast.

Good innovations may be delayed, not only because of costs or risks, but possibly by attitudes of groups that

are satisfied with existing technologies. Cures for such
delays include more competition, more exchanges of information, and possibly some legal actions. But experience suggests that too rapid innovation presents at least
as great problems as delayed innovation. Thus, the steam
engine was a major advance, but for years steam boilers
in factories, ships, and so on were prone to explode. The
doors of some early autos were hinged at their rear edges,
until experience with the effects of wind ended this dangerous design. Some innovations, such as dirigibles, were
simply abandoned.

Over time, such risks were usually reduced by some
combination of pressures from markets, governments, insurance companies, or others. Thus today, the Food and
Drug Administration controls risks in new medications,
and the Federal Aviation Administration requires an Ap-
proved Type Certificate to market aircraft with new technology. Such regulation does not prevent the introduction
of beneficial technology, although it may slow it.

Safety and health problems are not the only detriments of too-fast innovation. Quick innovations may
stimulate sales and offer improvements in quality or capabilities. But they often impose hard-to-measure burdens and wastage of consumers' time, energy, and money,
due to the obsolescence of good technology, or the need to
learn how to access the new benefits and then revise behavior patterns to adjust to new procedures, new formats,
terminology, and so on.

For example, today's telephones and TVs are better
than in the past, but older phones and TVs were relatively simple, standalone technologies whereas today's media technologies tend to be integrated. Naturally, when a

computing device becomes your television and telephone as well as something for internet searches and word processing, the "owner's manual" is going to be a lot more complicated than the manual for a simple television or telephone.

This nation has an increasingly older population, and the ability of older persons to participate in a wide range of activities is diminished by the burdens just noted. Some top executives turn these burdens over to their staffs, but most of us don't have that option. And while young people adapt more readily to new technologies, this too is far from an unmixed blessing. The devastating accident toll of text-messaging while driving cars and trucks includes young drivers, who already have far higher accident rates than other drivers.

The right and wrong tempo for introducing new technology may be more clear by comparing how new technology is often introduced in some fields with its introduction in cars. Cars over time are not only safer and more durable, but also much easier to operate. No longer are skills needed for cranking engines, adjusting chokes, and coordinated use of the clutch and gearshift. While modern cars have many innovations including computers, they rarely burden drivers. The basics of driving a car have become stabilized and increasingly the same regardless of make or model. A bit more of this KISS principle (Keep It Simple, Stupid) might be a benefit in other kinds of new technology.

While over-zealous innovation in technology is more likely to be burdensome than hazardous, it may present hazards in public transportation. Recent fatal accidents in the Washington, D.C., area's rail transit system and in a large airliner that crashed in the South Atlantic may focus attention on possible improvements in transportation equipment.

Finally, adjustments in technology might take account of the varying quality of work experiences. Assembly lines may be more efficient, but jobs on them could be boring for many people; the potential is to make the non-machine jobs "supervisory" of the technology, therefore, more interesting. That seems to be the direction many companies are going. After all, an interesting and satisfying job is part of the good life. Also, some jobs help develop qualities in workers that are generally beneficial, such as the work of doctors, nurses, pilots, and many others which tend to develop good judgment and responsibility, compared to jobs less likely to call for these qualities. Technological innovations might take some account of these considerations.

Entertainment

This subculture has many varieties, and is sometimes called recreation. It may be more important than some people realize. Despite recessions it is a large, and perhaps growing, part of modern economies. In the Great Depression, movie attendance increased because people sought escape from their daily struggles. In the words of theater people, there is great enjoyment in the "willing suspension of disbelief."

At one time, only the rich enjoyed much variety and quantity of entertainment. The 40 hour work week helped change this, and today some nations may come closer to a 30 hour week, at least for some occupations. With better technology and policies, and less waste, this trend might spread over time.

Despite its many varieties, entertainment can be grouped into some meaningful classifications. One is spectator versus participant activity. Another is according to value, which depends on direct and indirect costs and on satisfactions. These may be difficult to measure, especially since satisfaction varies greatly among persons.

Particular kinds of entertainment can have several effects: for example, participating in competitive sports may provide not only pleasure and health benefits, but also may help the young build self-esteem and teach them to play by the rules. Some recreation activities may affect land development patterns, the environment, various sectors of the economy, technological developments, educational effectiveness, and so on.

An activity that is work for some people may be entertainment for others. Thus, piloting for airlines is a job, but piloting is an enjoyment for those who pilot planes for personal or family travel. Fishing is both a commercial occupation and a popular recreation. Woodworking is a job for carpenters but a hobby for others. Reading may be part of a job, or of education, but it also may be recreation. These kinds of overlaps suggest interesting possibilities, for example, enhancing jobs or education by making some aspect of them more enjoyable.

Any serious approaches to improving entertainment must respect personal liberty in the pursuit of happiness. But that does not mean accepting the recreational use of illegal, addictive and dangerous drugs, or dropping efforts to modify some costly forms of commercialized gambling. It also should not exclude more attention to costs and benefits, the effects on health, on personal development, and on the economy or environment. After all, entertainment is a considerable part of the overall way of life in our country as well as elsewhere.

Education

In the long run, education is arguably the most important of the major subcultures. Although education itself is subject to influence by the other subcultures, since they are all inter-related, education is basic to all of them. Thus, it affects capitalism's competitiveness; the ability of religions to advance some of their generally accepted goals; the quality of our laws and how they are observed; the effectiveness of democracy in adapting to complex problems; the progress, quality and other effects of technology; and the costs and benefits of various kinds of entertainment.

Education means imparting the skills, knowledge and behavior patterns that best serve the individual, and also the society on which individuals partly depend. While education usually calls to mind the work of schools and colleges, education actually needs to be a lifelong activity. Thus it also depends on families and on various institutions such as news media. That's because education begins at birth, in how well or poorly a child develops readiness for school. It continues after graduation in adapting the individual well or poorly, and in helping society to adapt, to cope with a changing and perhaps confusing or threatening world.

What needs to be done about education? Chapter 12 explores the question in depth.

Practical Sociology in a Nutshell (that is, How the World Works)

8

So far, the key points in Part Two have all focused on solutions that relate to some aspect of human culture. Sociology takes a scientific, sometimes a clinical, approach to the development, structure, and functioning of human culture. It seems only fitting, therefore, to devote some space to a discussion of practical sociology—a term I've coined to describe how our knowledge of sociology can inform our behavior as a society.

Practical sociology is a basic guide for understanding what's probably one of the most important factors in your life: human behavior in today's complex world.

To understand human behavior well, you have to understand three things: the behavior of groups (teams and organizations, for example), the behavior of individuals, and the common pitfalls which may cause individuals or groups to fail.

I try to avoid technical jargon like that used by various specialists and experts, but unfortunately we have to invent two new words, both mercifully short: sorg and scult. I'll explain them shortly.

First, recognize that human beings are like little magnets, which attract and repel each other.

Next, focus on when they attract. Any attraction may have some consequences, but here we are only concerned with an attraction that succeeds in forming a group of some duration.

We're not concerned with, for instance, people who meet on a cruise ship, like each other, and chat and play cards with each other, but never see each other after the cruise. We're only concerned with groups that have some duration over time, even if the duration is indefinite. We will call all groups that have some duration "sorg" (short for "social organization", with the word "social" understood in a very broad sense, as including how two or more people interact with each other and with other people).

There are innumerable kinds of sorgs: a family, a nation, a business, a club, a school, a religion, some occupations, etc.

Frequently there are sorgs within sorgs, for example a business or other organization with several departments or locations, a religious denomination with many local groups, and within each local group a choir, youth group, trustees or elders, and others.

The defining characteristics of all sorgs (in addition to having more than a very brief duration) usually include (a) some known functions, (b) some internal division of labor, and (c) some degree of cohesion, meaning an awareness, by those who are in the sorg and those who aren't, of a sense of belonging, and sometimes an us – them attitude toward those who don't belong. In addition, (d) sorgs often seek to advance their own interests, at least as they perceive them, and to defend their interests.

For example, the federal government is a large sorg. So is its judiciary, the Senate, and each committee, agency, office, etc. The Marine Corps, Army, Navy, Air Force and Coast Guard each are sorgs, and they each contain numerous sorgs, including small units like a platoon, squadron, or ship's company, which typically have strong cohesion, comparable to that in well-functioning families.

It's important to recognize that most individuals belong to several sorgs, which in the aggregate absorb most of their energies. This usually enriches their lives and benefits society. But this sometimes results in the individual being faced with conflicting values and interests or conflicting demands on the individual's time and resources.

The other word, "scults," is short for subcultures. It means the group's attitudes and practices, sometimes called its culture. Most sorgs of the same general kind will be quite similar in their attitudes and practices. Thus, most upper-middle-class families in the 30 to 40 age bracket living in a suburb of a big U.S. city during a given timeframe such as the 1950s will have a fair amount of interests, attitudes and activities in common. The same could probably be said of most of the gas stations, geology departments, bowling clubs, etc. in a particular area and timeframe.

Yet it's important to realize that similar sorgs may have variations in their scults. This may be due to a variety of causes, such as different experiences or circumstances, an innovative or strong-willed person, pressures of competition, and so on. As a result, the scult of Goldman Sachs may differ from that of similar enterprises, the scult of a community college may differ from other such colleges, and of course families, clubs and other sorgs that have much in common may differ in some of their values and practices.

The thing to remember is that similar sorgs will usually have similar scults, but not always.

Since most individuals belong to several sorgs, it follows that individuals will have several scults, for example, as a parent, as a breadwinner, and as a member of various clubs and other groups.

Now that we have the basics of sorgs and scults—and thus of the behavior of groups—let's look at the basics of the behavior of what groups are made of, namely, individuals.

In a nutshell, the way individuals behave, including the values and attitudes which may be reflected in their behavior, is determined by a mixture of two kinds of factors, human nature and the culture and subcultures which the individual has learned or absorbed from other people.

Human nature, which is dealt with in more detail by psychology and other studies, reflects basic needs or drives such as for food, sex, rest, activity, self-esteem, greed, fear, and so on. A good part of human nature is common to almost all persons, but individuals may vary in such things as curiosity, aggressiveness, and empathy.

The important thing to remember about human nature is that it is almost impossible to change, although the way it affects actual behavior can be affected by self-control or social controls that reflect culture.

Although it's impractical to try to change human nature, it's often quite possible to change behavior by changing the culture. History provides abundant evidence of important changes in many fields, including government, finance, religious practices, courtship, social mobility, criminal justice, and care of the less fortunate.

However, changing culture can be a tricky business. Western subcultures in fields like economics and technology have spread globally with comparative ease, but Western subcultures like freedom of expression and gender equality find much less receptivity in various parts of the world.

Even within a modern nation, cultural changes that do not involve deep-seated feelings or values can nevertheless be difficult to effectuate. Advocates of the metric system in the United States were able to succeed in changing the packaging of distilled spirits, but efforts to sell gasoline and milk by the liter failed. A perception of inconvenience may block changes unless the changes are perceived to be necessary or at least worth the trouble.

Now that we've described the basics of how individuals and groups behave, let's turn to some common pitfalls that cause individual and group failures.

Elsewhere we have described the dangers of (a) group-think and (b) of prolonged or outstanding success. (See Chapter 5.) Now we'll describe four more common causes of failure, with their opposites representing approaches to solutions!

1. Overdoing, meaning too much of a good thing,
2. Assuming that what's necessary is sufficient for the desired result,
3. Overloading a good system, and
4. Maintaining a sick subculture.

Overdoing

Too much of a good thing is pretty common. Many persons enjoy an alcoholic drink before dinner to provide relaxation, cheerfulness and maybe stimulation of the appetite, but some folks take too much alcohol, creating highway hazards, liver damage, and other troubles. Most folks enjoy a good home and car, but some folks go for very pricey homes, pricey cars, or wrist watches costing thousands of dollars. (I know something about watches. In college I conducted tours of a watch movement factory. In World War II, I used chronometers for celestial navigation, in which an error of 20 seconds meant an error of up to five nautical miles in determining the plane's position. And believe me, today you can buy a watch for less than $50 that runs as well and looks as good as one costing thousands.)

Too much of a good thing affects sorgs (groups) as well as individuals. During the 1950s and 1960s Detroit's Big Three went overboard on style and power, with safety, reliability and value taking a back seat, thus creating openings for foreign car makers. Nations that had policies that led to economic, military or other successes, for example nineteenth century colonialism, sometimes pursued those policies to the point where the costs exceeded the benefits.

Assuming

Treating what's necessary as if it's sufficient is very common. Persons with various health problems may recognize the need to change something important – perhaps diet, or exercise, or medications – but overlook the fact that the desired results may require attention to several factors. Persons with financial difficulties may recognize a need to increase income or to reduce expenses when both may be needed.

Turning to sorgs, government officials or civic activists concerned about high levels of common crime may emphasize the need for more law enforcement, or new laws, or prisons that can handle longer sentences or provide better rehabilitation, or programs to alleviate poverty and increase family stability, or programs in schools or in faith groups or in playgrounds for supervised athletics, when the truth may be that a combination of several such actions is needed to obtain satisfactory improvement.

In dealing with problems in the national economy, various groups will advocate a particular approach to improvement, such as (a) encouraging entrepreneurship and private investment by reducing taxes and regulation, or (b) increasing the amount of credit or purchasing power, or (c) acting to reduce wasteful conditions such as monopolistic pricing (e.g., some state regulation of health insurance), environmental degradation (for example, deep water oil drilling spills), and disruptive financial activities (for example, corrupt Wall Street practices). But improvement may require a combination of such policies. And in dealing with something as complex as our country's foreign relations, where importing oil and exporting jobs are just two examples of important things to consider, it should be obvious that there is not likely to be a single action or program or policy, however worthy, that will provide general improvement.

A variant of assuming that what's necessary is also sufficient is assuming that getting rid of the cause of a bad situation will fix things. Actually, relief may depend on taking care that removing the cause of the trouble does not also involve removing or impairing related things that are necessary or useful. Failures to take such care are sometimes described as "throwing out the baby with the bath water."

Overloading

This too is a common mistake, by which a good system produces poor results. This problem seems more likely to occur in government and in small nonprofit activities than in competitive businesses, which can usually expand to meet, or even to anticipate, rising demand and rising workloads. In government, expanding to meet an increased need may wait until the next budget cycle.

Few illustrations should be needed to show how overloading operates on individuals. A parent with many children but few resources can break down under the strain or cut corners in child rearing. A parent whose earning power was destroyed in a depression may take a poor-paying job rather than none, supplementing the income by borrowing or moonlighting and jeopardizing health, longevity and family well-being.

A dramatic but little known case of a good system ruined by overload occurred in the federal government's handling of conscientious objectors. The military traditionally doesn't want a real conscientious objector, except for some who are willing to serve in work that doesn't require killing, such as being a medic. But when a draft is in effect – as it was in the Civil War, World War I, World War II and during the wars in Korea and Vietnam – public policy usually has drawn a sharp distinction between sincere C.O.s and persons who only claim to be, in order to avoid being drafted.

As you can imagine, it's often difficult for a local draft board, or any other authority, to decide who's a true C.O. and who is just trying to avoid the draft. At one time the test was membership in a so-called "peace church," with the Quakers the best known example. But some draft registrants were sincerely and religiously opposed to killing even though they weren't members of a "peace church."

Finally a system was devised that worked surprisingly well. If a man claiming to be a C.O. appealed to Selective Service from the local board's denial of his claim, the appeal was routed to a volunteer hearing officer (such as a retired judge) to interview the claimant, and also to the FBI to do a background investigation, which was usually not very time-consuming since claimants were young. Then the reports from the hearing officer and the FBI plus the claimant's statements were sent to the Justice Department, which reviewed it all and recommended granting or denying the appeal to Selective Service, which always followed Justice's recommendation.

For years the Justice Department assigned this work to a small Conscientious Objector Section, which had two lawyers, who became quite expert in this work. For some unknown reason the C.O. Section was placed under the Office of Legal Counsel even though its work had nothing to do with OLC's work. When I reported to OLC in 1958, my first assignment was to spend enough time in the C.O. Section to report to OLC on whether that section was doing a good job. (It was.)

Now fast forward to the late 1960s. Opposition to the Vietnam War had resulted in a great increase in C.O. claims that were denied by local boards and appealed. The limited numbers of hearing officers, of FBI agents available for this work, and of the C.O. Section's staff, combined to create backlogs and delays in processing the growing number of appeals. Finally, if a registrant filed an appeal, it had the effect of providing a year's deferment. This angered a congressional committee and the whole system was abolished. That may have aggravated the bitterness that developed about the war.

Some organizations cope with overloads by prioritizing who or what gets prompt attention. For example, when military medical facilities are overwhelmed by casualties, triage is used. Triage means giving first attention to those who both need and will benefit from immediate care ahead of those who will survive despite some delay and those expected to die regardless of care. Other groups, like fire departments, have arrangements with neighboring fire departments to help in large disasters.

There is probably no single answer to overloads except to try to anticipate and prepare for them.

Sick Cultures

It's not easy to define, or to agree upon, all the cultures or subcultures that might deserve to be called sick, but some are pretty easy to spot. They mostly fall into three main categories: excessively cruel, excessively crazy, or excessively greedy.

An example of the first type is the Nazis who controlled Germany between 1933 and 1945. They asserted that Germans, or at least those Germans who were deemed to belong to the so-called Aryan race, were the "master race" and thus were entitled to invade neighboring nations, subjecting their inhabitants to harsh treatment including forced labor or even death. Similarly deserving the sick designation are the cultures promoted by various other rulers, past and present, who imposed totalitarian conditions on their populations, depriving people of basic personal rights and subjecting them to harsh and unjust punishments.

A culture of cruelty does not necessarily involve governments. Some sports, some involving cruelty to animals and some not, may develop a following with such a culture. Various other practices, such as the once prevalent imprisonment for debt, or harsh methods of some bill collections, might also be deemed cruel.

Crazy cultures usually are fairly harmless, or they come and go as fads, but some are sick. The man involved in such a strong anti-tax culture in the Spring of 2010 that he flew a small plane into an Austin, Texas, office of the Internal Revenue Service had a mind detached from realities, like the fact that all nations have taxation because it's necessary, and that as a U.S. citizen he could vote and petition for changes in our taxes. Also in 2010, members of a small religious group reportedly demonstrated at funerals, explaining that God was punishing our nation because of something about sexual orientation, an explanation which seems equally detached from reality, at least in the absence of any indication that the deceased persons or their associates had been involved in sexual orientation issues. And Timothy McVeigh, who killed hundreds of people with explosives in Oklahoma City, may well have been involved in some culture crazy enough to be deemed sick. Similarly, the youthful terrorists involved in the 9/11 attacks and similar violence elsewhere have reputedly been indoctrinated in a culture that believes that their God wants them to destroy infidels, and that if they die in doing so they will be rewarded in heaven with a large supply of virgins.

Sick cultures of the excessively greedy type may not be as common as they were in the days of slavery and the early part of the industrial revolution. Yet they still

exist, partly because they can be made light of, or ratio-
nalized (there's a sucker born every minute, never give a
sucker an even break, and survival of the fittest is a good,
natural and necessary idea).

Bearing in mind that our competitive, profit-moti-
vated enterprises have proven quite productive, and that
a fair degree of greed usually motivates those who launch,
manage and invest in them, where do we draw the line
that makes greed excessive enough to be deemed sick?
Probably when consumers, employees, investors, competitors, the general public, including future generations,
are being seriously hurt by illegal, misleading, improp-
erly secretive or otherwise harmful conduct that's motivated chiefly by greed.

This would obviously include various gangs and
drug cartels, companies and con artists using fraud or
misleading sales promotion, and some characters in
the world of finance who gain large rewards by complex
transactions that are prone to injure not only those with
whom they deal but others (e.g., selling bad investments
to a pension fund, which injures not only the fund and its
managers but also the retirees who depend on the fund).
Such people reflect a culture of get the money, don't get
caught, and remember that good guys finish last. And
when they get a great deal of money their culture tends to
increase their self-esteem to the point of feeling that they
are the lords of the universe, and other people are "little"
people.

What should you and I and our nation do about sick
cultures, whether they involve cruelty, craziness or excessive greed? Be alert to them, try to discourage or modify
them as opportunity may offer, and join with other citi-

zens to support governmental or other actions to modify, discourage or terminate them. Yet also bear in mind that in a free nation that cherishes personal liberty, some degree of harshness bordering on cruelty, of craziness bordering on madness, and of greed bordering on rapaciousness may be protected behavior.

To summarize this short review of practical sociology, we have a great variety of "sorgs" (various kinds of groups and organizations), each with its own attitudes and practices (their "scults"). All sorgs consist of individuals, whose behavior is a mixture of human nature, which can't be changed, and their culture (the values and practices learned from other people) which can be changed, although sometimes with great difficulty. And the behavior both of sorgs and of individuals is at risk from the six common pitfalls that cause failures.

Reactivate Progress by Better Balancing

9

Despite the noble words in our Declaration of Independence, in the Bill of Rights of our Constitution and in Lincoln's Gettysburg Address, many years went by before our national ideals of liberty and equality were more fully recognized.

For years we had property ownership as a qualification for voting; for decades we had slavery, followed by more decades of official racism; and for over a century women did not have the right to vote. We have also made progress in economic matters, with laws against child labor and to protect the health and safety of consumers and workers. Yet today the increasing inequality within our population is a matter of growing concern. How can we put this concern into a helpful perspective?

First, let's look at how we have been changing and where we are, compared to other capitalistic nations. A report in Business Week of March 12, 2012 shows our trend toward increased inequality during about a half-century, compared to trends in other capitalistic nations. The report shows for seventeen nations (nine in Europe, three in the Western Hemisphere, and five in the Far East) the percentages of each nation's total income that went to the top 1 percent of its population, during 1949 and during 2005. In 1949, seven of the seventeen nations had more inequality than the United States. During the years between 1949 and 2005 eleven of the seventeen nations reduced their inequality and six, including the U.S. increased it. In 2005 the United States had 17.4 percent of its income going to its top 1 percent, the highest share among the seventeen nations.

No one argues that all should be identical in wealth or its benefits; rather that inequality has become excessive. Excessive inequality can damage our nation's way of life, including damage to our economy and to our level of national cohesion. We should also note the increasing pressures of economic and cultural globalization. Finally, we should recognize the long-standing conflict between our two most basic national values, personal liberty and equality. Since no one argues for total equality, perhaps our ideal of equality might in some respects be (better) understood as enough equality to achieve a better degree of fairness.

While our history shows repeated progress toward political and legal equality, equality is often subordinated to liberty in important fields like business, education, and personal and family activities. (Advocates of extreme equality were once referred to as levelers; advocates of personal liberties in almost all circumstances are sometimes referred to as libertarians).

Does our balance between liberty and enough equality to achieve more fairness call for some careful readjustment? Might it help to look at some other modern and successful capitalistic democracies?

Today we can identify at least seven successful capitalist democracies: Norway, Sweden, Denmark, Germany, Canada, Australia and New Zealand. (All of them except Denmark were included in the report about the seventeen nations described earlier in this chapter.) The citizens of these seven enjoy the same freedoms of expression, religion, travel, and so on as we do. But when it comes to poverty levels, crime levels, education levels, and health and longevity, they generally are ahead of us. Why? Part of the reason may be that they have more culturally homogeneous populations than we do, which may make it easier to reach agreements on public policy issues. But some of the reason may also be in a slightly different balancing of the two basic values of capitalist democracies, equality and personal liberty.

A comparison of such balancing is described in a new book from the Oxford University Press by historian David Fischer, *Fairness and Freedom: A History of Two Open Societies, New Zealand and the United States.* It was reviewed in *The Washington Post* (Feb. 19, 2012, p. B9) under the challenging heading "To Understand America, look at New Zealand."

In today's competitively globalized world, it would seem wise to pay some attention to what our competitors are doing—not just competitors like China which lack democracy and personal freedoms, but also nations such as the seven successful capitalist democracies listed above.

Ten Guidelines for Responsible Citizenship

10

Some Americans seem to pay more attention to their rights than to their responsibilities as citizens. In addition to the Constitution's Bill of Rights, we have rights to move, to change jobs, to drive cars and use other possessions, to start a business or other group, and much more.

Our national ideals put liberty first, equality next, and responsibility a poor third. The American Bar Association has a section on Rights and Responsibilities, but civic responsibility is a subject that goes beyond law. It involves our national culture in the broadest and most basic sense.

There are two kinds of responsibilities, those that are legally enforceable duties like serving on juries, paying taxes, and providing legally required information, and those that are not, even if they are equally or perhaps even more important.

Democracy, what Lincoln called "government of the people, by the people and for the people," depends on all these civic responsibilities. Yet even something as basic as voting is a right, not an enforceable duty. And as a practical matter, if democracy is to solve the problems facing our nation, much more than voting is needed.

Here is a short list that will help to identify what is needed from responsible citizenship today. It is a kind of bridge to Parts Three and Four, which examine specific solutions to problems and focus on things you can do to solve the problems, respectively.

Not every citizen can do everything listed, but more citizens are needed to do these and similar things:

1. List the subjects or problems facing your region, our nation and the world that are important enough to require serious attention. After some reflection a reasonably well-informed citizen should be able to list at least a couple of dozen.

2. Beware of extremism, distractions, and the carelessness that often results from apparent success. Read and listen to materials from sources that you generally don't agree with, for two reasons. Mixed with the advocacy stuff that you can just skim, you may find relevant facts bearing on the merits of an issue; also, if you're active on one side, you may find vulnerabilities or opportunities in either or both sides.

3. Consider the great variety of cultures and subcultures in our country and the rest of the world. Do this in relation to occupations, regions, religions, race, nationalities, ethnicity, past experiences, education, economic status, and so on. This is important because peoples' attitudes, values, assumptions and customary behavior can vary greatly, although people also have important things in common. Culture can be changed, but changing culture can sometimes be very tricky, and it helps to know what you might like to change or perhaps encourage.

4. Consider trends. Are they the kind that go back and forth like a pendulum or the kind that seem

to have continuity? What causes these trends, and what might their effects be? Be sure to consider trends based on technology.

5. Consider motivations, bearing in mind that individuals and groups often act from a mixture of motivations.

6. Consider possible or likely unintended consequences from particular actions, decisions, programs, policies, neglects, etc. These consequences can be harmful or beneficial or a mixture.

7. Consider the accuracy and adequacy of the information that you or others may have that influences policy positions and decisions.

8. Discuss problems with a variety of other people, to get broader perspectives of time (past, present, future) and of group attitudes (economic, political, occupational, etc.). Respect differences, and reserve the right to dissent or suspend judgment.

9. Invite others to join you in this process in a sort of informal civic club. Find interested people by announcements at service clubs, faith groups, business, labor, political, educational or other local groups, and through local media and the Internet.

10. Adopt as the central goal of your civic activity to help achieve and maintain our liberties and a range of sustainable beneficial conditions that will lead to

a peaceful and prosperous nation in a peaceful and
prosperous world.

PART THREE – MAJOR NATIONAL PROBLEMS WITH SOLUTIONS

As a preface to this Part, it's important to point out why eight major problems received attention in Parts One and Two, but only three get the spotlight in this section on solutions. It comes down to "stick to what you know." My academic credentials are chiefly in law and economics, and with most of my legal career spent in civil service in Washington, D.C., I feel qualified to offer insights on how to address issues plaguing our economic and political health. In addition, after retiring from the government, I formed a group called Citizens for Quality Civilization with other like-minded people. We targeted education as the ultimate public policy sector. Our work on education produced not only a civic handbook (a copy of which is included as Appendix B), but also tools for the classroom to support teachers in upgrading their approaches.

The Economy—
Some Solutions

11

In examining economic problems in Part One, I hinted at solutions. Three problems that received the spotlight are purchasing power—in some ways related to the diversion of job opportunities to offshore labor—shortage of certain specialized skills in our domestic labor force, and the effect of government regulations on business.

As I said, it is elementary economics that purchasing power is the desire plus the ability to buy what's offered for sale. Advertisements can stimulate desire and build brand affinity, but the ability to buy depends on having money to spend. Credit can only do so much. It provides purchasing power for various periods of time, but it ultimately depends on either wealth or income. And since purchasing power directly or indirectly depends on income, purchasing power will not be adequate in the long run to buy what's produced unless income is sufficient and sustainable. So, as recent U.S. presidents have all said in one way or another, the issue is jobs. To be more specific, greater harmony is needed between the skills people have and the skills needed in jobs.

This brings us to the second point. The need for people with specialized skills in fields such as robotics and genetic engineering relates to problems of education. Some solutions to them are covered in Chapter 12. But not all specialized skills imply a PhD. In the manufacturing environment, for example, people need to be trained to "supervise" robots. And in the arena of genetic engineering, or any other field of biological science, we need lab technicians. The economy benefits when we take people who want to enter or remain in those environments and educate them to move into a more specialized position.

Finally, we cannot overlook long-standing disagreements about the effects of governmental regulations on businesses. Sometimes, these regulations are a burden on business; they prevent businesses from being fully productive, which might also create more jobs.

In general, the regulations that burden the profitability and productivity of businesses were designed to improve safety for employees and protect consumer interests. The solution is not to do away with them, but to determine—devoid of a political agenda to whatever extent possible—how those objectives could be achieved with less red tape. The evolution of the Energy Star program, providing incentives to companies to produce energy-efficient products, is a model of relatively low red-tape, non-regulatory action by the Environmental Protection Agency and the Department of Energy. Compliance with the standards established earns the product an "Energy Star" seal of approval. The program was so effective that Australia, Canada, Japan, New Zealand, Taiwan and the European Union have also adopted it.

I will continue with a discussion of solutions by introducing three kinds of economic problems to complement the discussion in Part One.

First, swings of mood, between exuberance and discouragement, by consumers, investors, business managers and others, can create economic problems. This can be addressed by agencies such as the Federal Reserve and by educating young people in money management. S e c -

ond is the increasing vulnerability of our national economy to problems in the economy of some European or other nations. This can be addressed by some combination of international agreements and some limitation on risky foreign investments by large financial institutions. Our national economy should not become excessively dependant on the global economy.

Third is the growing impact of increases in the already large amount of health care spending on our economy. The growth of these costs is partly driven by the increase in our elderly populations, partly by improved but expensive developments in medical technology, partly by lifestyle deficits, and partly by economic practices not unique to health care.

These costs must be met by some combination of governments, businesses and consumers. Especially in the case of governments these increasing costs may mean increased debt and/or increased taxes.

Controlling the rise in health care costs without impairing the quality and availability of health care is not a simple matter, as evidenced by the confusion and resistance over implementation of the Affordable Care Act. Leadership should rely heavily on medical professionals who have detailed knowledge of the subject and who reflect the ethics and culture of the profession, as well as persons who reflect business cultures and representatives of consumers.

Education in school and later in support of preventive medicine, such as minimizing obesity and substance abuse, should also help. In addition, solutions to control rising costs should not overlook the fact that the health care sector, unlike some other sectors, includes a lot of personal services. It thus helps reduce unemployment and increases our nation's purchasing power.

Finally, economic problems should be viewed not only from the perspectives of businesses, workers, investors and taxpayers but also from the perspective of consumers. Today consumers often enjoy a broad range of choices, and they also have some protection from fraud and from products that may be dangerous to health or safety. At the same time, consumers are increasingly burdened by the need to spend more time in order to make choices that best serve their own interests. Today, marketing and other experts present consumers with an increasing blizzard of novel offers and inducements that can take considerable time and skill to evaluate.

Here are just a few examples: Consumers used to buy electricity from their local utility company, which was regulated by the state public utility commission. But we have recently received solicitations from three other companies to sell us cheaper electricity to be delivered by our local utility. Two of these companies are outside our metropolitan area. How much can we expect to save? What is our recourse if the new supplier fails to deliver electricity? Will the loss of sales impair our local company's ability to maintain its distribution facilities? How much of our time could this new arrangement involve, both to start it and possibly to change it? Wouldn't it save a lot of the public's time if our local utility and/or the regulatory commission handled this, or at least clarified and simplified our decision?

Supermarket shopping used to depend on the skill of a consumer in choosing household products. Today, supermarkets often quote different prices depending on whether the buyer is a regular customer. Other retail chains, airlines and credit card companies offer customers "points" which can be converted to certain goods or services depending on a variety of terms, conditions, formulas, circumstances, procedures, time limits, and so on.

These marketing programs cost the company money to sustain and add a level of complexity for consumers that causes many of us to disregard the "opportunity." Consumers are often too busy to invest their valuable time in evaluating, monitoring and obtaining these inducements.

A long-standing consumer problem has been owner's manuals that aren't clear. I recently bought an electronic device that didn't work, although I had followed the manual's instructions to the letter. Then a friend noticed a small object in the device, removed it and it worked. The manual didn't say anything about this object.

A growing problem, especially for our increasingly aging population, is plastic or other packaging that's difficult to open, particularly of food products. This is partly due to the great variety of packaging designs and partly because of the strength or dexterity required to open and close the package. So far, market forces haven't done much to curb these irritations.

As to the tremendous speed of never-ending improvements in consumer electronics (computers, smart phones, and so on), many consumers are burdened with providing the time and money to adjust to frequent changes. This is okay for heavy users of such products and for young people who don't have many established habits to modify. But it's burdensome for occasional users and for elderly persons, who are an increasing part of our population. At some point, consumers should be offered more standardization and stability, at least as an option. Today, the auto industry makes cars which almost any driver can easily drive, regardless of make or model. Hopefully makers of consumer electronics will provide a user-friendly product like the auto makers.

So how do special offers, packaging, technological advances, and owner's manuals get to be part of the discussion of solutions to economic problems? An economy thrives when those contributing to it have a clear sense of what's going on, how things work, why choose x over y. We have lost that simple element of engaging the population in economic stability and growth by making so many things obscure. This problem was an impetus for the Occupy Wall Street and other global Occupy protests. People were protesting "not knowing" as much as they were protesting what they perceived as greedy behavior.

As a general matter, the solution to our economic problems should include paying attention to the following five factors:

1. consider all the groups and interests involved;
2. consider the experience of our own economic history and that of other capitalist nations;
3. relate our economic policies to the cultures of the people involved, to the environment, and to the particular characteristics of each industry;
4. maintain economic freedom coupled with civic responsibility, and
5. maintain our own national interests with due regard for other nations.

In addition, priority should be given to the following four objectives:

1. the responsible control of debt;
2. the maintenance and enhancement of purchasing power;
3. the responsible management of investments; and
4. the effective education of consumers, workers, managers, investors and voters.

Upgrading the Ultimate Policy Sector—Education

12

Both personally and as a nation we choose our priorities. If there is a natural disaster, an epidemic, an invasion, a rebellion or an economic collapse, priority will probably be given to policies to cope with the emergency.

But to maintain our ability to cope, and to avoid emergencies if possible, and to anticipate new kinds of dangers, and to counteract the slow decay of capabilities that are seldom exercised, emergency policies are not enough. Far-sighted policies are needed.

There is usually much public support for such general long term goals as protecting the environment, achieving a stable peace, maintaining personal liberties and assuring good standards of living. But experience shows that proposed actions to advance these goals often run into complexities and disagreements. In a democracy, such complexities and disagreements are less likely to be resolved effectively if education falls short. Therefore the most important of our long term policies is education policy.

Education means learning, plus an activity to assist learning called teaching, with both learning and teaching designed as a preparation for life. But life, taken as a whole, has become extremely complex, and in some respects it changes rapidly. How do we prepare for that?

There are two basic approaches to education policy. The first is to support what works in our schools and colleges and try to remedy what doesn't. The second is to look at what actually occurs in both formal and informal education, in order to determine whether what occurs is adequate for present and foreseeable needs.

Both of these approaches are needed. This means that we must recognize that education is not limited to what occurs in schools, colleges and similar institutions. Beginning in infancy it occurs, well or poorly, in the home and the community, including the extended community of television and other outside sources. Education continues through adulthood with a wide range of possible learning, some occupation-related and some not, from the news media and many other sources.

What belongs in planned educational "content," that is, what educators and others have agreed should be learned? It includes a wide range of skills, habits, knowledge and attitudes for dealing with both the human and the non-human parts of the individual's surroundings. Hopefully this will help the individual deal with what he or she may encounter in the future. Education also normally includes content for personal pleasure.

But actual educational content (what, in fact, is learned) naturally depends on a broader context, the sources of what is learned. Much of what is learned, even if it is new to the individual, is taken from what is observed in others, or taught by others (teachers, textbook writers, family, friends, the media, et al). But this is complemented by experiential and discovery learning.

What this actually means is that the source of what is learned is the prevailing culture. That's important, especially since our culture has a considerable amount of variation, by region, economic status, ethnicity, and other factors.

At this point we confess that we're using the jargon of cultural anthropology, in which "culture" means the total way of life or civilization of a tribe or nation. Culture thus includes all generally shared practices such as use of soap, a common language and legal system, plus many subcultures of various age groups, occupations, clubs, faiths, and more. It also includes not only customary patterns of behavior but also shared attitudes and values.

What does this mean for education policy? It helps make clear that education, broadly viewed, necessarily transmits large parts of our massive cultural inheritance, which includes all academic subjects but much more. And it helps explain, for instance, why so many of our "best and brightest" graduates from our most selective colleges go into Wall Street to earn as much and as quickly as possible by any legal means, or go into Madison Avenue to earn lots of money in commercial advocacy aimed at consumers. That was not true during the Great Depression and the New Deal, but when the emergency was replaced by the long years of prosperity after World War II the earlier culture pattern reemerged.

How should education policy mesh with our complex culture? Education policy is also complex—no surprise—but the following eight guidelines can serve as springboards to what needs attention. These eight are (a) pre-school concerns, (b) family involvement during school and college, (c) curriculum, (d) teaching, (e) colleges, (f) developing responsibility for the future, (g) news and entertainment media, and last but not least (h) motivation for learning.

(a) Child-rearing from birth to the start of schooling needs more support. The rights of parents to control their child-rearing practices must be respected, but these rights do not include gross neglect, because adequate parenting is a civic responsibility that affects the community in many ways. Beginning in maternity wards or perhaps in some high schools or other venues, helpful information should be attractively presented. Babies must receive early stimulation by being talked to and played with by parents or other caregivers. Child care facilities for working mothers should be assisted in encouraging such things as basic literacy and familiarity with numbers, using storytelling, games, and so on.

(b) Parental involvement should not end when school begins. Two kinds of involvement are necessary. First, parents and schools should stay in touch. Schools should regularly send parents report cards on their children's academic progress and conduct, and parents should sign an acknowledgement that the report has been received and reviewed. Given the options on digital document security, it may be better in many cases to do this electronically. Second, parents should enrich education by discussing some of their own experiences and opinions with students. Education is, in part, based on and a substitute for experience, and is enriched when experiences are added. If both parents work full time, a special effort should be made to discuss things, including current events, with their children during school and college.

(c) A hardheaded and sophisticated curriculum for K through 12 schooling is essential. It should include three things: essential skills, essential knowledge, and personal enrichment material. And to whatever extent is necessary, these three things should be reinforced in college. There are six essential skills: English, math, critical thinking (including common logical fallacies), the art of deliberation in decision-making, managing personal health, and managing personal finances.

In teaching the skills of critical thinking it is important to go beyond describing the techniques of critical thinking such as testing ideas and beliefs by experiments or observation plus logical analysis. Teaching critical thinking should also include common illustrative situations where critical thinking may benefit the individual or society. These situations generally involve subjects in which political or commercial salesmanship may outweigh the actual merits of competing products or policies. Most citizens, whether as consumers or voters, seldom have the time or information to evaluate carefully large amounts of advertising and advocacy. While mistakes resulting from successful advocacy may later be corrected, for example Prohibition and its repeal, much damage may result. Presenting our war in Vietnam as part of our fight against communism, when to many natives it was a war by foreigners against national independence, also illustrates the power of salesmanship.

Teaching students to question the sources, motivations, accuracy and balance of puffery and propaganda is not radical. It is rooted in both ancient and American wisdom. "I'm from Missouri" is a short way of saying don't believe everything you hear or read. "Caveat emptor" (let the buyer beware) is an older expression of the same healthy attitude. And "there's a sucker born every minute" and "never give a sucker an even break" shows that some people in the world of entertainment agree.

Closely related to developing alertness to puffery and propaganda is teaching basic sophistication about the functions of words, sometimes called semantics. This can be easily taught. Some types of words clearly function as symbols that serve to identify things, like "chair" and "turnip." Other types of words have multiple or shifting meanings, like "liberal" or "conservative," or "delicious" or "suspicious." Students should be made aware that this second category of words are often used by political or commercial advocates to create a positive or negative emotional response by their intended audiences

It should also be made clear that advertising and advocacy that plays on emotions is not necessarily bad, only that decisions are likely to be better when emotions do not overcome adequate attention to pertinent facts.

Finally, as a practical matter, critical thinking requires some ability to make preliminary judgments about what kinds of experiments or observations might be useful. Especially in dealing with complex public policy issues, this requires some degree of common sense or uncommon sense, based partly on familiarity with the subject of inquiry and partly on broader perspectives. In today's era of specialization, broader perspectives may be in short supply. Thus, to some extent, the practical value to society of teaching critical thinking may depend on a good general education, covering the major sciences, plus in-depth knowledge of world and national history and of trends affecting the future.

Essential knowledge has two principal categories, the natural world (basic physics, chemistry, biology including basic human anatomy, physiology and pathology, geology, astronomy, and physical geography), and the world of human behavior, including the economic, political, technological and general history of the world and the United States, basic psychology, basic cultural anthropology, basic economics and political science, basic civics including the structures, procedures, rights and responsibilities in American government, and political geography. Essential knowledge also includes knowledge of the methods for acquiring additional knowledge.

Recent discussions of American "exceptionalism" as a tool in American politics call for special attention to the importance of history. Knowledge of both American and world history in reasonable depth (economic, political, demographic, military, technological, philosophical, and so on) is essential for a successful democracy in today's partly globalized world. It is vital in avoiding the blunders of the past, in competing with other advanced and advancing nations, and in resolving public policy issues effectively. Yet most educators have neglected history, perhaps because teaching it more than superficially might lead to controversy. The federal No Child Left Behind Act supported learning English, math and science, but not history.

Properly taught, history will give students plenty of reasons to take pride in our nation's impressive accomplishments and in our capacity for future accomplishments. But to proclaim we're uniquely the world's best and greatest nation, as a political argument for brushing aside discussions of what others have accomplished or what needs improvement in our country, is unwise. It tends to turn people in other nations, including our friends, against us, because it may sound like boasting we're the master race. After all, there are other successful nations that have a lot to be proud of too, and from whom we have borrowed large parts of our culture, including our language and much of our law. And political exceptionalism diverts attention from experiences that may be helpful in solving our problems, and even from the problems themselves.

Personal enrichment materials include sports, music, art, literature, foreign languages, travel, and various extracurricular activities, which should supply good role models and types of recreation that can be enjoyed in later life. Personal enrichment materials might also include some assistance for students to consider in choosing, at least tentatively, a general direction for their journey through life. Successful people have often done this between their mid-teens and age 25. The rights listed in the Declaration of Independence could be used as a springboard for this assistance. Life and liberty will hopefully be reasonably secure, but the pursuit of happiness is obviously a real challenge. Schools and colleges can help students understand that happiness is, in fact, a real challenge. Schools and colleges can help students understand that happiness has two broad components, pleasures and satisfaction. Pleasures involve the use of the five senses and other capabilities plus the gratification of biological drives, which together include a huge variety. Satisfaction arises from a sense of worthwhile personal accomplishment, alone or as part of a group, especially when the accomplishment receives recognition from others. Together pleasures and satisfaction support a choice of personal goals, giving the student a stronger motivation to acquire the skills and knowledge to help overcome the shoals that may lie on the path to the goals.

While this may seem a lot to expect from schools, it needs to be done, for the benefit of the students and of the country. Some major subjects—for example, basic world history—might be covered adequately in thirty or forty class hours, provided the material is carefully chosen, well presented, and students are reminded that they are learning the main features, but with some important details omitted, for possible study in the future. The basics of some important skills, such as managing personal finances, could be helpfully covered in ten or fifteen class hours, which would help prevent future debacles like the recent costly and painful sub-prime mortgage mess.

No discussion of curriculums would be complete without some reference to fads and subject advocacy. The emphasis on "new math" and on math and science in response to Sputnik and to economic globalization comes to mind, as well as the rise and fall of "character education." A comment by a professor of mathematics at the University of Illinois captioned "Do We Really Need All This Math?" *(Washington Post*, October 23, 2010) warrants attention. My own wartime experience reinforces it; in 1943, when I asked about becoming an air navigator, I was told to forget it because I had no math in college. Fortunately this was overruled and I had no trouble learning overwater air navigation. The main thing to remember about curriculums is not to let too many electives overshadow the importance of the basic academic skills (language and math) and of basic knowledge (the sciences and in-depth history). These skills and knowledge are essential to prepare for the future.

(d) The teaching profession needs to be further professionalized. Prior to WW II, schools benefited because bright young women had few career opportunities besides teaching and nursing. But today, women have seized the opportunity to go into a broad range of careers. Also, schools have become parts of larger school systems. In some large systems teachers often seem subordinated to a large headquarters bureaucracy, instead of partnering with these staffs on the basis of respect and shared objectives. In other advanced countries the teaching profession is generally on a par with professions like medicine and law.

The necessary upgrading means providing more status, authority and compensation for teachers, and of course it means greater teaching effectiveness in bringing about learning. This in turn requires that teachers are well qualified in the subjects they teach, in how that subject relates to other subjects, and in how to teach effectively. The Teaching Company offers a 24-lecture course of DVDs on "The Art of Teaching" by Emory University Professor Patrick Allitt, designed for more effective teaching in high schools, colleges and other groups. And upgrading the teaching profession means ending the indiscriminate scapegoating of teachers for poor test results, when responsibility is partly with home conditions or school system administration. It also is essential that teachers have the authority to control their classrooms by terminating disruptive or inattentive behavior and when necessary communicating with parents.

Sparked in part by the success to date of Washington, DC's initiative called IMPACT, discussions of the teaching profession have criticized the longstanding domination of seniority to determine teacher pay and tenure. In an October 17, 2013 article in *EdSource* entitled "Stanford Professor finds Michelle Rhee's teacher evaluation system effective," author John Festerwald opens with this:

> Score one for Michelle Rhee and performance pay.
>
> A study released Wednesday [October 16, 2013] of the controversial teacher evaluation system that Rhee initiated when she was chancellor of the District of Columbia Public Schools has found that both its threats of dismissal and big pay incentives worked as intended. Within its first three years, the system led to increases in the retention and the performance of effective teachers while encouraging ineffective teachers either to quit or improve.

Historically, the federal civil service gives limited recognition to seniority as a factor in determining compensation, but promotions to a higher pay grade within a particular professional field depend on how the employee's performance and abilities are evaluated in relation to the needs of the group in which he or she works. If teaching included several pay grades, reflecting both basic and additional contributions to improving education, seniority might be continued but as a less dominant factor.

Rhee, who now heads a group called Students First, recognized that factors beyond seniority had to be taken into consideration in determining compensation. Her triumph was in going beyond improvements in standardized test results as a measure of success. Festerwald's article notes that IMPACT also includes:

...five observations by principals and master teachers of classroom management and instruction, a teacher's impact on the school community and other measures of student achievement not involving standardized tests. Three other elements distinguished IMPACT from other pay-for-performance programs, the researchers said:

- Strong incentives of dismissals after two straight "minimally effective" reviews and substantial monetary rewards, including first-year bonuses of up to $27,000 and permanent raises of as much as $25,000 for two consecutive "highly effective" ratings;

- Instructional coaches to assist teachers in improving performance;
- Recognition that the system would be neither small-scale nor temporary.

Since education budgets are usually parts of government budgets supported by taxes, it is not likely that all teachers can promptly be upgraded as described above. But over time this can be accomplished to a considerable extent. The rest of the educational gap can be closed by such things as carefully developed programs of guest lecturers, by various methods for increasing the motivations of students to learn, and by rooting out disincentives to learning, such as disruptions, bullying, badmouthing learning on an ethnic basis, or other distractions.

No discussion of the teaching profession can ignore the role of teachers colleges, which now tend to be entities within larger university systems. These colleges, which have often been closely linked to state teacher certification requirements, have been the object of various ideas for improvement. One suggestion is that their students should be given "clinical" training by teaching in actual classrooms. In addition, teachers colleges could assist schools in taking advantage of community resources for enriching education. Many people who aren't teachers have a natural inclination and aptitude for teaching, have done it as part of their jobs, and find it an enjoyable and rewarding activity. Our increasingly aging population contains many retired members of the learned professions and experienced leaders and practitioners in many aspects of business, government and other sectors. Schools of education should develop short courses to help these resources adapt to classroom audiences, which can contribute greatly to student motivations and development. If teachers colleges won't or can't do this successfully, others in the community should.

An encouraging development occurred in New Orleans during the recovery from Hurricane Katrina in 2005. The city embarked on major changes in the public school system, including a conversion to charter schools, freedom of parents to choose among those schools, and greater freedom of teachers and principals[1]. The result was a significant improvement in students' test scores, compared to the text scores before the hurricane and the test scores in the rest of the State of Louisiana.

(e) Higher education should be expanded and should be more than trade schools. "Our Underachieving Colleges" by Derek Bok, a former Harvard president, points the way. In many cases even supposedly well-educated persons with Bachelor and Masters degrees are not well educated except in the specialties of their work. When they rise to policy and management levels in business or government they often face situations they can't understand. Apart from their weakness in leadership positions, these products of specialized education may not even understand policy issues enough to vote intelligently unless they have broadened their education independently. While specialized and vocational education and training are necessary in the world of today and tomorrow, they are not substitutes for good comprehensive education.

Nevertheless, to many businesses and to many young adults, the term "higher education" clearly means preparation for particular jobs. This has had some effect on four-year and community colleges. But it has spurred a very rapid expansion of for-profit colleges. An article in the November 22, 2010 *Business Week* report that one for-profit college chain received three-quarters of its revenue from U.S. taxpayers and that its CEO was paid $41.9 million in 2009, more than twenty times the compensation of Columbia University's president. Yet students at for-profit colleges default on loans at three times the rate of students in private nonprofit colleges. In addition, the graduation rate for four-year degree students in for-profit colleges is only 22 percent, compared to 55 percent at state colleges and 65 percent at private nonprofit colleges. These differences may be partly due to the fact that the for-profits often serve a more disadvantaged population.

(f) The entire educational process must be oriented toward responsibility for the future. It is natural and often laudable to pursue a fair degree of personal wealth in various ways, but the pursuit is sometimes carried on in a manner or to an extent that's damaging to the pursuer and to others. Education can focus on various role models, and can point out that the law of diminishing utility applies to most acquisitions. Education can also point out that survival of the fittest often means not the fittest individual but the fittest group. Finally education can point out that experience shows that success without responsibility usually ends in failure.

While education alone probably cannot correct misallocations or misapplications of talent in our nation, it can certainly raise the issue, and other institutions can help readjust the range of inducements for a better balance.

(g) The so-called infotainment industry can contribute greatly to schools and lifelong education, in various ways. Over the years many excellent movies and fine historical and biographical documentaries have been made. They are both entertaining and useful. They should be exhibited in schools and other places to stimulate interest and searching discussions. These discussions should focus on the causes and effects of important events, and should also be alert to distortions of history, which are quite common. Local groups based on neighborhoods, faith groups, service clubs, and others could be helped to organize such activities, and modern computer technology could encourage participation without the time and cost of travel. College level materials, taught by leading professors and other experts, can be added to such activities with the help of materials from groups like The Teaching Company and the outreach activities of colleges and universities.

It is especially important that citizens have a better grasp of history (economic, political, military, demographic, technological, philosophic, and so on) as it bears on major policy concerns, present and future. In today's complex and partly globalized world, high school and college graduates should be able, for both world history and U.S. history, to identify the most important events and developments, and for each of these landmarks to list its probable causes and its effects.

Better public understanding of the background of major national issues—taxes, health care, energy, transportation, foreign relations—would mean more light and not just more heat in our democracy.

(h) An absolutely critical element for the success of any educational activity is the motivation to learn. This applies at all ages, but especially in growing up.

The preceding discussion refers to motivation twice, first under subheading (c), curriculum, where the motivational value of including personal enrichment materials is noted, and second, under subheading (d), the teaching profession, where it is recognized that upgrading the profession, while necessary, is not sufficient to close the educational gap, which will require, among other things, "various methods for increasing the motivations of students to learn."

What are these "various methods"? A column by Robert J. Samuelson, "Why School 'Reform' Fails" (*Newsweek*, September 13, 2010, also in *The Washington Post* of September 6, 2010) stirred a useful discussion of these "various methods." To summarize these methods: (1) take advantage of student curiosity or student ambition where it exists, (2) stress development of student responsibility and organizing skills, (3) cut truancy and tardiness, (4) cut time spent on TV and/or video games, (5) increase time on homework, (6) increase books, magazines and newspapers read in the home by adults, and (7) increase the authority of both parents and teachers. The first of these methods was emphasized by the writer Anatole France who said, "The whole art of teaching is only the art of awakening the natural curiosity of young minds for the purpose of satisfying it afterwards."

A useful way to apply these motivational methods in selective and effective ways is to bear in mind the ancient wisdoms of "the carrot and the stick" and the value of "setting good examples." But first it is important not to discourage curiosity and to welcome students who raise their hands with a question about the subject, something easier to do in small classes. Other motivational methods include giving good to excellent grades with praise and recognition, covering both academics and conduct, and even recognition of class rank at or possibly before graduation, with lower grades accompanied by counseling on how to improve. These valuable practices should not preclude some pass-fail or ungraded activities that maintain the motivation of late-blooming or academically slower students. However, a general practice of social promotion will dangerously undercut the motivation of many students. Attention to the motivation of slower students might be along the lines of the Army saying "be the best you can be." Assistance can take the form of tutoring, summer school, or a limited use of a track system. And schools should not be bashful about telling families that parents or older relatives and friends can serve as important role models for student development, as well as seeing that more student time is shifted from things like media-based recreation to homework. (Homework itself should be interesting enough to encourage motivation. For example, solving problems collaboratively or engaging in discussions with students in another state or country is a way to turn the computer into an exciting homework tool.)

Of course, neither the "carrot or stick" nor the "setting good examples" approaches always succeed. Carrots often fail to work if youngsters in well-heeled homes feel that success can be taken for granted. Sticks don't work if they are so severe as to cause deep discouragement. Setting good examples doesn't work if competing patterns of behavior and attitudes have a dominating power of attraction. So success in applying the various methods for improving the motivation to learn requires good judgment and an awareness of various influences in the cultural environment.

Finally, at several points in a K-12 education, students should be given an explicit, direct presentation of why they are in school and why they may later go to college. This presentation should feature four reasons: First, to learn how to earn a living, including what to do if one's family situation or job environment has unexpected changes. This does not mean vocational or specialized education for existing jobs, which may be added later. Second, one's rights and responsibilities as a citizen. Third, to learn about one's relationships, both direct and indirect, with other persons and organizations. Fourth, to learn various ways to enjoy life while avoiding health or financial difficulties. It should also be made clear that learning these things is the student's responsibility, not the teacher's, although the teachers are there to help the students learn.

The above guidelines do not explore all the complexities that may be involved in applying them to particular communities, school systems, or other segments of our population. But please feel free to add to or modify them as circumstances may suggest. Our future depends on it.

Here's an important postscript to the summary of the many ways American education needs upgrading. When Michelle Rhee took over as chancellor of the District of Columbia's public schools, which with very few exceptions provided inferior education, she had full authority to fix the mess. As mentioned above, she made enormous strides, but at the cost of much unhappiness in the teachers union and in some parents with children in schools that were closed. As a result, the mayor who appointed her lost a primary election. Rhee resigned, only to be vindicated later by studies such as the one cited by Stanford Professor John Festerwald. When she resigned she wrote an insightful piece called "What I've Learned" *(Newsweek* December 13, 2010). Among her reflections were these:

> The truth is that despite a handful of successful reforms, the state of American education is pitiful, and getting worse. Spending on schools has more than doubled in the last three decades, but the increased resources haven't produced better results. The U.S. is currently 21st, 23rd, and 25th among 30 developed nations in science, reading, and math, respectively. The children in our

schools today will be the first generation of Americans who will be less educated than the previous generation.

She added that the teachers' union "spent huge sums of money to defeat (Mayor Adrian) Fenty." But she then (perhaps sarcastically) goes on to say that teachers' unions shouldn't change, because "they're doing a great job" of their purpose, "to protect the privileges, priorities, and pay of their members."

Instead, she urges that education's "reform community" must exert countervailing influence on behalf of school children and our nation's competitiveness. She implies that some teachers would support the reform community, stating that "So many great teachers in this country are frustrated with the schools they are working in, the bureaucratic rules that bind them, and the hostility to excellence that pervades our education system." She started Students First to energize the reform community.

While it's unrealistic to expect excellence in all students or all teachers (remember the joke about the place where all students are above average), it's vital to encourage excellence wherever possible, and to encourage an approach to it everywhere else.

Politics—Solutions of Responsibility

13

> *"Let us not seek the Republican answer or the Democratic answer, but the right answer. Let us not seek to fix the blame for the past. Let us accept our own responsibility for the future."*
> John F. Kennedy

In terms of "fixing" politics, let's start with a fundamental responsibility as citizens: voting. Voting is a more complicated topic than many people realize, however. For one thing, where you vote has bearing on the outcome, not just for whom (or what) you vote.

Justin Levitt, a professor at Loyola University, wrote a piece about redistricting for the law school website entitled "Why Does It Matter?" In it, he gives some interesting background on the historical roots of the redistricting controversy, as well as its significance in terms of American politics.

American attempts to tailor district lines for political gain stretch back to the country's very origin. Patrick Henry, who opposed the new Constitution, tried to draw district lines to deny a seat in the first Congress to James Madison, the Constitution's primary author. Henry ensured that Madison's district was drawn to include counties politically opposed to Madison. The attempt failed, and Madison was elected—but the American gerrymander had begun.

Ironically, the man who inspired the term "gerrymander" served under Madison, the practice's first American target. Just a few months before Elbridge Gerry became Madison's vice president, as the Democratic-Republican governor of Massachusetts, Gerry signed a redistricting plan that was thought to ensure his party's domination of the Massachusetts state senate. An editorial artist added wings, claws, and the head of a particularly fierce-looking salamander creature to the outline of one particularly notable district grouping towns in the northeast of the state; the beast was dubbed the "Gerry-mander" in the press, and the practice of changing the district lines to affect political power has kept the name ever since.

In most states, the gerrymander is alive and well. Politicians still carve territory into districts for political gain, usually along partisan lines. This can lead to some serious consequences for the health of the democracy[1].

Levitt cites those serious consequences as

- Cherry-picking voters
- Eliminating incumbents
- Eliminating challengers
- Skewing statewide representation
- Diluting minority votes
- Splitting communities
- Destroying political goodwill

In principle, redistricting should perhaps be done by an expert, independent commission, and/or be subject to judicial review. The new district boundaries should (a) be reasonably compact, (b) should reflect some community of social and economic interests, and (c) should not discourage political balance, in the light of the history of party registrations and past voting. The goal should be to avoid discouraging voters who may stay at home because they feel, quite reasonably, that the outcome has been fixed by gerrymandering.

Let's now turn from the blame game to encouraging various kinds of civically constructive conduct. First, let's recognize that politicians sometimes show true statesmanship, both in emergencies and in taking action on chronic and long-term problems. Political skills are often necessary, just as they might be for parents when their children start to fight with each other. If President Woodrow Wilson had used more political skill at the end of WW I, he might have achieved a more durable peace. And often it isn't easy for a political leader to get support for what he or she believes is necessary, if the public isn't well informed, doesn't pay attention, or isn't ready to change things. And even a politician whose political career developed in a very corrupt political machine, like the Thomas "Boss Tom" Pendergast machine in Kansas City in which Harry S. Truman served, may be totally free of the machine's corruption, as Truman was.

Second, let's encourage participation in politics by independent-minded, civically responsible citizens. Political parties tend to neglect such folks until shortly before an election, especially a close election. Choosing the candidates and taking positions on policy issues is usually done largely by (or for) the party's "base" or "core," meaning those voters who usually can be counted on for support.

Independent-minded voters may or may not be registered as members of a party. In either case they may be able to alert party leaders to concerns and ideas that warrant attention. Some might volunteer to join search committees to find candidates better than some recent Illinois governors. (As of this writing, four of the state's last seven governors were convicted and imprisoned.)

The recent fashion of "surveys" in political fundraising letters does little to attract serious independent comments. Such comments require thoughtful preparation, clear presentation, and of course competent listening and discussion.

Now, for the encouragement of each of our two political parties and the benefit of our country, here are some thoughts to help both the Democrats and the Republicans to attract independent-minded, civically-oriented voters.

The Democrats, at least at the national level, might tone down their elitist image, which is associated with an apparently excessive reliance on a meritocracy of people with prestigious academic credentials. Meritocracies are necessary and are better than aristocracies, but they certainly are not immune from group-think and some "us-them" attitudes. Bring in some can-do people like Harry Hopkins, one of the architects of the New Deal under Franklin Delano Roosevelt, plus some people who question long-held assumptions. A contemporary example of a can-do politician is Governor John Hickenlooper of Colorado. When the federal government experienced a shutdown as part of Congressional action (or actually, inaction), Hickenlooper realized that efforts to rebuilt parts of Colorado devastated by floods could grind to a halt. He needed to keep certain federal workers—primarily 120 soldiers working on roads and bridges repair—on the job so he told the federal government he would pay them out of state funds to stay on the job. The Department of Defense then deemed the soldiers "essential" and let them keep working.

The Democrats have tried to reform Wall Street, as they once did in the 1930s, but they still suffer from a widespread feeling that Wall Street will manage to prevail again in one way or another.

The Democrats have long enjoyed labor union support. But they need to persuade union leaders to be more sensitive to not alienating public support on various issues, like the 60-year-long slide in U.S. auto manufacture, secret ballots in union representation elections, some form of merit pay for teachers, and so on.

The Democrats must show that they are serious about budget deficits and the national debt. When they correctly point out that this partly depends on improvements in our sluggish economy, they must make clear that they will bring about such improvements, even if it requires some curbing of exporting of our jobs and some curbing of some imports.

The Democrats must attack bureaucratic hassles of all kinds, including one-size-fits-all policies. Ten years after the 9/11 terrorist attacks, the TSA (Transportation Security Agency) still treats all airline passengers as potential terrorists, using radiation, groping body parts, removing shoes, belts, and water bottles. This even applies to retired naval reserve officers carrying official armed services photographic identification, like me. The FBI has had over a half-century of experience in doing background checks; TSA should seek its advice in developing a trusted traveler program for persons who demonstrably aren't terrorists.

The Democrats should go easy on "politically correct" policies that (a) discourage free discussion and (b) substitute one kind of discrimination for another. Some affirmative action may have been necessary temporarily. Americans generally support religious tolerance, but they also may have legitimate concerns about groups which include persons who express intolerance toward "infidels," or which reject our constitutional separation of church and state in favor of a government that enforces the "laws" contained in their own religion.

The Democrats should be careful about seeming to be in sympathy with groups that oppose all private ownership of guns, as do some in the District of Columbia, or oppose the private ownership of cars, as do some Sierra Club environmentalists.

The Democrats should suspend their lawsuits against state laws on illegal immigration until they have made every reasonable effort to negotiate federal-state cooperation on this important aspect of law enforcement.

Now let's turn the independent spotlight on the Republicans. First, they should make up their minds on whether or not they really are populists. With the Tea Party successes in the early 2000s, they have projected themselves as populists. Yet many of their policies clearly favor the very wealthy, who largely are an elite group, somewhat like the aristocrats of the past. Are Republicans seriously concerned about the great and growing inequality in our country? If so, what do they plan to do about it?

Second, Republicans suffer from being linked to extremists, such as the "no new taxes" variety. All those who have given serious thought to correcting our large federal deficits and national debt recognize that some kind of a 3 – part solution is needed: (a) cutting some kinds of government spending, (b) increasing federal revenues with some mixture of higher tax rates, better collection of existing taxes and curbing various legal loopholes from taxes, and (c) a sufficiently healthy national economy to reduce the need for some kinds of government spending and to increase the revenue yield of existing taxes.

On global problems, including national security and economic globalization, the Republicans offer a confusing picture to independent-minded voters. Where do they stand on military budgets, involvements in places like Afghanistan, Mexico, The Middle East, and so on? What about economic and diplomatic relations with Iran, China and its neighbors, Russia and its neighbors? What about the role of the World Trade Organization (WTO) and North American Free Trade Agreement (NAFTA) and of multi-national corporations, which under the banner of "free trade" have shifted jobs and taxes from the United States to other countries? (It's only fair to note that Democrats also are not too clear on these matters.)

On domestic policies, to what extent will Republicans give priority to various parts of the business community (big business, small business, and Wall Street) and to what extent will priority go to tradition-minded groups concerned with so-called social issues?

Whom do some Republicans have in mind when they call other Republicans "RINOS" (Republicans In Name Only)? Does that apply to people like Michael Gerson, who served in the Bush administration, but who expressed concern about a prominent Republican who opposed pasteurization of milk and accused Lincoln of violating the ideas of our founders? (*Washington Post*, July 1, 2011).

Finally, independent-minded voters who are familiar with U.S. history wonder why some Republicans constantly glorify Ronald Reagan as the great Republican president. It's true that Reagan's Hollywood background may have helped him project a politically successful image. But his job performance in the White House certainly rates no more than a B.

On the Cold War, Reagan can take some credit for its successful end after he left office. But Reagan basically followed the policies of containment with co-existence laid out by Truman, Eisenhower, Kennedy and the rest of Reagan's predecessors. Reagan correctly fired the striking air traffic controllers, but then he put them all on a permanent backlist against possible re-hiring: not just the leaders but ordinary employees who simply went along with their co-workers. Reagan blocked sensible measures to help poor people in poor nations to control overpopulation, thus helping to keep them in poverty and more prone to radicalism and terrorism. And his policies helped to bring an end to our country's long post-war prosperity, cutting taxes on the wealthiest Americans. Thus, in some fashion, he paved the way for our long slide into our large and increasing inequality, our sluggish economy, and the large increases in our national debt. Reagan does, however, deserve credit for upgrading the national mood, after the depressing experiences of Watergate and President Jimmy Carter's misfortunes.

With this record, it puzzles independent-minded voters why Republicans constantly point their spotlight on Reagan. After all, Republicans might point with pride to some other Republican presidents like Lincoln, Teddy Roosevelt, Eisenhower and others to show what Republicans can do for our country. (Of course, if they did that, the Democrats might engage in something similar with regard to some of their own presidents, a competition that might be enlightening.)

Both parties also suffer from blind spots. Democrats have a blind spot on passenger travel on both short and long distances, for example. In 1978, they repealed the Civil Aeronautics Act in favor of free and open competition for anyone to start an airline. This blind spot is also exhibited by their negative attitude toward former president Dwight Eisenhower's interstate highway system and roads to serve cities with rapidly growing suburbs. On local transportation, Democrats sometimes seem to feel that bicycles, busses and rail should replace private cars.

One of the Republicans' big blind spots seems to be neglect of the important dependence of our economy on sufficient purchasing power to match productivity.

PART FOUR—HOW YOU CAN HELP

Overview of Options 14

This entire Part covers practical ways to exercise your civic responsibility, and to have satisfaction in doing it.

There are two main ways to exercise civic responsibility. One is in the course of some feature of your life that you engage in anyway, such as your occupation or your family activities. This can be very important, depending on various factors. Jobs vary greatly in opportunities for civically-related activities. Families often can raise children with a sense of responsibility and an interest in newsworthy matters. But you can judge better than I how civic responsibility might fit, or already does fit, into those parts of your life.

The second way to exercise civic responsibility is as distinct projects or activities. This Part Four will deal chiefly with that way.

Let's start with the most basic questions about getting involved:

- How much time and/or money can you devote to this? The answer usually depends on what's free after the demands of job, household and family.
- Do you want to act alone or as part of some group?
- If you lean toward acting with a group, is there a group you might join, or would you like to start a new one, perhaps with some friends? Of course, a new group might cooperate or federate with other similar groups.
- To what extent can you expect volunteers or resources of various kinds: from neighbors, the Inter-

net, news media, or academic, political, business, labor, professional, faith, seniors, veterans or other groups?

- If your thoughts turn toward starting a new group, how should it be established? Possibly just as an informal association? But if it might engage in various activities, perhaps as a membership corporation, to limit personal risks?

- What about the group's finances? Can you keep expenses low by using your homes instead of renting office space? Perhaps some school, church, or other institution can provide free or inexpensive space for occasional larger meetings. Can you rely on volunteers, only rarely paying for special help? Can you qualify under the tax laws as a 501(c)(3) group so that dues and contributions to the group are tax-deductible?

- How will the group's work be arranged? Will there be a central team plus teams for particular projects or functions? What about newsletters, meetings, records, checkbooks, and related items?

- When the group decides to deal with particular problems, what products might be developed to address those problems, and how will those products be distributed?

Now let's look at acting alone instead of in a group. You can engage in advocacy for solutions to problems (a) by speaking to individuals or to groups at various hearings or gatherings or by calling in to some broadcast talk shows, and by writing letters, emails, and so on to newspapers and other periodicals, to your Congressman or other public officials, or to the Internet audience, perhaps by starting a blog.

To obtain facts to guide or support your advocacy, you can use your own experience, engage in experiments or observation, or obtain information from libraries, the Internet, various organizations or governmental agencies (which may routinely publish some information and may provide more under the Freedom of Information Act or similar open-records or open meetings laws). A further method to obtain certain kinds of information is by "discovery" procedures in civil litigation, but even when this is available it is likely to be costly.

All these methods of advocacy and of obtaining facts to support or guide advocacy are generally available to groups as well as to individuals. Also, it may be easier for a group than for an individual to do these things because groups usually have more capabilities or resources. On the other hand, an individual often has some advantages over a group in being able to make decisions and to act more quickly. For similar reasons small groups, which usually are less formal than large groups, may have similar advantages over large groups.

At this point, let's stop before it seems that exercising civic responsibility to solve problems is only a matter of advocacy. Solutions to some problems require direct actions like supplying resources, changing behavior patterns, undertaking research, or arranging for ongoing activities. Providing your time or money to meet public needs is civic responsibility with or without advocacy.

Nevertheless, in a nation like ours, which is a democracy with a free market economy, both of which function in a world of great complexity and rapid change, a high quality of advocacy is often essential in focusing attention on problems and their possible solutions.

But by "quality advocacy" I don't mean the kind of salesmanship that sometimes produces results in commerce or in politics. I mean the kind that puts the spotlight on what's important, and does so in ways that don't let either ideology or undisclosed financial interests distort the picture.

This means being alert to the fact that some so-called "think tanks"—and Washington is full of them—may actually be advocacy groups. This also means that their think-tank activities are in support of their advocacy objectives.

I'll end this overview with a few thoughts about exercising civic responsibility by joining some existing group.

- What are the admission criteria, if any, in terms of background, experience, and/or credentials?
- What will it cost you in time and money?
- Could you make friends there, and would you like to?
- Who started the group and who runs it now?
- Which national or community public policy problems fall within the group's possible range of interests?
- What does or could the group do about such problems?
- Would the group welcome your ideas as well as your support?
- Would you enjoy yourself and perhaps improve or advance yourself by participating in the group's activities?

Zoom for a Better Future

15

To increase the chances that the efforts of you or your group in dealing with a problem will be successful, it's important to bear in mind two basics: first, that we live in a world of increasing complexity and specialization, and second, that we also live in a world that needs good generalists, meaning persons who try to monitor the overall picture of the conditions, cultures and trends within which the various specialties function.

Acting on good intentions in today's complex and changing world often ends in disappointment, because the actions were taken without enough information, or with misleading information. Bear in mind that most successful people in any profession or job seldom embark on major actions without first trying to get enough pertinent information.

It's a pity that some voters cast ballots, and some consumers spend money, without adequate information. It was a pity that the well-meaning opponents of alcoholism a century ago, as well as the well-meaning opponents of war during the 1930's, put in a lot of hard work and seemed to be succeeding, but ended up making things worse.

To get a better picture of what you or your group may encounter when trying for improvement in some community, national or global problem, you need two kinds of information.

The first kind of information is similar to the view you get when you move a zoom lens to its wide-angle position: a broad picture which includes the things that surround the object of your concern. This broad picture gives you two useful kinds of perspectives: of time and of place. Time perspective includes past experience, current trends, and future possibilities. Space perspective provides information on how the problem that concerns you is dealt with in other communities, organizations, nations or cultures.

Perhaps the easiest way to get these wide-angle perspectives is a broad education, not one chiefly designed to prepare for a particular kind of job. A broad education includes the basics of the natural and social sciences, plus in-depth world and national history. Such history will include enough technology, demographics and developments in economics, law, government, religion and other aspects of Western and other cultures to show how we arrived at where we are today.

But this kind of college education is not the only way to get the big picture. Remember that former president Harry Truman, who never went to college but read a lot of history, coped quite successfully when he suddenly was faced with the dangerous emerging reality of the Cold War in a nuclear world.

Some universities offer a variety of on-campus and off-campus courses for those past their college years. And the Teaching Company of Chantilly, Virginia offers a great variety of recorded lecture courses by professors well qualified both in their fields and in teaching skills. The 30-minute lectures in some of these courses provide a solid understanding of our present situation and how we got here.

The Price of Civilization by Jeffrey Sachs of Columbia University is a book published in 2011 that helps illuminate the broad picture. Sachs has a long history of advising governments and other institutions on serious economic and social problems. The first part of the book describes various causes of the 2008 crash and the sluggish economy. The second part suggests remedies for these causes.

Taking advantage of resources such as Sachs' book, plus use of reliable newspapers and magazines, should help fill in the broader, wide-angled picture. The fact that some outstanding newspapers have strong biases on some issues does not destroy their value, so long as readers are aware of the biases and the newspaper presents news and opinions contrary to its own views. An especially helpful magazine is *Current History*, a monthly which covers a different part of the world each month, but covers "Global Trends" in its January issue each year.

But getting a broad, wide-angle picture for your problem is only part of the information that you or your group should have. As someone once said, getting the broad picture only means that you know something, not a lot, about a lot of things. Now you or your group needs to shift your zoom lens from wide-angle to telephoto, to get a more detailed and thorough picture of the problem itself. As someone once said, the devil is in the details.

There are many ways to get more detailed information on a problem. Here are some:

- Use a library with help from a librarian, and use the Internet. Some websites are useful but others may be less reliable, possibly due to advocacy, secret funding, or other reasons that may be difficult for users to evaluate. At the very least, go to the "about us" page and find out something about the history and founders behind the website.

- Use FOIA (the federal Freedom of Information Act), and similar state open-records and open-meetings laws. There is no specific form to make a FOIA request, and most agencies now accept the requests electronically by web form, email or fax. You don't even have to be a citizen to make a FOIA request. The basic criteria are that the request must be in writing, reasonable describe the information sought, and it must comply with any specific agency requirements. This points to the reality that there is no single office in the government that handles FOIA requests; they are handled by the individual agencies. All of the agencies do have FOIA sections of their websites, though, so guidance on approaching them should be readily available online.

  The kinds of records available through FOIA requests are all records that belong to an agency unless they are exempted from, or prohibited from, disclosure. This may include records about yourself, events, public or private organizations and their activities, and people who are alive or dead. If you want information about yourself, be prepared to prove that you are who you say you are. The government has a duty to protect your privacy and won't release records about a person unless it's crystal clear that the person asking for the records has a right to know, either because it's the individual himself asking or because an individual has given explicit permission for someone else to ask.

Under usual conditions, the agency has 20 days to respond to a request. There are unusual conditions, however, in which research might be required. Those requests take longer, but the person requesting is supposed to be notified about what's going on and why it's taking longer than usual.

In 2007, Congress created the Office of Government Information Services (OGIS), which is an organization within the National Archives and Records Administration (NARA). To some extent, OGIS does what we used to do in the Office of Legal Counsel, which is a review of agency compliance and support in the resolution of FOIA disputes.

FOIA applies to all records, paper and electronic, of all federal agencies, including cabinet-level departments. But it doesn't apply to records of federal courts and of Congress and its agencies, such as the Congressional Research Service and the Government Accountability Office. (However, the office of your Member of Congress or Senator may be able to give you access to some records of these legislative-branch agencies.)

If you aren't sure which agencies may have records that interest you, you might get help at your local library or the local office of your Member of Congress. And you can see for yourself what each agency does by using the U.S. Government Manual. You can buy the latest edition of this 600+-page book for $30 from the Government Printing Office,

P.O. Box 979050, St. Louis, MO. 63197-9000, or by phoning GPO's Washington Office at (202) 512-1800 and paying by credit card.

Of course FOIA doesn't provide access to all records. FOIA contains several "exemptions" from compulsory disclosure. Chief exemptions are for (a) classified national security information (mostly military and diplomatic matters), (b) confidential business information such as trade secrets, (c) personal privacy information such as medical records, (d) records of law enforcement, (e) records of internal advice and assistance which might be inhibited by fear of disclosure, and (f) information the disclosure of which is prohibited by some other federal law.

When an agency gets a request for records containing exempt information, it may deny access or when practicable grant access with the exempt parts deleted. It also may make a discretionary release of some kinds of exempt material, which is sometimes done with records of internal advice or assistance, to enhance the public's right to know. However, there are other federal laws which prohibit the release of certain kinds of information, and FOIA must respect those laws.

Agencies are authorized to charge fees for some of the work in responding to requests. But agencies are also authorized to waive all or part of the fees, and they frequently do so, especially when the request isn't burdensome or will provide information that will benefit the public. Therefore a request letter might include something about how the requested information will benefit the public, perhaps noting if the request is on behalf of a charitable or educational group operating under section 501(c)(3) of the Internal Revenue Code.

If your FOIA request is denied, you can appeal to a higher authority in the agency, and you can sue the agency in federal court. There have been thousands of court decisions in FOIA lawsuits.

FOIA has been the law of the land for more than 40 years. It was originally passed by Congress largely due to the efforts of the nation's journalists. Public awareness of FOIA was stimulated during the 1970s by Ralph Nader and other consumer activists, and by public concern about unjustified government secrecy in the Watergate crisis. FOIA has been amended several times, usually to strengthen it, and has been the subject of some important court decisions.

For all these reasons, a person or group planning to use FOIA might be well advised to consult the latest edition of "Guide to the Freedom of Information Act." This is published by the Justice Department's Office of Information Policy. The 2009 edition can be bought from the Government Printing Office (GPO) for the current price of $29. Like the U.S. Government Manual referred to above, it can be ordered from the GPO by phone, (202) 512-1800 and paid by phone with a credit card.

The latest edition of this Guide can be accessed without charge on the Justice Department's website, www.justice.gov. The home page of the

Justice website has a link to FOIA, which leads to the website of the Office of Information Policy, which includes the Guide. In addition, take advantage of the free video information online. The Department of Justice in the Obama Administration has produced a multi-part video on YouTube explaining what the law provides and what you need to do to take advantage of it.

- Naturally there are other ways to obtain the "telephoto" kind of close-up, detailed information on the problem that concerns you or your group. In this age of specialization you may be able to contact persons whose work provided direct contact with that problem. Such persons might be recent retirees, or persons who have changed jobs, or "whistleblowers." You also may find journalists or scholars with useful experience. And, if you have a large budget for your civic activities, you may be able to find a private detective agency or some accountants that can develop useful information to support your efforts.

- Finally, you may search for other organizations that have concerns and experience that may enlighten the problems that concern you or your group. This country has large numbers of trade associations, scholarly and scientific groups, and other groups that deal with major or specialized aspects of various public policies (for example, environment, poverty, education, law enforcement, taxation, and immigration). Such groups can be found through various graduate schools, some government or journalistic sources, or the Internet. These sources of help may often be limited to information that the organization has already made public. That's partly because the other organization may not be sure about you or your group, as to whether to expect cooperation or competition or even opposition.

Here's a short example of how the success of problem-solving may depend on zooming to get a better picture—both the macro (that is, the big, wide-angle picture that surrounds your problem) and the micro or telephoto picture (that is, the details of your problem).

Problem; increased obesity, leading to several serious diseases and running up the nation's costs for health care, which burdens the national economy and increases the level of governmental and private debt.

Important part of this problem: increased obesity among school children.

Proposed Solution: Improve the nutritional quality of the school lunches that are provided by schools.

Macro Insight: The late Professor of Anthropology Ralph Linton said "men act from mixed motives." Here the act is eating. There are several motives for eating, such as (a) satisfying hunger, (b) enjoying tasty food, (c) improving nutrition, (d) being polite to your hostess, (e) obeying your parents and (f) conforming to culture-based habits such as preferring beer over wine or the opposite, avoiding pork or other foods, and so on.

Micro Insight: How can we motivate the kids to eat more nutritious school lunches? Start with making them taste better or have a more pleasant texture: some like vegetables cooked to be soft, others don't. Careful choices of fruits and vegetables by school cafeterias would seem to be important, given that consumers in supermarkets are often faced with fruits that look nice but aren't ripe. Canned fruits seldom taste or feel unripe. And consider the judicious use of condiments or different methods of food preparation to make food taste better. And consider cultural motivation, such as making known the fact (if it is a fact) that role models such as star athletes eat nutritious food. Consider obtaining or making a powerful training film on the effects of various kinds of food on various health problems. Cafeterias might also launch a "taste test" program, offering free samples to students of various foods and various ways of preparation that the cafeteria might serve.

This example may make the process sound simplistic, but let's look at how it has actually worked in certain locations. Some states have laws in place to restrict the types of food that can be served to schoolchildren at lunchtime primarily to improve their nutrition. The macro perspective on the situation is that children have to eat something to satisfy their hunger and if they have something that tastes good, so much the better. In attempting to conform to the law, schools and school districts have tried to take a micro approach to make the law work.

The result, according to a study published in the June 2013 issue of *JAMA Pediatrics*, is this:

> [There is] an association between more stringent school meal standards and more favorable weight status, especially among low-income students.

The study produced one other noteworthy result. Students did not compensate for the healthier school meals by buying more snacks or sodas on school premises. . . . students in states with stricter standards governing competitive foods—those sold in competition with federally supported school meals—consumed fewer calories and less fat and sugar at school and did not gain as much weight as students in states with less stringent standards.[3]

The CQC Story–
Can You Adapt it?

16

While I was working full-time on a variety of national problems from 1950 to 1980 my family and I lived in suburbs of Washington. During these years I used some of my spare time on civic projects at the community level, such as starting a branch library and a community swimming pool and working on zoning disputes to protect our neighborhoods.

After I retired from the Justice Department in early 1981, I divided my working time three ways: work at a Maryland law firm, consulting for an American Bar Association committee that was concerned about Soviet publicizing of America's Freedom of Information Act, and with the help of a few friends starting Citizens for Quality Civilization, Inc. (CQC). We planned to select a few of our many national problems for attention and action.

CQC began by considering a list of 32 national problem subjects, in order to choose one or two for first attention. Here they are:

- Education
- Abuse of alcohol and drugs
- Criminal justice systems
- Transportation systems
- Health care and its financing
- Balancing personal freedoms and public interests
- Balancing nationalism and (what's now called) globalization
- Underpaid occupations

- Environmental issues
- Energy issues
- Substandard management in business, government
- Misallocation of talent (for example, top graduates of top schools heading for Madison Avenue and Wall Street in lieu of civil service positions)
- Immigration and other demographics trends
- Pressures on working mothers
- Self-esteem problems of various groups
- Coping with increasing specialization and complexity
- Terrorism and nuclear war
- Assorted bigness issues: cars, houses, cities, corporations
- The no-one-in-charge perception
- Balancing competition with cooperation in various situations
- Effects of sports on schools, values, and other aspects of life
- Corruption, not only in business and politics but also in academia, faith groups
- Proliferation of hassles in everyday life
- Problems in child-rearing practices
- Updating national security
- Revisions of land-use policies
- Impacts of violence in entertainment
- Political machinery, including campaign financing
- Overhaul of financial services as to risks, debt, stability, meeting economic and public needs
- Effects of migrations on rich and poor countries, on urbanization, and on coastal areas

- Tax policies and their effects
- Privatization of government functions and trends as applied to various services.

We picked education and decided to create a classroom program to stimulate learning, both in academics and in what later became known as character education. We tested our prototype materials for a year in eight public schools, which urged us to continue, but with stronger materials. We upgraded our materials (a poster for students, a guidebook for teachers, and a letter to parents on how they could help) with teachers who volunteered, plus some paid help.

Teachers, principals and state officials praised the materials, which were placed in about 300 classrooms, and an education organization bought 2,000 of the posters. The poster illustrated eight elements of excellence and success: responsibility, role models, skills, knowledge, peer pressure, critical thinking, self-control and broader interests.

But CQC had little capability to distribute what it had produced. A salesman for a big textbook company once expressed interest in our materials, but when he heard the price we charged, about $20 per classroom, he said we would have to increase it to a package priced at $200 or $300 to make it worthwhile for his company to distribute. He suggested we add something to justify a higher price. In retrospect, I should have followed his advice. We had tried to make our materials affordable, but we should have given distribution realities more careful attention.

In 1998 CQC turned to the nation's healthcare problems. With a team of volunteers we wrote and published
our first citizen's handbook in 1999. We arranged to have
our final draft reviewed by a professor who had served
as the late Senator Daniel Patrick Moynihan's expert on
healthcare economics. This handbook was 17 pages long
and was titled "What Every Citizen Should Know About
Healthcare Policy: Answers to 12 Basic Questions."

In the following years, building on our experience
with our health policy handbook, CQC assembled volunteers to create civic handbooks on several other areas of
public policy. These handbooks featured readability, cov-
erage of the whole subject with references to related subjects, objectivity, lists of names and qualifications of the
drafters and of a spectrum of experts who reviewed the
draft before publications, and sources of further information. These handbooks are attached as appendices to this
book, and are also available as free downloads at www.
GamePlanPress.com; in order of publication, they are as
follows:

(a) "Metropolitan Transportation: What Every Citizen
Should Know," subtitled "This civic primer is a condensed
analysis of traffic congestion, its relation to other public
policy concerns, and its possible remedies." First published in 2004 and then reissued in 2014, it is 17 pages
plus appendices.

(b) "Education Policy: What Every Citizen Should
Know," first published in 2008 and then reissued in 2014.
It is 53 pages long, including an outline covering 5 basics

and 4 problem areas, plus 8 appendices, including material on curriculums, websites, parenting education and schools in other advanced nations.

(c) 'Globalization And The Economy: What Every Citizen Should Know," first published in 2009 and then reissued in 2014. It is 24 pages long, covering the types of globalization and their causes and effects, with 5 appendices including websites, a glossary, and a list of major players in globalization.

For many years CQC mailed a short newsletter to interested persons. CQC also solicited annual dues of $30 each December and some folks contributed more. The contributions were enough to sustain activity that generated these readable, focused handbooks for citizens.

Our CQC experience has some lessons for groups that seek to address national problems. First, it may seem easier to find volunteers for such a group around Washington, which, as you would expect, has many persons, including retirees, with a lot of experience in various national and global concerns. But other parts of our country, including some major cities and some places with universities, also have people with these interests and backgrounds. And, of course, the Web makes it much easier for people who don't live near each other to work together.

Second, it may be easier to recruit volunteers for specific areas of concern, something which CQC's name fails to do. Part of the cure for a civic group with broad interests may be to publicize specified teams for specific projects. Third, an ability to create useful products should be matched with a good plan to distribute them. Fourth, a group should be aware of its aging members and work to involve younger people. The latter two points spotlight the serious weaknesses of CQC: Failure to attract young professionals and insufficient focus on distribution. At least to some extent, the distribution problem is being addressed by making the material available as free downloads.

Getting Specific
about Action

17

You can take a couple of rather immediate actions, as well as couple of longer-term actions, to improve conditions in your community and your country.

The first is providing help to people in need. This means finding who needs help and providing it as a volunteer. Well known categories of those in need are (a) children in poor or incomplete families or foster homes, or in need of day care or Head Start, (b) elderly or disabled persons who need assistance in transportation, shopping or other activities, and (c) persons who have suffered a major loss, tragedy or misfortune and need help until they adjust or recover.

In many communities you can find services that help meet such needs, perhaps through a local United Way or a Volunteer Center operated by your local government, or faith groups, which may have their own pastoral care activities and may know of other sources of direct help. Some groups, such as Meals on Wheels and the Visiting Nurses Association are well known. Some parts of local governments may also know of needs where volunteers can help, for example using volunteers to mentor juvenile delinquents.

In many situations you may be better off providing help as a volunteer in an established group, rather than by acting alone. The group will generally have experience on where the needs are greatest and on how to provide help more safely and effectively.

It's also important to consider, in case something goes wrong during your volunteer efforts, that the risk of legal liability may be handled by the group, rather than falling upon you.

In addition, if your volunteer work entails some incidental expenses such as travel, the group may pay them, and if you donate money to cover such expenses to the group, or pay for those expenses yourself, the donation or expenditures may be tax-deductible.

It's worth noting that experience in providing direct help may produce some useful insights into the problems which contribute to various needs for direct help, and may even give you some useful ideas for helping solve the problems which give rise to various kinds of needs.

By providing direct help to people in need, you exercise your humanity. By joining a political party, you have a chance to exercise your cognitive thinking skills and values.

While politics and politicians often have a bad name—sometimes deserved and sometimes not—don't write off affiliation with a political party. Getting involved in politics has its pros and its cons; your involvement can perhaps boost the pros. (Before discussing them, let's be clear that by "joining" a party we mean more than just registering so you can vote in a party primary; we mean also joining a local political party group and putting in some time and/or money.)

The first pro of joining is that it can enhance your role as a responsible citizen. A great range of issues—about possible changes in our laws, policies, taxes, spending, and activities within and beyond our borders which are engaged in, or influenced by, various levels of government—may be affected by politics. In other words, politics is one of the most important links between the people and governments. (The other links are the actual conduct of government activities, lobbying, education, litigation, information systems, and political fundraising.) So becoming a member of a party in good standing may give you more clout than just as a voter.

The second pro is that you might advance yourself, perhaps by being elected or appointed, or by becoming part of the party's leadership team, or by gaining some recognition in connection with some governmental functions such as contracting, zoning, school board, and so on. Naturally this pro depends on a large number of variables. America has had many great presidents, legislators, governors, mayors, and other officials and almost all of them were able to enter into those positions through politics.

A third advantage is that if you or your family or friends have some problem or concern in which some part of government might play a role, your party connections might save you time and trouble in threading your way through various bureaucracies. This help, sometimes called constituent service, is often given by elected officials or their staffs to any citizen regardless of politics. However, party officials may provide similar assistance. This assistance, often called access, is generally not improper and it can help save time and avoid mistakes.

Fourth, you and maybe your spouse or partner might have fun. In some places political parties engage in a lot of recreational and social activities such as dinners, fairs, outings, and receptions. These might enrich your life, and might broaden your range of friends and contacts.

The cons largely depend on where you live. In general parties welcome volunteers. But in some places, one party or even both may be less than welcoming, possibly because a local party group feels it's a sure thing, or a hopeless thing, or has poor leadership.

Another con is that parties depend on workers and money, so you might be expected to spend time in a fair amount of local precinct work, helping to build support by visits to voters, especially helping or encouraging those who support your party to get to the polls on Election Day.

Another con is that parties try to avoid discussions that could lead to internal divisions. This means that you can't just express your policy opinions as freely as you might in other places if that might cause friction or distract the group from other priorities.

Finally, serious involvement in politics can lead to disappointments that aren't your fault. This can have several causes, such as (a) a deep public mood of unhappiness resulting in a reaction to throw out all incumbents, (b) a political leader's voicing of an early warning about something unpopular such as a need to raise taxes or (c) scandals involving some people in the party.

However, politics are not the only activities in which one can have disappointments that are not one's own fault. This also happens in business, sports, and churches. And while politics may often be an uncertain activity, uncertainty sometimes offers excitement and even opportunity. In addition, there are some periods of time and some parts of the country where the fruits of political activity are fairly secure.

You might also consider how politics can affect our way of life. Throughout our history, developments which have improved the American way of life have been possible because our culture contains a wise mixture of freedom and progress, a mixture in which politics has often played an important role.

Before joining a political party, you might want to consider why there is so much public dissatisfaction with both parties. A commentary captioned "We need a third Party" by Matt Miller (Washington Post, 9/26/11) offers possible reasons for this dissatisfaction, especially among independent and civically-minded citizens. Miller says that citizens should not have to choose between a party that offers timid half measures to solve our problems and a party that offers extremism and fanaticism. He says this unsatisfactory choice has three reasons: First, the chief aim of both parties is to win elections, not to solve problems. Second, both parties are prisoners of special interest groups and are thus subject to ideological tests. Third, neither party trusts the public enough to lay out the facts and to explain the steps that are truly needed to fix things, some of which would be unpopular.

When George Washington was president he feared that the rise of political partisanship would injure our country. But political parties soon arose, and parties are also a feature of other successful democratic nations. So maybe Miller's concerns are curable, if not by a third party, then by more responsible conduct by our two present parties. Could you help with this problem in one way or another?

The more long-term actions you can take are to start a candidate appraisal group, which could be formal or informal, and as a corollary, popularize quizzes on civic issues for present and future voters.

When we vote for rival candidates in an election, what are we really doing? Naturally, we are choosing between parties, personalities and programs, which is important. But we're also deciding between rival applicants for the same jobs. And we can do better if we improve the process.

As voters, we need to act like an experienced executive choosing someone to fill an important job. Two things the executive would want to make clear are: (a) what are the job's responsibilities? (b) What qualifications of abilities and experience should we look for in each applicant for the job?

The group could start with a formula for choosing a president. That job has four main responsibilities

1. to conduct our foreign relations, which includes diplomacy and economic and military concerns;
2. to lead politically in order to maintain the support of the public and of Congress for his party and his policies, both domestic and foreign;
3. to manage the executive branch of the government so that its departments and agencies function properly, thus carrying out his constitutional duty to see that federal laws are "faithfully executed"; and
4. to provide the Congress and the people with forward-looking recommendations in his State of the Union and other reports in order to help meet the nation's foreseeable needs and opportunities, including the health of our national economy. There-

fore candidates should have the knowledge, experience and abilities to perform these four functions.

Candidates should also have two additional qualifications. The first is personal health: President Woodrow Wilson was largely disabled by a stroke during a critical part of his presidency. The second is sensitivity to people's feelings: President Jimmy Carter alienated many federal workers and their families by charging them to park at their jobs on government property—something private sector employers rarely do—in effect cutting their compensation at a time of inflation.

The group could then specify what kinds of education, experience, knowledge, skills and temperament are needed in a job with those responsibilities.

To warm up for applying agreed-upon qualifications to rival presidential candidates, a good exercise for the group would be to write report cards on each president from the years 1900 on, perhaps even including an incumbent. And if the group is sufficiently free of partisan loyalties, it might do prospective report cards on rival presidential candidates.

To start a candidate appraisal group, it might be helpful to involve one or more teachers or professors of American history and perhaps of political science. It might also be helpful to have some people with experience in filling important jobs both in the government and in the private sector. But a large part of the group should be independent-minded citizens with a strong interest in the success of our democracy.

Obviously, the value of the group would largely depend on spreading its work-product. The group could probably expect help on this from candidates whom the club found well-qualified, particularly if the club found the rival candidate to be less qualified.

The jobs of other elective officials are also quite important. Senators and Congressman don't have many executive responsibilities but they must deal with a wide range of domestic and foreign policy issues, using their powers of the purse, of legislating, and of oversight. State and local elected officials also have a broad range of important responsibilities.

This idea of groups to evaluate persons for important governmental functions is not without some precedent. For many years, the qualifications of persons being considered for appointment to federal judgeships have been reviewed and reported on by a committee of the American Bar Association. And some newspapers publish their choices among candidates, sometimes with their reasons for their choices, before Election Day.

But a more rigorous and impartial report, based on a systematic appraisal of the qualifications of candidates for the job to be filled, and which describes the candidate's experience and abilities, not just his or her policy and political positions, should help voters in deciding whom to support.

This does not necessarily imply that a conscientious voter should vote for the best qualified candidate. A voter might justifiably vote for a less qualified candidate whose position on major policy issues seems preferable to the position of a better qualified rival, but at least qualifications and policy positions would be separately considered.

Now let's turn to quizzes, which have proliferated so much since the advent of the World Wide Web. There are thousands of quizzes online about personalities, relationships, literature, fashion, food, and every other subject you can imagine. There are even quizzes on civics. So the issue is not so much that you need to create quizzes for present and future voters, but that you can take action to help popularize them.

Readers of this book know that one of the most important sectors for our nation's future is education. You also know that in-depth history is a vital part of education, to help make wise choices on issues of public policy. However, year after year, surveys indicate that too many of us know too little history, especially the kinds that show how problems develop and how they are dealt with. To help address this weakness, here is a short quiz that turns the spotlight on the most important parts of U.S. and world history.

You may prefer to use and popularize this quiz rather than the lengthier ones online: It has only two questions:

1. What are the ten most important parts of U.S. history, with a brief indication of why each is important? The indication may refer to the causes of the event or development, to its effects, or to both.
2. What are the ten important parts of world history, also with an indication of why each is important? The indication may refer to the causes of the event or development, to its effects, or to both.

As you can see, the contest is subjective. Some would argue that the election of an African-American as president was one of the ten most important things to happen, whereas others would not put that on the list.

You can have fun with this in a school setting or even at a social gathering by turning the quiz into a contest—maybe one that even involves prize money. Allow contestants, or teams of contestants, a given amount of time to construct their answers to both questions. The winning answers can be judged either by a designated panel of judges or by the contestants themselves.

In suggesting that other people take this two-question quiz, either as part of a contest or just as a thoughtful review of what they already know, it occurred to me that maybe I should take a dose of my own medicine. So here are my tentative answers, which I'm sure others can change and improve upon.

Ten Important Developments in U.S. History:

1. The Declaration of Independence in 1776. Several of its causes were listed in the document itself, but its effects, which flow from its bold opening statements about individual rights and democratic government, set standards for the U.S. and impressed people in other nations.
2. The Northwest Ordinance of 1787. Cause: need for government in territories not yet organized as states. Effects: limited spread of slavery and established public schools as basic feature of American life.
3. Adoption of the U.S. Constitution, 1787 – 1788, and its Bill of Rights. Cause: the inadequacy of the weak national government

under the Articles of Confederation. Effect: cured the inadequacy.

4. The Louisiana Purchase of 1803. Cause: concern about European barriers to westward expansion. Effects: removal of cause for concern, and setting a precedent for presidential actions in foreign relations not specifically authorized in the Constitution or by Congress.

5. Civil War, 1861 – 1865. Causes: Southern fear of growth of industrial north and northwest, coupled with Southern reaction to violent extremism of abolitionists such as John Brown. Effects: widespread destruction in South, increased productive capacity in North, stronger national unity by foreclosing secession, and ending slavery. (Note: the British also had slavery in their colonies, but ended it without war, by a law in 1833 compensating slave owners for their loss.)

6. Federal initiatives for better transportation, such as supporting transcontinental railroads in the 1800s, building the Panama Canal in early 20th Century, expansion of airlines beginning in 1938, and the interstate highway system, begun in the 1950s. Causes: mixture of economic, political and national security factors. Effects: increases in national unity, wealth, power, and standards of living.

7. The Great Depression, started in 1929, hit bottom early 1933, improved during 1930s,

ending in World War II. Multiple causes: growth of productivity exceeding purchasing power, credit practices inducing instability, etc. Effects: programs of federal relief, recovery and reform, including insurance of bank deposits, regulations protecting investors and workers, extension of electricity to rural areas, etc.

8. World War II, 1939 – 1945, with U.S. at war from 1941. Causes: defective peace settlements after World War I; ambitions of Germany, Italy and Japan; aggressive expansion by Hitler, Mussolini and Japanese militarists; and failure of the Western democracies to curb aggression. Effects: 50 million dead; increased U.S. military and economic power; Cold War with the Soviet Union; establishment of U.N. and NATO; advances in atomic and other technologies; increased cohesion in U.S., aided by G.I. Bill of Rights, etc.

9. Major changes affecting U.S. population in 1965, with new civil rights laws ending discrimination against African Americans and new immigration law increasing Hispanic and Moslem immigrants. Causes: political action. Effects: faster population growth, problems of assimilation

10. Relaxation during last quarter of 20th century of nation's concern about domestic and foreign policies. Causes: long period of prosperity, ends of Vietnam War and Cold War.

Effects: Reagan era budget and tax changes and involvements in several smaller wars.

Ten Important Developments in World History:

1. Invention of agriculture. Cause: hunter/gatherer economy made people move when local edibles became scarce. Effects: cities became feasible, and part of the populations became available for occupations other than obtaining food.
2. Invention of writing. Cause unknown. Effects: preservation of knowledge without total dependence on memory.
3. Development of classical Mediterranean civilizations (Greece, Rome, Israel and Egypt). Causes: surpluses and human nature. Effects: advances in government, engineering, warfare, religion, etc.
4. Development during last six centuries of maritime technology and industrial capitalism. Causes: multiple. Effects: more trade and productivity, exploration and exchanges of ideas and practices with Asia, Africa, the Americas, etc.
5. Development of printing. Effects included more diffusion of information and ideas, plus religious differences in Europe and America, with some local practice of democracy.
6. Development of scientific knowledge in astronomy and other fields. Effects: advanced technologies, greater productivity, and

weakening of the authority of some religious teachings on questions of fact.

7. Development in Europe of firearms as weaponry for war. Effects: Western nations expanded worldwide, increasing their wealth and spreading major segments of their culture, ultimately establishing English as the international language.

8. The Enlightenment. Effects: spreading the influence of science and individual freedoms in economic and political matters to supplement or supplant established authorities.

9. Development of totalitarian governments. Causes: communist reaction to early industrialization, capitalist reaction to communism, etc. Effects: more nationalism in Europe and Asia, with political repression and aggressive wars climaxed by World War II.

10. Establishment of capitalistic democracies after World War II and after the Cold War in Eastern Europe and elsewhere, with international organizations such as the U.N., NATO, the WTO and the European Union, coupled with the rise of the Chinese economy and turbulence in the Middle East. Effects: increasing populations, especially of the elderly, and rising living standards, but with growing pressure on natural resources.

Of course, your quiz contests for students or voters or perhaps other categories of citizens can focus on subjects other than U.S. and world history. You might ask for the five most important trends affecting the U.S. future, and the same for the world's future. You can ask to identify the kinds of players who will try to affect our future or the world's. You can ask about the roles of groups that share a common history, nationality, education, religion or occupation in shaping our present and future. You can ask for the greatest dangers that will face us in 2025, 2050 or 2075. You can offer a prize for the best short essay, for example, 1,000 words on "If I were President I would ..." The point is to stimulate attention to solving problems that cry out for more civic responsibility, and perhaps have fun in doing so.

Seven Icings on the Cake

18

"Cake" refers to the book up to this point. I thought it needed a little finishing touch, so here are the icings.

First Icing: This book has a lot of detail in some places and not as much in others. Like the work of map-makers, some elements are left out, and some may change by the time the map is used. The best we can do is to make this book as accurate, balanced and useful as we can at this point in time.

Second Icing: Consider the possibility of civic responsibility in careers. Since most people have or will have established careers or established families or both, we have chiefly dealt with civic activity as an avocation. But it's a mistake to overlook civic opportunities in family or occupational activities. For example, good parenting can help develop a sense of responsibility and a broad range of interests in young people.

Many careers contain opportunities for exercising civic responsibility. To summarize them under three big categories:

- The world of business. Although the basic goal of a business is to benefit those who own or manage it, history shows that businesses have developed and provided a remarkable range of goods and services which are huge improvements over the past. Today, despite the problems of capitalism, the average citizen of a developed nation has better food, clothing, shelter, transportation, health care, entertainment, longevity, etc. than the royalty and nobility of earlier centuries. The problem, of course, is to find or make careers in business that serve the business, serve your personal interests, and advance the interests of our nation.

• Public service in government. This category is full of variety, including many kinds of research, law enforcement, emergency and other assistance, and so on. It includes not only the federal, state and local governments but also inter-governmental bodies, some of which are international.

Currently there's much sentiment that governments are often wasteful or ineffective. But, as is the case of business, history shows that governments have had various successes in dealing with wars, crime, natural disasters, depressions, dangers to health and safety, inadequacies in transportation and education, etc.

Causes for concern about these and other policy sectors have not disappeared. The problem, as in the case of business careers, is to find some job in which you can provide service to the place where you work while also serving your own interests and those of our nation.

- Category three is careers in what may be called the "enlightenment sector." This includes (a) education at all levels, (b) print and electronic journalism that keeps the public informed of important conditions, trends and issues, and (c) some nonprofit groups, including some so-called "think tanks", which give the public useful information with or without advocacy. The variety of careers in the enlightenment sector, like choices in business or public service, is also quite large.

It also should be noted that careers in any of these three categories may encounter evidence of corruption or other wrongful situations. Persons who help correct such conditions, as whistleblowers or in some other way, may thereby serve civic interests and of course a career in charities also is likely to serve civic interests.

Third Icing: This is a toolkit of five short reminders which improve the chances that well-intentioned civic activity will succeed.

Tool One: The *mix* reminder. Almost every person, organization, policy and subculture is a mix. Good ones have faults and bad ones may have some good aspects. This applies to businesses, unions, nations, religions, educational and political groups, policies, programs, etc. It's risky to assume that someone or something is totally good or totally bad.

Tool Two: *Stereotype control.* It's impossible to know everyone well. Stereotyping is almost inevitable when most people who may affect our lives are strangers to us. We usually know them only by their reputation and the news media.

We may be careful not to discriminate against an individual because of race, religion, sexual orientation, or any other reason, but at the same time we probably have opinions about some groups that have particular ancestral, regional, educational, financial, occupational, political, life-style, or age-group characteristics. Such stereotypes can vary greatly in accuracy, and a group or its reputation may change over time. Therefore reliance on stereotypes should be controlled.

There is a duality to such control. One aspect of it is that individuals should be judged as individuals, not as members of a stereotyped group. At the same time, in screening for matters such as terrorism, common sense permits some attention to stereotypes, but only for preliminary attention.

The second control is to bear in mind what a great teacher said about most stereotyped groups: "Some do, some don't." This was said by Professor Ralph Linton, who trained the WW II staffs which helped convert populations of Germany and Japan from supporters of warlike autocracies to citizens of peaceful democracies. It means there is usually some variation within a stereotyped group.

Tool Three: *Passion control.* History shows that in counteracting some public policy problems (slavery, some types of crime, foreign aggression) passion may be part of the formula for success. But history also shows that unless passion is controlled, a worthy cause can end in trouble. Compare two revolutions against monarchies, the American with the French Revolution, which ended in the Reign of Terror and in Napoleon's dictatorship. And compare England's peaceful abolition of slavery with the war that followed the violence of abolitionist John Brown. And compare the postwar plans of Lincoln for "binding the nation's wounds" with the passion aroused by his assassination, resulting in the harsh and unsuccessful "reconstruction" that followed. And remember the passionate fight against the abuses of alcohol that led to a victorious overkill—Prohibition—that soon proved to be a disaster.

Tool Four: *Checklists.* This started years ago in aviation to reduce accidents. Today several kinds of aviation checklists are used as standard practice.

In today's increasingly complicated world, checklists have been developed for various important activities that involve things that a person might not remember, for example, performing operations in hospitals. Checklists are also developed for major decisions and for periodic reviews of operations and inspections of facilities and resources. (Checklists may not be called that; they may be "standard operating procedures" or something similar)

Reducing mistakes and oversights in the civic activities of your group or yourself (as well as in some of your personal activities) justifies the time to obtain or create good checklists.

Tool Five: *Your can for spraying some good cheer.* For some time there's been a lot of gloomy news, nationally and globally: a sluggish economy, high unemployment, foreclosures, bankruptcies, heavy debt burdens, adverse balance of trade, governments stymied by political gridlocks, and failures to provide needed upgrades in transportation, education, health care, environment, and more, plus worries about rogue nations and terrorists with nuclear ambitions and uncertainties about the Middle East and other areas.

But don't let gloom and doom become dominant. Use a squirt from your can of good cheer. Remember, things were much worse in the past. The Black Death killed half the people in Europe; long-drawn out religious wars took a bloody toll; the Great Depression had much worse unemployment than today and there was no unemployment insurance; and many millions of servicemen and civilians in various nations were killed in WW II. And remember the grim threat to even the survival of civilization, starkly evident in the summer of 1940 after Hitler crushed France, when the overwhelming power of the three fascist aggressors (Germany, Italy and Japan) was confronted only by the weak army of England, which had lost its weapons at Dunkirk, and of the United States, which was still at peace and had not begun to re-arm.

Now "cheer up" doesn't mean relapsing into our years of being "fat, dumb and happy." That attitude in our country started after WW II and it became stronger with many years of prosperity, putting a man on the moon, and the end of the Cold War. We mean cheering up because our history strongly suggests we can overcome our present problems by facing up to the realities and agreeing to work together for needed improvements.

Fourth Icing: Consider a clear and simple personal philosophy to help guide your life. It can be a great benefit to you and to others and perhaps a key to success.

A personal philosophy is more than a series of beliefs and opinions, although it may include them. It's largely an attitude toward life and the world.

A good place to start is "pursuit of happiness," a right asserted in our Declaration of Independence, and one most people accept in one way or another.

The next step is to be clear about "happiness" and also about the methods for "pursuing" it. Happiness has two main parts, pleasures and satisfactions. There are innumerable pleasures, all of which relate in some way to our bodies and especially to our senses. Pleasures include both active and spectator kinds. Pleasures come with various benefits, risks or costs to one's self and perhaps to others.

The satisfaction kinds of happiness usually arise from some activity or decision that is worthwhile in the judgment of one's self or of others. This might include completing routine or even unpleasant but necessary tasks. An especially potent kind of satisfaction happiness can come from solving a problem that has plagued your family, community, work-groups, nation or others, particularly if one's solution is recognized by others.

Turning to the methods for the "pursuit" of happiness, they are innumerable. But successful pursuits can be easily summarized. They generally have three qualities: self-control, good judgment and responsibility. Self-control needs no explanation. Good judgment means using some knowledge or experience, skill and good sense, without excluding new ideas. Responsibility is the most basic. It includes exercising self-control and good judgment, but it also includes an awareness of, and concern for, how one's "pursuit" may affect other people.

This awareness and concern is important not only for others, but also for the pursuer. A successful thief may use self-control and good judgment in performing thefts, but in time he will probably come to suspect that stealing is a dubious method for pursuing happiness.

To put a serviceable personal philosophy in a nut-shell, try this: "the responsible pursuit of happiness."

Fifth Icing: Be careful with tricky words, such as words with multiple meanings and words with fuzzy meanings. Bear in mind words have two functions, to convey meaning and to produce human reactions.

Words like "conservative" and "liberal" have several meanings, with a dominant meaning that varies from person to person and also from time to time as conditions change. Civically-minded problem-solvers may be able to get conservatives and liberals to cooperate by offering solutions that recognize both the openness of liberals to new ideas and the concern of conservatives about negative effects of new ideas. Such solutions may offer new ideas that include provisions for monitoring and controlling the effects.

Fuzzy words often arouse curiosity and sometimes attract people, at least temporarily. Examples: existentialism, postmodernism, and transcendentalism. These kinds of words seem to attract people who are dissatisfied with modern life or with rational attitudes and who long for the romantic values of nature, beauty, art, glory, status, dramatic leadership, loyalty, and more.

Some persons who seek to build a following in political, religious, artistic or other circles may use fuzzy words and sometimes accent their appeal as leading to "peak experiences," possibly enhanced by use of certain substances, some of which may be behavior altering.

A responsible civic group will avoid such methods of attraction. Nevertheless, experience shows that a coldly rational approach to policy issues may actually be unrealistic. Therefore it may be wise to be aware of all kinds of dissatisfaction, including those based on unsatisfied personal interests and tastes.

Sixth Icing. We need to monitor the ingredients of a successful democracy, which are civility, responsibility, access to information, education for effective citizenship, and a healthy sense of belonging.

Civility between rival political and policy advocates is essential for the debates, discussions and election campaigns that help voters choose good leaders and good policies.

Responsibility means that voters will balance their own interests with those of their community and nation, and it usually also means keeping ideology and extremists on tap, not on top.

Access to information has been improved by the Freedom of Information Act, which shows how our laws are administered, but it doesn't provide information on how our laws are made, including the effects of lobbyists for big political contributors.

A healthy sense of belonging to one's nation is vital, and similar to identifying with one's family or with one's work group when it is blessed with a good team spirit. But with our nation's many subcultures, including various kinds of "populists" and various kinds of "elitists," our cohesion may be weakened. An interesting tell-tale of this weakness is the reported comment by the late wife of a New York City hotel magnate. When someone working for the hotels spoke to her about a possible tax problem, she replied "We don't pay taxes, little people pay taxes." If such divisive and destructive attitudes spread, our nation's future will not be bright. There is some historical evidence that one of the causes of the decline and fall of the Roman Empire was a spreading avoidance of taxes

.

Seventh Icing: Can we agree on an ultimate national goal for our nation? Would it be to achieve a good life for all our people and our descendants as free citizens of a prosperous and peaceful nation in a prosperous and peaceful world?

Most people would probably agree with this goal, but there would be disagreements about how to reach it, and perhaps some disagreement about what a "good life" is like.

A new approach to this subject is a worldwide public opinion survey undertaken by some economists and psychologists. They apparently thought that the widely accepted national goal of growth in a nation's productivity should be accompanied by a goal of improvement in the happiness of a nation's people.

The results of their worldwide survey were released in a "World Happiness Report" ranking 156 nations on the happiness of their people.

The columnist Robert J. Samuelson expressed doubts about the limits of public policies in promoting happiness (Washington Post, Apr. 16, 2012). Yet he recognized that the survey report contained some very interesting results.

Dramatically, the top ten nations in happiness (Denmark, Finland, Norway, Netherlands, Canada, Switzerland, Sweden, New Zealand, Australia and Ireland) were all small in population and all but two were also small in territory. All of them are also capitalistic democracies and all have cultures derived from European sources including the Enlightenment and Western religions. And, although most of the world's population and most of the world's nations are in Asia, Africa and South and Central America, none of the top ten were in those regions.

The United States ranked eleventh among the 156 nations, making us the top rank among large nations in the happiness of our population. That sounds both realistic and encouraging.

So something like the national goal stated at the beginning of this Seventh Icing would seem to be attainable and worthwhile. And if we accept it we should bear in mind Samuelson's warning about the limits of public policies in promoting happiness.

But that doesn't mean that trying to promote happiness by some mixture of private and public efforts would be impracticable. It only means that, like a good navigator, we should have a pretty clear idea of our destination and should be aware of the rocks and shoals that may complicate our choice of courses to reach that destination.

Americans have a good record of two vital qualities needed to reach national goals. One is pragmatism or common sense that takes account of realities. The other is the imaginative idealism that takes account of new possibilities and opportunities for progress. With these two qualities we should be able to further define our goals and the methods to achieve them. In fact we should be able to do this with a fair degree of justifiable confidence.

Perhaps we can summarize the discussion of our national goals with a short equation: Passion (for improvements) times Pragmatism (awareness of realities) equals Progress.

APPENDICES

Appendix
On Capitalism

A

What is capitalism?

It is the use of money (owned or borrowed or a mixture), together with certain skills and activities, to acquire more money.

What were the prerequisites for starting capitalism?

The three chief prerequisites were

(a) The invention of agriculture, which freed part of the population from food-gathering,
(b) The invention of money, which superseded barter as a method of exchange and as an incentive, and
(c) The invention of writing, which facilitated various capitalist activities.

Did capitalism become dominant as soon as those three prerequisites were established?

No. In ancient times there was limited capitalism, followed by feudalism after the collapse of the Roman Empire. But some cities, such as Venice and Genoa, engaged in certain kinds of capitalism.

What are the three main kinds of capitalism?

They are (1) merchant capitalism, which is buying wholesale and selling retail, (2) industrial capitalism, which is using costly facilities such as factories plus relatively unskilled labor to create products (goods or services) at lower cost and often of better quality, and (3) finance capitalism, which is (a) providing money to businesses and governments in return for stocks and bonds, (b) providing various kinds of insurance, and (c) providing investment opportunities to the public and to various institutions such as pension funds.

Are there other kinds of capitalism besides those three?

Yes. For example, investing in land that one expects will become more valuable, or in commodities such as wheat, oil, etc. for the same reason, are forms of capitalism.

What's the difference between communism and socialism?

There are two main differences. Communism means government ownership and control of all the means of production (that is, factories, mines, and so on), while socialism means government ownership and control of selective parts of the economy, such as courier services (for example, the postal system) or protective services, such as police.

The second difference is that communism is autocratic (that is, the dictatorship of the proletariat), while socialism is limited and is compatible with government in a democracy.

What explains the rise of communism as an alternative to capitalism during the 19th and 20th centuries?

Communism was largely a response to the rapid growth of industrial capitalism in 19th century Europe. This growth often involved treating labor in factories and mines with great harshness. Surprisingly, however, communism first took hold in 1917 in Russia, a largely agricultural nation, not in nations where industrial capitalism was well-established. During the early 20th century, communism spread to some nations in Eastern Europe and to China. During the Great Depression (1929-1933 and to some extent for some years after that), a few Americans became interested in communism because of the near-collapse of our own capitalist economy during that depression.

What explains the end of communism, which occurred near the end of the 20th century?

The leaderships of the Soviet Union and of China both finally became convinced that a communist economy, which involves 100 percent top-down control of all economic activity by the government, was unable to compete with capitalism, because capitalism includes entrepreneurship and competition, which result in more and better productivity, leading to a higher standard of living for most of the population. (The Chinese government still calls itself "Communist," but it is communist only in the sense that the government continues to be autocratic, while nevertheless welcoming capitalism.)

What caused the Great Depression in the United States?

Several causes. It was triggered by the stock market crash in October 1929, which caused a change in the mood and spending habits of many Americans. It was worsened by credit practices, some far too loose (for example, selling stocks for 10 percent down) and others far too rigid (for example, selling homes on a two-year-mortgage). Monopolistic pricing in certain industries such as steel and a high protective tariff were also factors. But the greatest weakness may have been that, despite the illusion of the prosperous 1920s, purchasing power had not kept up with productivity. This was largely because of the crash of major crop prices during the 1920s, which crippled a large part of the U.S. economy, including various businesses that depended on a large, but no longer prosperous, agricultural sector.

Does capitalism always promote entrepreneurship and competition?

No, in at least three situations. One is where businesses try to increase profits by reducing or eliminating competition. The antitrust laws are designed to prevent this. The second is in some businesses that require a lot of capital, and where investors hesitate to provide it unless the business has some protection from competition. Examples include railroads, airlines, and electric and other kinds of utility services. A third situation may be regulatory laws to protect consumers or workers, and patent laws designed to encourage invention, which nevertheless may discourage newcomers from entering particular kinds of businesses.

Based on capitalism's history and current condition, what improvements should be considered?

First, provide more stability. This became evident in the big boom-and-bust tulip speculation in Holland centuries ago in which investors drove up the price of tulip bulbs higher and higher until the price collapsed and the investors lost their money. Since then, capitalism has suffered from boom-and-bust cycles, which hurt many and benefit few.

Second, capitalism must recognize it depends on adequate purchasing power, for which easy credit is only a temporary substitute.

Third, capitalism must cooperate more effectively with the rest of society, including governments, in recognizing present and future problems and responsibilities. One area is necessary attention to the depletion of natural resources. Another is sharing with educational systems the responsibility for job-related training, perhaps through apprenticeships. Industries should also share responsibility for reducing various risks to public health and safety.

Appendix
Globalization and the
Economy

B

What Every Citizen Should Know

Citizens for Quality Civilization (CQC)
6603 Lone Oak Drive
Bethesda, MD 20817
www.citizens-quality-civilization.org

Do you know that we are all, in some ways, citizens of the world? While our allegiance belongs to our own country, our actions can seriously affect people in other countries. Also, their actions can affect us, as history and recent economic developments clearly show.

Globalization is not a strange concept, to be dealt with only by professors. Ever since the first airplane took to the skies and ships began sailing to other lands, what occurs in the world can impact the lives of everyone, everywhere.

The material that follows will provide a clear review of the basics of globalism. It will explain why you need to understand the importance of this subject for you and for people living now and in future generations.

From the CQC task force on globalization (the participants are described in an appendix.)

Outline

I.   The Economic Downturn

Although world trade quadrupled over the past 25 years, the economic downturn that began in 2008 has slowed the rate of globalization to the degree that trade is declining faster than production. Plummeting demand for goods and services has been accompanied by falling global water and air traffic, national bailouts of financial institutions, and measures designed to protect home country workers and business firms. Many observers see only a temporary slowdown of globalization, noting movement of government funds across borders to help prop up teetering economies.

The future rate of globalization is likely to be affected by the rate national economies recover and by the degree to which nations use protectionism (high tariffs, quotas, subsidies to domestic producers) to protect their domestic economies. In early 2009, the Inspector General of the World Trade Organization (WTO) warned its members against the perils of competitive protective policies. Many nations, however, were concerned about the outsourcing of jobs to places with cheaper labor and the spread of unsound financial products into global markets.

When the downturn has finally ended, the causes and effects of globalization as described in this Handbook will require increasing attention. A focus on ways to forge closer collaboration between nations on global problems will also emerge.

II.   Globalization Summarized

A.   *Definition:* Globalization, broadly understood, is the worldwide integration of markets, finance, commerce, communications, technology, and law, which transcends national boundaries. It also includes the outsourcing of work in manufacturing and service industries, the increasing movement of people across national borders, and worldwide trends affecting the environment and natural resources.

B.   *The Importance of Globalization:* Globalization increasingly affects the livelihoods of people everywhere, the use of the earth's resources, and the viability and cohesion of both nations and of international organizations. It is therefore not surprising that globalization generates controversies. The 2007 Pew Global Attitudes Survey of 47 nations reported the United States as the country in which opposition to globalization has risen the most. Opposition in the United States grew from 24% in 2002 to 41% in 2007. Problems associated with globalization have been simplified into sound bites, but are also discussed in hundreds of articles and scholarly books. We seek to explore the subject factually in order to provide a balanced picture.

C.   *Overview—Causes, Effects, and Options:* Since globalization is chiefly driven by economics, technology, and trade policy, we first discuss trade, investment, transnational corporations, and international organizations. We then take a worldwide look at the effects of globalization on labor, on distribution of incomes, and on national security, sovereignty, democracy, the environment, and culture. Finally we discuss how globalization will help or harm you and your descendents, and what might be done about it.

III.   Major Globalization Issues

A.   *Causes of Increasing Globalization—Free Trade, Technology, and Global Problems:*

1.   Basic Causes: The spread of free trade and multinational businesses has been a major stimulant of globalization. Free trade means few if any barriers to trade between nations, such as quotas or tariffs. Tariffs are taxes on imported goods that increase their price. Tariffs impede imports and international trade.

During the 19th century international trade expanded until World War I halted it. As the same time, the United States used tariffs to help build its industrial facilities, standard of living, and national power. After World War I, the United States erected higher tariffs, other nations retaliated, and trade diminished. This was one of the causes of the worldwide depression in the 1930s.

At the end of World War II, the United States and other nations acted to restore and encourage international trade, largely by reducing or eliminating tariffs. This free trade policy followed the principle of *"comparative advantage"* described in the early 1800s by the economist David Ricardo. That principle says nations gain more than they lose if each nation specializes in producing and exporting what it can make best, with consumers in the importing countries benefiting from lower prices.

Today, huge retail chains that sell products made in low-cost countries exemplify the consumer part of this principle. However, "comparative advantage" no longer reflects natural factors, like a warm climate for growing bananas, or plenty of coal to power factories. It also reflects acquired factors, such as new technology, investment of capital, often from outside sources, and especially an educated but much cheaper workforce.

Since World War II international trade has grown rapidly. Among the factors driving trade expansion are tariff reductions by advanced and some less developed countries, cheaper transportation and communication, foreign direct investment (FDI), and outsourcing.

The second main stimulant of globalization has been technology. This means more than just cheaper transportation. It also includes new goods and services that are faster, more capable, or more attractive. Examples: containerization of shipments, jet flights for persons and cargo; electronic transfer of funds; flash freezing of seafood; medical imaging for services far from the patient's residence; and products that are attractive in many countries (e.g., cars, cell phone).

The third main stimulant of globalization is the accumulation of primarily global problems. These include global warming, nuclear proliferation, terrorism, and depletion of ocean fisheries, fossil fuels, and other resources. Such problems call for some form of international cooperation, often by creating new international organizations.

There may be other factors stimulating globalization. Thus, the increase in transborder travel—itself a form of globalization—may stimulate other forms of globalization. If the traveler is a tourist, student, or other visitor, the economic effect on the country visited is similar to an export. If the traveler is a migrant, legal or illegal, the economic and other effects are more complex. (For further information on migration, see the April, 2009 issue of *Current History*, listed in Appendix A.)

2.   **Foreign Direct Investment (FDI):** Foreign Direct Investment (FDI) means that a company from one country invests its money in facilities or businesses in other countries to benefit financially. The following illustration helps to explain FDI.

Traditionally, international trade has been primarily a matter of exports and imports. A supermarket may import fruit from another country, buying it from foreign farmers or wholesalers. If the supermarket then finds it can make more money by actually buying the fruit farms, this decision is a form of FDI.

FDI is conducted largely through transnational corporations, which are companies that produce goods or services in a country other than that of their origin, control, and ownership. (Sometimes the term multinational corporation is used interchangeably with transnational corporation.)

Thousands of transnational corporations and many foreign affiliates are located around the world and engage in various industries. These corporations provide foreign capital and expertise to the countries where they operate for facilities, equipment, mergers, and acquisitions; their investments are often protected by treaties that safeguard the rights of foreign investors.

The total worldwide value of FDI has been estimated in trillions of dollars, a large amount but less than the world's investment in domestic businesses. FDI boosts production and the division of labor, primarily between advanced nations. Poorer nations receive less than 20% of the world's FDI.

For many years U.S. corporations were leaders in FDI, developing various facilities in many countries, such as oil wells in the Middle East. However, since the U.S. has become a debtor nation, there has been increasing FDI by foreign investors, including "sovereign investors" controlled by foreign governments, who are buying up income-producing properties in the U.S.

3.   Outsourcing: Outsourcing is a rapidly growing trend, shifting work previously performed within businesses in advanced countries to countries with lower labor costs or other advantages, especially to countries in Asia or Latin America. Outsourcing can cut production costs by 50% or more, making possible lower prices that will increase sales and profits. Originally used by manufacturers for making or assembling parts, outsourcing now includes such work as accounting, debt collection, data processing, personnel office work, and customer service. In response to labor's concern that outsourcing affects U.S. jobs, government statisticians have stated that the U.S. has experienced overall economic gains. However, the statistics showing such gains are now under review.

By 2004, China emerged as the leading manufacturer of televisions, automobile parts, and computers. The Indian outsourcing sector is rapidly expanding, and is unique to the degree to which Indian businessmen have bought out Western firms. Indian companies specialize in service call centers, transcription services, tax returns, and insurance claims.

Other countries in Eastern Europe, Africa, and elsewhere have begun to challenge China and India with bids to outsource for them as well as for advanced Western nations. Both advanced and developing countries are increasing competing in outsourcing.

4.   International Organizations

   a.   Worldwide Economic Organizations Created by Treaties: After WW II three worldwide organizations were established by treaty to encourage international trade and development. There sere the World Bank, the International Monetary Fund (IMF), and the General Agreement on Tariffs and Trade (GATT), which in 1995 was replaced by the more powerful World Trade Organization (WTO).

The World Bank provided funds to help nations rebuild and reduce poverty. The IMF was created to help stabilize exchange rates among various international currencies. It also lent money to poor nations for development, sometimes on the condition that the poor nation changes its economic policies. The WTO promotes international trade and discourages discriminatory trade practices.

The WTO's rules are established by its member nations and must be agreed to by applicants for membership. The WTO also includes a tribunal to enforce its rules. WTO requires that any advantage in trade gained by changing tariffs or quotas, which one country grants to another, must generally be extended to all member countries. But this requirement does not seem to apply to regional arrangements such as the European Union and NAFTA (the North American Free Trade Agreement between the U.S., Canada, and Mexico.)

The WTO conducts "rounds" which are negotiations to reduce tariffs and other trade barriers. But these reductions sometimes do not affect farm products, because of objections by agricultural interests in wealthy nations. These interests fear competition from poor countries such as Morocco and some West African nations. Farmers in poor countries are also disadvantaged by subsidies like those which the U.S. Congress provides to American cotton farmers. These subsidies allow U.S. cotton farmers to sell cotton at a price lower than the world market price. The WTO declared the subsidies illegal in 2005 but cannot enforce this ruling.

When trade disputes are brought to the WTO, they are referred to a panel of experts; panel decisions can only be appealed on legal grounds. Countries are expected to either comply with the decisions or compensate the injured parties. Most countries provide compensation in one way or another. The trade ministers from a majority of nations believe WTO's activities benefit them, but many participants and observers express dissatisfaction with the lack of openness that surrounds decisions and the effect of compliance on national sovereignty.

b.   *Regional and Bilateral Agreements:* WTO members are free to enter bilateral trade agreements with another nation or regional agreements with several nations. The U.S. has agreements of both kinds, including NAFTA, mentioned above. For some years, Congress gave American presidents "fast track" authority to help achieve these agreements. "Fast track" means that Congress agreed to suspend its authority to modify these agreements as a condition of its approval. It now appears questionable that this "fast track" authority will be renewed.

c. *Other International Organizations*: There are many kinds of international and regional organizations that affect trade and other aspects of globalization, in addition to the ones discussed above. First, and of greatest economic influence are the large commercial and financial corporations that are heavily engaged in international trade and investment. Second, there are specialized international organizations, typically created by international agreement and in some cases affiliated with the United Nations, which deal with such subjects as labor standards; postal services; health; telecommunications by satellite or other means; nuclear energy; and crime. Third are various privately established nonprofit groups, often called NGOs (Non-Governmental Organizations), which deal with an assortment of humanitarian and other concerns that transcend borders. Fourth, the United Nations itself has some effect on globalization. Although originally created to prevent wars of aggression, the UN has taken various actions of global significance, such as refugee relief, the Universal Declarations of Human Rights, and the work of UNCTAD, the UN organization for trade and development.

The European Union is somewhat unique. It is a regional organization established by the European nations which acts as a free trade zone among its member nations. However, its scope is more than purely economic. It includes political, security, and other features, such as free immigration within the union for citizens of its member nations. The European Union may still be evolving, although voters in several member nations have rejected proposals for its further development.

B.   *Effects of Globalization*
1.   **Effects on Labor**

 a. *Trends:* There is no global labor market comparable to the increasingly unrestricted global capital market. Labor, restricted by family ties and immigration barriers, in nonetheless also affected by international trade, outsourcing, and the ease with which businesses can change locations to obtain cheaper labor or other advantages.

  Many improvements in communication, transportation, business organization, and technology produce greater productivity (output per hour). Greater productivity, however, can create overcapacity and unemployment. The pressure to privatize government activities can also contribute to the loss of public employment. The bargaining power of labor is also diminished because of the deterioration in the right to organize, the weakening of protective labor legislation, and the immigration of cheap labor.

All of these trends, sometimes reinforced by the international lending institutions and changes in national labor policies, tend to weaken labor. Recently, however, union leaders from 64 nations formed a Council of Global Unions in an effort to counteract the globalization of capital. Some U.S. unions have merged with others (e.g., the U.S. United Steelworks with a British union). The International Trade Union Conference, headquartered in Brussels, represents several hundred union organizations worldwide.

b.   *Labor In Less Developed Countries:* The condition of labor in less developed countries is important to Americans for several reasons: it affects the amount of outsourcing of U.S. jobs to other countries and it can improve the market for American exports. It may also have humanitarian or foreign relations significance.

In less developed countries it is difficult to achieve labor standards similar to those in advanced countries. Labor unions in advance countries have urged that poorer countries adhere to the labor standards of the ILO (International Labor Organization). The ILO, founded in 1919 and now a

United Nations affiliate, researched economic conditions and publishes desirable labor standards, including the right to bargain collectively and discouragement of gender discrimination. However, the ILO has no enforcement power.

But manufacturers in some poor countries assert that low wages offer a comparative advantage for them. They also view demands for labor standards as a form of "protectionism" by advanced countries. In Sri Lanka, China, Thailand, Malaysia, and Guatemala workers who tried to unionize have been jailed.

Some observers advocate worldwide labor standards. Non-governmental groups (NGOs) may be allowed to conduct factory audits or promote the boycott of goods and services made under substandard conditions.

The U .S. Congress has begun to insist on labor standards in trade agreements with less developed nations. But such standards are hard to enforce, as shown in Guatemala. The *Washington Post* reported that workers there who complained and tried to form unions often were fired or even killed. Hundreds of labor organizers were murdered in Colombia. Guatemalan managers and higher wages meant higher prices. As prices rose, company owners threatened to move their operations to China.

Agricultural workers in poor countries have also suffered. In Mexico, under NAFTA, several thousand Mexican farmers were displaced. Imports of corn from the U.S. may have aggravated their distress.

Assembly plant laborers have other complaints. Some assembly plants in Mexico, operated by U.S. corporations employing thousands of workers, have been termed sweatshops due to poor working conditions. NAFTA has "side agreements" pertaining to labor but these agreements lack effective enforcement codes. Another concern is that Mexican products may be unable to compete with Chinese exports. Despite such problems, a U.S. Congressional Research Service report indicates that in Mexico under NAFTA, gross domestic product has quadrupled and poverty has been reduced by 10%.

Many experts believe that globalization offers the most practical means for achieving higher wages and living standards in less developed countries. The average wage in such countries has risen over the past 30 years to 30% of the average U.S. wage. Economists believe that as poor countries buy technology and equipment with their export earnings, the new technology will lead to better labor standards. Others maintain that the removal of agricultural subsidies by advanced countries can be the key to economic health in poor countries.

c.   Labor in Advanced Countries: The effect of globalization on labor in advanced countries varies. To achieve an effective competitive price, business firms often cut back on employment and employee benefits. Some advanced countries with strong labor unions, however, have been unwilling to permit such reductions.

In the United States, globalization is estimated to be responsible for a relatively small percentage of job losses. According to experts, U.S. unemployment largely results from better technology that has increased productivity, so that less labor is requires. Some experts also expect these changes to create new jobs to replace those that have been lost.

The U .S. Federal Reserve Board reported that one in seven U.S. job losses result from U.S. technological growth, compared to one in fifty job losses created by foreign competition and outsourcing. United States unemployment statistics remained steady or declined during the first five years of the 21st century. However, these statistics do not indicate the shift from jobs with good pay, security, health insurance, and pensions to jobs with lesser benefits. Also, even relatively small job losses can adversely affect thousands of workers and their families as well as entire communities in which factories shut down. The recent downturn has aggravated these job losses.

Recommendations to address these job losses include the availability of greater worker assistance; education and retraining; government investment in science and technology; wages and benefits for workers that compare more favorably with executive compensation and corporate profits; and modernization of employment sectors such as health care, education, energy, and infrastructure.

2.   **Effect on Incomes**

a.   Income Distribution Among Nations: Despite long-term gains in global income, two factors in the distribution of global income stand out: the persistence of poverty and great inequality of income between the world's major regions. The scope of international income inequality is illustrated by vast differences in per capita GNP between high and low income countries. In 1999 average income per person was $7,000; this breaks down to $26,000 for high income nations and $1,900 for the poorest countries.

b.   Income Distribution in Less Developed Countries: The distribution is also unequal throughout the less developed world. Wages as percentage of total income dropped in India, for example, from 35% to 20% over the past 25 years and in Mexico from 40% to 20%. The greatest degree in income inequality it is in Latin America, where the top 10% of the population receives 48% of the total;

the bottom 10% receives only 1.6%. Nevertheless, two research projects in 2008 found a link between globalization and the reduction of poverty but did not establish that globalization is a cause of income inequality.

c.   *Income Distribution in Advanced Countries:* In the United States, despite the growth in total U.S. incomes in recent years, U.S. incomes and wealth are also very unevenly distributed, with 94% of the estimated wealth held by 20% of the top households. Over the past 25 years, the top fifth of U.S. households received incomes 9.8 times that of the bottom fifth. The United States wealth and income disparities are greater than those in European countries. These disparities have been accentuated by reductions in progressivity of tax rates in the United States and worldwide, and by the decline in labor union power in the United States.

d.   *Income Protection as a Key Social Factor:* A study conducted by the ILO based on data from 102 countries concluded that only one in three countries offer protection covering eight social risks—sickness, maternity, old age, survivors, family allowances, work injury, disability, and unemployment. One in six countries cover at least one-half of these risks. Only one in two pay unemployment benefits; some of these may be sparse. With regard to eligibility for and adequacy of risk protection worldwide, only 17 of 102 countries satisfactorily met ILO criteria while 34 countries, located primarily in Africa and Latin America, met none of them.

Retirement benefits in the U.S. have eroded as many corporations have shifted pensions from defined benefits to investment plans. Other trends in at least 40 countries surveyed by the ILO include raising the legal retirement age and increasing the number of years to acquire eligibility for retirement benefits.

Unemployment benefits are provided primarily in industrial countries. The ILO study found that income insecurity caused by unemployment has increased over the past 25 years. Contributing to the insecurity are the following: lengthened qualifying periods to become eligible for benefits; a reduction in the duration of benefits; restricted conditions for initial entitlement; and declining income replacement ratios.

e. *Economic Growth:* The World Bank and academic research institutions have published statistical evidence that poor countries that open their economies to trade achieve greater economic growth than countries with less open trade policies. Statistics also seem to demonstrate that economic growth is required as a first step to reducing poverty. However, these statistics rarely reflect the food and shelter consumed without monetary exchanges in stable communities with subsistence economies. But whether economic growth leads to greater income equality and less poverty depends on government policies and other factors such as removal of industrial country agricultural subsidies.

The percentage of people worldwide who live in poverty, measured as $1.00 per day, has fallen from 17% to 6.7% in the last 30 years. The largest gains in poverty reduction, achieved in China and India, contrast markedly with negative or static results in Africa.

3. **Effects on National Security, Public Health, Sovereignty, and Democracy**

National Security and Public Health: Increased movement of visitors, migrants, and traded goods across borders, accelerated by globalization, threatens the security of nations. Considerable inspection and enforcement measures may be required to protect against the entry of terrorists and illegal weapons into a country. The importation of toys, pet and human foods, and medication have recently presented serious health problems. In addition, the increasing movement of people across borders has put more pressure on public health authorities to develop defenses against new types of pathogens.

National Sovereignty: National Sovereignty can be defined as the legal and political independence of a nation from outside control. Nations voluntarily surrender a degree of control when they join international organizations and agree to abide by majority decisions. Although international trade and investment may weaken the economic viability of some nations, these nations normally do not lose their sovereignty rights.

However, regional and global trade tribunals can jeopardize a degree of sovereignty. For example, Guatemala faces a lawsuit from a transnational mining corporation under the provisions of the Central American Free Trade Agreement (CAFTA) for trying to protect the public water supply jeopardized by the mining firm's operations.

Anti-globalization political forces in France and the Netherlands were instrumental in defeating referendums on an expanded European Union in 2005. The opposition forces, led by labor unions, believed that greater success in obtaining their economic goals could be achieved within their own individual nations rather than through a stronger European Union. The views were echoed in Italy and Germany.

Upholding national sovereignty has been the justification for nations that refuse to permit transnational corporate ownership in local business firms. France, for example, issued a decree protecting eleven industrial sectors from foreign purchases. Spain asserted power to prevent foreign takeover of utility firms. The European Commission in Brussels is empowered to decide whether such takeovers are legal.

The United States has experienced an increasing share of its economic activity coming under the World Trade Organization. Since the WTO has power to issue binding rulings in trade disputes, and to require nations to change their laws, many critics view it as a threat to national sovereignty. Others respond that WTO membership is voluntary, since nations agree to exchange a degree of national sovereignty for a system of binding rules that should ultimately benefit all.

Some U.S. state governments have experienced legal restraints within the current international framework. California was told by the NAFTA tribunal to stop its efforts to exclude a foreign gasoline additive that pollutes drinking water. Utah's prohibition of gambling was declared illegal by the WTO as discrimination against foreigners.

Democracy. There is no clear relationship between a nation's degree of democratic government and its participation in globalized trade and business. However, it has been observed that democracy seldom exists in countries with such features as low per capita income, a low education level, an ethnically divided population, or a high degree of wealth obtained from oil or other natural resources. The World Bank Governance Report of 2006 found no evidence of either positive or negative trends in the development of democratic government.

An assumption is often made that if an underdeveloped nation profits from economic growth spawned by globalized trade, a rising middle class will demand democratic institutions. Analysts have been surprised to discover that this assumption is not correct. Political economic elites may be able to suppress the process.

Globalization may encourage democracy by facilitating travel and education that help spread information on the benefits of democracy. But globalization may undermine democracy if it shifts power away from elected governments to international tribunals or to multinational businesses.

4.   **Effect on Government and Culture**

Environment: The growth of new and expanded industries as a result of globalization can have a pronounced effect on the environment. Industries seeking fresh sources of oil, timber, water, croplands, and other natural resources often wipe out grasslands, forests, farmlands, rivers, and lakes. Also, the ability of oceans to sustain valuable fisheries may be impaired.

Additional problems include global warming and impact on wildlife. The build-up of carbon dioxide from vehicle tailpipes and coal burning plants may increase the danger from disasters such as tsunamis, floods, and droughts. Although trees remove carbon dioxide from the air, forests are being cut down in Brazil and other places. Some experts predict that one-third of all wildlife species could be extinct by the middle of the 21st century.

Nigeria is classic example of the impact of globalization on the environment. An important source of oil was discovered in the Nigerian delta in 1956. At that time, palm oil, cacao beans, and other agricultural products were Nigeria's principal exports. Today, oil accounts for 95% of its exports.

Nigeria's 130 million people, no longer self-sufficient in food supplies, must import much of the food they eat. In one instance, the village of Finima lost its main source of income, fishing, because the village was relocated to make room for fuel storage tanks and a liquefied natural gas plant. A *National Geographic* article concluded that, "From a potential model nation, Nigeria has become a dangerous country, addicted to oil money; half a century of oil extraction has failed to make the lives of people better."

The dangers to wildlife are not limited to impairment of their habitat or other environmental changes. They also include commercial harvesting and depletion of valuable species such as salmon, cod, swordfish, oysters, and whales. Some nations have taken disputes over efforts to protect whales from commercial depletion to the WTO. Improved fishing technologies and international markets for seafood have increased these problems. Efforts to preserve threatened ocean fisheries include aquaculture, the work of environmental groups, and stronger international protection of ocean resources.

Culture. Culture can be defined as the shared values and customs of the persons in a community or nation who have adapted to their history and environment through a sharing of a common language, traditions, norms, folkways, and livelihoods. Culture provides people with roots and a sense of belonging and security rather than monetary values. Culture may also greatly affect how people behave toward other people. Subcultures based on particular interests form within larger cultures. According to author Thomas Friedman, globalization can threaten the sense of distinctive place and community that give persons their bearings. He warns that, "Institutions, habits, cherished values of social cohesion, religion, and national pride that make up our identities could also be threatened."

Family farms throughout the world are multifunctional: they provide a living, give sustenance to families, and foster child-rearing cooperation. Agricultural practices developed over time and found to be consistent with sustainability do not depend on new technology but do protect natural resources. Globalized agriculture industrialization disregards local practices such as using plants for medicine or developing grain from local grasses.

The introduction of cheaper foreign food into less developed countries may displace foods that are grown on family farms and sold locally. Globalization and development bring higher production per acre, an increased size of farms, and modern technology to local areas. In the process, however, resources may be exploited, family units broken up, and local knowledge and culture norms lost. This may also affect village craftsmen and their families who have served nearby farmers. In addition, as has recently occurred, nations that become dependent on cheaper imported food are vulnerable when food prices go up.

Globalization creates a social stratum of dominant people who have an advanced knowledge of economics, administration, and technology. As their expertise begins to prevail in national and local life, treasured values of cultures and subcultures may be threatened. Concern about the wearing of headscarves is one example of a cultural conflict. The mixed reaction in France to the spread of American fast food is another example.

Following the historic importance of the British empire in spreading Western culture, the United States has grown to such economic dominance that English is the prevailing language worldwide. U.S. standards, customs, and popular culture, transmitted by motion pictures and the Internet, are often accepted or adapted to various other cultures. However, some features of Western culture, such as the freedom expression, gender equality, and separation of church and state, are not welcomed in certain parts of the world.

Immigration, which has increased with the advance of globalization, affects the culture of the societies into which it moves. Assimilation of immigrants may vary, depending on such factors as citizenship status, host country attitudes and policies, and the compatibility of the cultures of the places of origin and residence. The failure to effectively assimilate immigrants has sometimes led to severe culture clashes, terrorist-type activities, and financial burdens borne by the host country.

One important effect of globalization on cultures has been to focus attention on cultural competition and conflict. Some culture elements spread easily from nation to nation, such as technology, the use of mon-

ey, and even foods (witness the U.S. adoption of pizza, sushi, tacos, etc., as well as the
foreign adoption of American fast foods). But
other culture elements of a more intangible
nature, such as personal liberty, equality,
democracy, opportunity, and openness, are
not accepted or are even condemned in some
societies.

Even within advanced Western countries there are significant cultural clashes.
Examples included the clashes between traditional religion and secularism, and also
between the U.S. economic philosophy of
growth and opportunity as opposed to the
European philosophy of security, sustainability, and balance. While globalization ac-
centuates such clashes, they are not new.
In fact, history can be viewed as an ongoing clash of cultures. According to *New York
Times* columnist David Brooks, the major
challenge of the future will be to understand
how cultures change and how destructive
cultural conflict can be turned into healthy
cultural competition.

IV.   Conclusions

General Conclusion: Globalization, like international
trade which drives it, produces winners and losers, benefits and detriments, and some serious problems that
require adjustments. The speed and extent of globalized
trade, however, make adjustments more difficult for the
losers who must turn to their national governments or to
non-governmental organizations to seek redress.

A. *Significant Trends*

1. Globalized trade has spurred economic growth in both rich and poor countries.
2. Globalized trade is often accompanied by an increase in inequality of incomes and wealth within nations, although direct causation has not been proved.
3. Outsourcing may resume its acceleration after the global downturn is reversed.
4. There is growing recognition of the need to develop stronger safety nets for globally displaced workers. European nations with strong labor unions and protective legislation provide greater workforce security than most other nations.
5. Labor has begun to establish international labor unions.
6. Non-governmental organizations and scholars have had some success in bringing globalization to public attention.
7. Long-term environmental and demographic issues have been disregarded both nationally and internationally by manufacturers and the business community. Populations continue to increase in most countries, while resources to support good standards of living are rapidly depleted.
8. Some prosperous emerging nations are becoming less dependent on the need for aid from rich industrial nations.
9. Globalization has increased the number of economically powerful nations. Several nations may, in time, share economic dominance, instead of the U.S. being viewed as the single dominant power.

B.   *Favorable and Unfavorable Effects of Global-*
       ization

       The favorable effects of globalization appear to be

1.   Citizens in all countries will benefit (a) if each na-
       tion does what it can do best and the results are
       exchanged in a mutually positive way, and (b) if
       companies in other nations can compete effectively
       with industries that lag in quality or value, e.g.,
       the auto industry in the United States from the
       end of World War II and for decades thereafter.

2.   Standardized practices and improved technology
       promote efficiency and productivity. These may
       best be spread by management that crosses nation-
       al borders.

3.   People and nations have been making progress,
       especially in technology, as they learn from others
       throughout the world.

4.   Globalization has highlighted the need for better
       international cooperation and for global solutions
       to global warming and other global problems.

5.   Globalization increases opportunities for healthy
       cultural exchanges and competition.

6.   Globalization may provide a valuable additional
       source of supply if domestic supplies are disrupted
       by natural disaster or are unsatisfactory in quality.

       The unfavorable effects of globalization appear to
       be

1.   Globalization may tend to favor the rich and pow-
       erful, who may have little regard for the effects on
       the less advantaged.

2.   Globalization often creates disruptions that impact businesses and employees whose jobs can be moved to places with cheaper labor. Such disruptions can also destabilize the local communities that lose employment.

3.   Globalization encourages a degree of economic growth that threatens such vital elements of the environment as rain forests and ocean fisheries.

4.   Globalization increases the consumption of fossil fuels needed to transport large volumes of bulky products over great distances.

5.   Globalization may increase dependence on distant sources of supply that are subject to disruption, price increases, or lack of adequate quality controls.

6.   Globalization may undermine democracy by shifting power away from voters in states and nations to international tribunals.

C.   Policy Suggestions

These are for consideration and are not necessarily recommendations.

1.   The World Bank, IMF, and WTO should be reviewed for their current impacts and for possible changes. This should be done by an independent international commission representing all stakeholders, after public hearings. A similar review should be made of NAFTA.

2.   A way should be sought to rebalance U.S. trade policies to reduce adverse effects on the U.S. economy and, as appropriate, on the economy and environment of other nations.

3. Displaced American workers and adversely affect-
    ed small businesses should be assisted by retrain-
    ing, research, preservation of pensions and health
    benefits, and new job-creating projects.

4. Emergency legislation should be developed to pro-
    vide prompt assistance to American businesses and
    their employees facing immanent shutdown due to
    severe foreign economic pressure. Such assistance
    might include financing and expert advice on new
    business methods and opportunities.

5. The U.S. should analyze potential job losses or
    gains in advance of any future trade agreements,
    arrangements, or modifications.

6. After receiving full public input, Congress should
    enact legislation on a comprehensive, long-range
    program to restore and maintain American eco-
    nomic competitiveness, with due regard to educa-
    tion, health care policy, research, infrastructure,
    energy, and the more efficient allocation of finan-
    cial, natural, and human resources.

7. New or strengthened international agencies should
    be developed to meet global concerns such as envi-
    ronment, labor, nuclear proliferation, global warm-
    ing, terrorism, and conserving natural resources.

8. The responses to globalization suggested in 2, 3,
    and 5 above present questions of how they might
    be funded, particularly in a time for sizeable feder-
    al deficits and debt, plus major claims for funding
    several major national needs. One idea might be
    a modest revenue-type (i.e., not "protective") tariff
    on all or most imports of perhaps 2 percent, which
    should raise much revenue. Another idea might be

a fee or tax to cover the costs of screening imports for health hazards, terrorist weaponry, or violations of the law.

9. Citizens should educate themselves on globalization's complexity. Globalization cannot be blamed for every problem.

D. *What You As a Citizen Can Do*

1. Review the suggestions above, plus other ideas, and express your views to elected officials, to the news media, and to business, labor, civic, and community organizations.

2. Join with friends and neighbors in discussions and actions that reflect the ideas above. To facilitate this, organize informal groups and invite participation by persons with professional, business, academic, government, and other backgrounds—including both retirees and students.

3. Keep informed about developments. Consider both the short-term and the long-term effects of new developments and of proposed policies.

4. Be skeptical of over-simplified solutions.

5. For the protection of yourself and your family, explore education and training opportunities that will help you cope with possible job losses by shifting into different kinds of work.

V.   Appendices
Appendix A—Globalization Resources (Books, Web-sites, Etc.)

During the more than four years of work in creating this handbook, CQC's globalization group examined many reports and commentaries in newspapers, periodicals, books, and other sources. Since it is impractical in a civic handbook to deal with all aspects of globalization, we encourage the use of the following additional sources.

Books

Bergsten, C. Fred and the Institute for International Economics. *United States and the World Economy: Economic Policy for the next Decade.* The Peterson Institute, Washington, DC, 2005.

Bhagwati, Jagdish. *In Defense of Globalization.* Oxford University Press, New York, 2004.

Chua, Amy. *World on Fire.* Doubleday. New York, 2003.

Dorgan, Senator Byron. *Take This Job and Ship It: How Corporate Greed and Brain Dead Politics Are Selling Out America.* Thomas Dunne Books, St. Martin's Press, New York, 2008.

Friedman, Thomas L. *Hot, Flat, and Crowded.* Farrar, Straus and Giroux, New York, 2008.

_____ *The World is Flat: A Brief History of the Twenty-First Century.* Farrar, Straus and Giroux, New York, 2008.

_____ The Lexus and the Olive Tree. Farrar, Straus and Giroux, New York, 1999.

Halper, Stefan and Jonathan Clarke. *America Alone: Neoconservatives and the Global Order*. Cambridge University Press, New York, 2004.

Harrison, Ann. *Globalization and Poverty*. University of Chicago Press, Chicago, 2007.

Hufbauer, Gary. *NAFTA Revisited*. Peterson Institute of International Economics.

Krugman, Paul. *The Return of Depression Economics and the Crisis of 2008*. W. W. Norton & Co., New York, 2009.

Larsson, Tomas. *The Race to the Top*. Cato Institute. Washington, DC, 2001.

Lynn, Barry. *End of the Line: The Rise and Coming Fall of the Global Corporation*. Random House, Inc. New York, 2005.

Mishkin, Frederic. *The Next Great Globalization*. Princeton University Press, New Jersey, 2006.

Perkins, John. *Confessions of an Economic Hit Man*. Berrett-Koehler Publishers, Inc. San Francisco, 2004.

Singer, Peter. *One World, the Ethics of Globalization*. Yale University Press, New Haven, CN, 2004.

Stiglitz, Joseph E. *Globalization and Its Discontents*. W. W. Norton Company, New York, 2003.

_____, *Making Globalization Work*. W. W. Norton Company, New York, New York, 2006.

Thurow, Lester. *Fortune Favors the Bold*. Harper-Collins Publishers, New York, 2005.

Tonelson, Alan. *Race to the Bottom*. Westview Press, Boulder, CO, 2002.

Weisbrot, Mark. *Globalization: A Primer*. Center for Economic Policy Research, Washington, DC, 1999.

Wolf, Martin. *Why Globalization Works*. Yale University Press, New Haven, 2004.

Zakaria, Fareed. *The Post-American World*. W. W. Norton Company, New York, 2008.

Publications

Business Week, 1222 Avenue of the Americas, New York, NY 10020

Current History, 4225 Main Street, Philadelphia, PA 19127

The Economist, 111 West 57th Street, New York, NY 10019

Foreign Affairs, 58 East 68th Street, New York, NY 10065

Foreign Policy Magazine, 1779 Massachusetts Avenue, NW, Washington, DC 20036

National Geographic, PO Box 63001, Tampa, FL 33663-3001

Websites and Other Information Sources

The American Enterprise Institute (publications, debates), 1150 17th Street, NW, Washington, DC 20036. www.aei.org

The Brookings Institute (research and policy papers), 1775 Massachusetts Avenue, NW, Washington, DC 20036. www.brookings.edu

Carnegie Institute for International Peace (publications on issues such as web-based globalization 101), 2008 Massachusetts Avenue, NW, Washington, DC 20036. www.carnegieendowment.org

The Center for Strategic and International Studies (CSIS) (recommends policy solutions for global problems), 1801 K Street, NW, Washington, DC 20006. www. CSIS.org

The Council on Foreign Relations (sponsors studies and public forums on foreign policy), 1779 Massachusetts Avenue, NW, Washington, DC 20036. www. cfr.org

The Heritage Foundation (sponsors research promoting conservative public policies), 214 Massachusetts

Avenue, NW, Washington, DC 20026. <u>www.heritage.org</u>

The Institute for Policy Studies (develops recommendations for progressive policy solutions), 1112 16th Street, NW, Suite 600, Washington, DC 20036. <u>www.ips-dc.org</u>

Peterson Institute of International Economics (research and publications by Director Fred Bergsten and other economists), 1750 Massachusetts Avenue, NW, Washington, DC 20036. <u>www.petersoninstitute.org</u>

Appendix B —Global Acronyms

AEI   American Enterprise Institute

BOP   Balance of Payments

CAFTA   Central American Free Trade Agreement

CFR   Council on Foreign Relations

CIA   Central Intelligence Agency

CQC   Citizens for Quality Civilization

CSIS   Center for Strategic and International
                Studies

DHS   Department of Homeland Security

DNI   Director of National Intelligence

EHM   Economic Hit Men

EU   European Union

FAO   (UN) Food and Agriculture Organization

FISA   Foreign Intelligence Surveillance Act

FOIA   Freedom of Information Act

FPA   Foreign Policy Association

GATT   General Agreement on Tariffs and Trade
            (Replaced by the WTO)

G-8   Group of Eight (United States, Great Brit-
            ain, France, Germany, Russia, Canada, Ja-
            pan, and Italy)

G-20   Group of Twenty (the G8 nations plus Ar-
            gentina, Australia, Brazil, China, European
            Union, India, Indonesia, Mexico, Saudi Ara-
            bia, South Korea, Turkey). It was formed
            during the Asian financial crisis of the 1990s
            to provide a forum that would include devel-
            oping countries.

GNP   Gross National Product, now sometimes re-
            placed by GDP—Gross Domestic Product

HRW   Human Rights Watch

IAEA   International Atomic Energy Agency

IDB   Inter-American Development Bank

IBRD   International Bank for Reconstruction and
            Development (World Bank)

ICE   (U.S.) Immigration and Customers Enforce-
            ment (agency)

IIE   Institute for International Economics

ILO   International Labor Organization

IMF   International Monetary Fund

NAFTA   North American Free Trade Agreement

NGO   Non-Governmental Organization

OAS   Organization of the American States

OPEC   Organization of Petroleum Exporting Coun-
            tries (Algeria, Indonesia, Iran, Iraq, Kuwait,
            Libya, Nigeria, Qatar, Saudi Arabia, United
            Arab Emirates, Venezuela)

SDR   Special Drawing Right (currency of the IMF,
            drawing its value from a combination of dol-
            lars, pounds, Euros, and yen)

UN   United Nations

UNESCO   United Nations Educational, Scientific, and
            Cultural Organization

UNTAD   United Nations Organization for Trade and
            Development

WHO   World Health Organization

WTO   World Trade Organization (Replaced GATT,
            General Agreement on Tariffs and Trade)

Appendix C – Information About CQC and Its Globalization Project Participants

Citizens for Quality Civilization (CQC) is a volunteer civic organization under Section 501(c)(3) of the Internal Revenue Code. CQC's mission is to safeguard and improve the quality of life. CQC has a 19-year record of working in important policy areas such as U.S. education, health care, transportation, and globalization. CQC operates informally and checks its drafts with outside experts.

 Robert L. Saloschin, founder of CQC, is a lawyer and civic leader. He graduated Phi Beta Kappa from Columbia College with honors in economics. In World War II he served in the Navy Department and in the Pacific. In the Justice Department's Office of Legal Counsel, he worked on oil import regulations, the communications satellite program, the Cold War aspects of the Olympic Games, expatriation, overhaul of immigration laws, and in the U.S. Delegation to the 1970 Hague Conference on extraditing hijackers. He chaired the Department's Freedom of Information Committee, providing guidance to all federal agencies on secrecy issues. After retirement he consulted on national security for the American Bar Association, practiced law in Maryland, and worked on the projects of the Citizens for Quality Civilization.

 Dr. Ann McDonell, coordinator and editor of CQC's globalization handbook project, earned her Ph.D. in government and politics at the University of Maryland, writing her dissertation on U.S. foreign investment policy. She received an M.A. in international relations from the Fletcher School of Law and Diplomacy, administered by Tufts and Harvard Universities, followed by a Fulbright scholarship to the School of Oriental and African Studies at the University of London. Her professional background includes university teaching, social science textbook editing, and administrative positions. She currently serves on the Board of the United Nations Association-National Capital Area and other policy groups.

Suzanne Buckler graduated from Miami University in Ohio, and gained a wide reputation as a social activist on human rights and affordable housing. She was also active in urging nuclear freeze, sanctuary movements, and providing shelter for Central American refugees. In 1996, the Unitarian Church and the United Nations Association honored her for her work on human rights issues. Suzanne Buckler died in October 2007.

Horst Brand is an economist, formerly with the United States Department of Labor Statistics office. He has written for the *Monthly Labor Review* and other publications on the problems of labor and productivity.

Donald Cleary was awarded a Bachelor of Arts degree in economics from the University of Massachusetts and a Masters of Arts degree in economics from the University of Florida. He also completed a graduate study program in natural resource economics at the University of Michigan. He was employed as an engineer with the Unites States Marine Fishery Service and the Nuclear Regulatory Commission. After retirement, Mr. Cleary served as a consultant in the fields of energy economics and environmental policy.

Emanuel Karbeling, an editor and information consultant, graduated from Kent State University in Ohio with a Bachelor of Arts in journalism and public relations. As an editor and information specialist with the Department of the Army and various civilian publications, he developed and edited materials for military and civilian audiences on subjects including East Germany, Africa, outer space, Turkey, Syria, China, technology transfer, and the Civil War. He also worked with the Army's Freedom of Information Program and the Army Materiel Command, and served as a White House volunteer from 1993 to 2000.

Other important contributors during the drafting of this handbook have been *Herbert Stone*, a civilian engineer retired from the Department of the Navy, and *John Aitchley*, a retired foreign service officer.

Outside Reviewers

It is CQC's practice, before finalizing a handbook on a major area of public policy, to invite comments from a broad variety of knowledgeable outside reviewers. We seek comments on readability, objectivity, and constructiveness, plus any other comments the reviewer may offer. These comments are carefully considered for possible changes in our draft.

We received comments on this draft from eleven reviewers, whom we now wish to thank, as follows:

James Bean, Foreign Service Officer, U.S. State Department

Joan Bunning, author and Cornell Bachelor of Arts in psychology

Dale M. Hill, economist and consultant, Global Partnership Programs, formerly with the World Bank

John R. Hubbard, retired banker, organizer of program donating schoolbooks to developing African nations

Timothy Mack, President World Future Society

Louis Ricciardi, Senior V.P, the Ricciardi Group, Chair, Board of Trustees, Bridgewater State College

James Weaver, Professor Emeritus of Economics, American University

We also thank the remaining four reviewers who provided us with incisive and helpful comments, but requested they not be named. One was with the World Bank, the second is a retired executive in a national labor union and a volunteer leader on international human rights, and the last two serve in a federal agency involved in international economics.

Appendix D—A Short History of American Foreign Policy (Diplomatic, Military, Economic)

1. 1776 to 1783: Obtained foreign help against England.

2. 1786 to presidency of Theodore Roosevelt: Avoided foreign policy entanglements, fortified by the Monroe Doctrine, high tariffs after the Civil War. Welcomed foreign investments to help in building railroads.

3. President Theodore Roosevelt to President Woodrow Wilson: Acted like a major world power as United States interests were perceived.

4. 1919 to Pearl Harbor: Isolationist; high tariffs; weak military forces. Development of aviation, which facilitated the movement of peoples.

5. Pearl Harbor to the end of the Cold War (about 1990); Acted like a major world power; protected the United States and the free world against Nazi and Soviet threats; ended high tariffs; increased immigration. (The failure to cite the Vietnam conflict and reaction to it does not change the overall characterization of this half-century period. From Pearl Harbor to the end of WW II, the policy was to defeat Fascist aggressor nations; after WW II, the policy was to contain Soviet expansion but without another world war.)

6. 1990 to 2001: Foreign policy on the back burner because of general prosperity and the absence of perceived major foreign threats.

7. 2001 to date: Outlook unclear. So far, our foreign relations have largely been related to the "war on terrorism" and to Iraq. Growing problems in the fields of immigration; international trade; transition of the United States from a creditor to a debtor nation; dependence on imported oil; various kinds of global cultural diffusion and polarization. The United States still has a strong military force, asserts a mission to spread democracy, freedom, and market economies around the world. The present and future of U.S. foreign policy may also be affected in some ways by the economic downturn in the U.S. and elsewhere.

Appendix E—The Major Players in Globalization

1. Nations seeking to increase their exports in order to increase their wealth and/or power.

2. International organizations with treaty authority to overcome trade restrictions by signatory nations (WTO, NAFTA, etc.).

3. International organizations supporting the above but without treaty authority (G8, etc.).

4. Regional organizations such as the European Union (EU).

5. Groups within nations seeking to protect their market positions against cheaper imports (French and Japanese farmers, U.S. sugar beet growers, etc.).

6. Labor union members and non-union employees concerned about outsourcing jobs—or reducing compensation or employment levels when industries outsource to obtain cheap foreign labor.

7. Business and agricultural organizations that seek cheap foreign labor and marketing advantage by either outsourcing or encouraging the influx of "guest workers" or illegal immigrants.

8. Religious and other organizations that favor opportunities for poverty-stricken workers regardless of nationality.

9. Corporate or financial leaders whose first concern is growth and gain.

10. Economists, academics, and media pundits who promote the benefits of globalization as sufficient to outweigh its problems, who stress the problems as outweighing the benefits, or see it as an inevitable process that needs to be monitored. (People with strongly opposing views sometimes call their opponents elitists, or populists, or protectionists, etc.).

11. Scientists and environmentalists. They emphasize subjects such as global warming and they warn of the depletion of natural resources unless public policies balance growth with sustainability.

12. Politicians, diplomats, military leaders, and citizens in various nations who view globalization as either tending to undermine national cohesion and national security—or as an improvement over narrowly focused national concerns which they deem unsatisfactory or obsolescent.

13. Other groups with specific interests, including those concerned with national or international terrorism; language education and media; and financial service businesses that benefit or suffer from currency exchange transactions and other international economic activity.

Appendix
Education Policy

C

What Every Citizen Should Know

Citizens for Quality Civilization (CQC)
6603 Lone Oak Drive
Bethesda, MD 20817
www.citizens-quality-civilization.org

PURPOSE OF THIS PRIMER: Today, an objective look at America's situation, and at global trends, strongly suggests that the strengths and weaknesses of American education are critical to our future. This civic primer is a condensed analysis of American education from early childhood through high school, its problems, and options for improvement. The primer's purpose to help develop public understanding in support of better education.

READING TIME: No more than necessary, in light of the following quotation:

"One of the most important aspects of the way of life of any society, primitive or advanced, is their child-rearing practices."

– Ralph Linton, president of the American Anthropological Association, head of the United States School of Military Government in World War II, professor of anthropology at Columbia University, the Sterling Professor of Anthropology at Yale University, and author of *The Study of Man.*

Outline

Page

Overview

This primer is designed for parents and other citizens who are concerned about the quality of education in America. The future of our children depends in large part on their education. And the future of America, in a turbulent world, also depends in large part on the quality and financing of American education.

The ongoing and accelerating development of technology in most fields–medicine, warfare, computers, economic production, communication–offers all of us a higher material standard of living, but at the price of a world of daunting complexity.

To cope effectively with the many choices and problems of today and tomorrow, and for society to identify and manage successfully the benefits and risks in major areas of policy and subcultures, individuals will require a very high level of education.

Lacking high quality education, society may be increasingly dominated by the few, and those few may have inadequate competence and values. Their leadership will thus be questionable, yet the rest of society will be poorly equipped to question them. History suggests that a contributing cause for the decline and collapse of some empires and nations may have been the weakness of their educational systems, compounded by the incompetence of their leaders. More recent examples are the incompetence of both leaders and citizens in the great Western democracies in the 1920s and 1930s, which led to the Great Depression and World War II.

American education today has many important strengths. These include many excellent, dedicated teachers, administrators, librarians, and support staff; a greater range of educational choices for most than in many other nations; a sufficiency of actual or potential resources for better education; and democratic traditions and procedures that give parents, other citizens, and the media a high degree of open access to the policies and operations of educational organizations.

But along with these strengths are weaknesses that demand attention. Both the strengths and the weaknesses depend on many factors. These factors vary from system to system, from school to school, and even from classroom to classroom.

Recently, public and private advocates have stressed the need to improve our weak science and math education, in order to remain economically competitive with foreign nations. We agree on this need, but we believe that three other weaknesses are equally, if not more, important: weakness in developing early childhood readiness for school, weakness in literacy, and weakness in preparing students for civic responsibility.

In a democracy, citizens and parents have the ultimate responsibility for public policies, including the scope and quality of education and the schools' civic mission. At the same time education, as actually conducted in this country, is a very complex process, which needs the best efforts of professional educators and of researchers on education. As a practical matter, progress in education depends on cooperation among all the concerned groups.

This primer is intended to help in the exercise of civic responsibility for education. It is not a scholarly thesis, dissertation, or research report. Its practical value can perhaps be judged by its contents, and by the appendix which describes the nine persons who drafted it and the many and varied outside experts whose comments on the draft were taken into account before publication—a process that took over three years.

THE Basics (Parts 1 through 5)

Part 1: What are the three components of education and what are its five goals?

Education is the development of students' skills, knowledge, and character. These three components are produced by schooling and other activities. "Character" refers to an individual's attitudes and values, which are important for personal well-being and good citizenship. Education should include the whole person, not just academic proficiency, and should moderate any innate aggressiveness.

The five major goals that justify spending time and money on education are

(a)   Productivity—to help develop knowledge and skills to work in order to earn a living;

(b)   Identity—to foster bonds and transmit knowledge needed to support responsible citizenship;

(c)   Socialization—to provide a basis for successful participatory relationships within families, schools, communities, and other groups;

(d)   Perspective—to preserve some of the beneficial knowledge and skills from the past, thus "transmitting the cultural inheritance" and providing a database to help with problems affecting the individual and society;

(e)   Maturity—to enable the individual to engage in effective personal planning and decision making, based on available information with regard to health, finances, and other major concerns, and to support the responsible and effective pursuit of happiness for self and for others in an increasingly complex and volatile world.

The most important knowledge needed to support these five goals is knowledge of the real world, both natural and social, as it was, is, and may become. The most important skills needed to support these goals are reading and critical thinking. Critical thinking requires that students develop not only analytic skills but also enough personal self-reliance to resist peer pressure and similar manifestations of conventional wisdom and herd behavior. Critical thinking also requires that students be made aware that words are symbols which may refer to very specific or very general things, and which may also be used to stimulate emotions or actions. This awareness should include the limitations of stereotypes.

Part 2: What are the main elements of quality in education?

(a)   Effective parental involvement, starting in early childhood. When this is missing, some kind of family or community substitute may be an alternative.

(b)   Full professionalism for teachers, in status and compensation, reasonably comparable to other learned professions that play an important role in the well-being of society.

(c)   Effective learning of basic skills, particularly to reach a sufficiently high degree of literacy to function productively and responsibly in a complex and competitive democratic society.

(d)   Effective learning of basic knowledge, particularly the natural and social sciences, and all the major aspects of history, presented as objectively as possible, to understand the world in which the student lives.

(e)   Academic programs, including the analysis of role models drawn from history, literature, and other sources, that develop character education and civic responsibility.

(f)   Adequate preparation to meet the risks, opportunities, and uncertainties of a large, interdependent, and volatile society.

(g)   Adequate and reliable financing for all of the above.

Part 3: What six kinds of curricular subjects should students learn?

The development of knowledge and skills is traditionally the task of schools, and the kinds of skills and knowledge that schools provide is largely determined by the curriculum. (The development of "character education" should be the home, the school, and other institutions.)

A complete curriculum has six major parts, all of which are essential:

(a)   Reading and other language skills, such as effective writing and speaking. These are basic to all education and are generally essential for success in life. An important tool to develop literacy is the humanities, particularly fiction and biography, carefully selected for both intrinsic value and reading pleasure, without censorship by special interest groups. Class discussions and homework essays based on such books also contribute to character education by helping students strike a better balance between the popular or celebrity culture and a more critical evaluation of possible role models. Well-written stories about historical characters are also excellent material for critical thinking and civic responsibility. In an increasingly globalized world, literature can also improve awareness of the way of life in other times and places.

(b)   Mathematics, to the extent needed for effective living and for occupational advancement.

(c)   The sciences, both natural and social, including the scientific method.

(d)   History and civics as needed for effective civic participation in a modern democracy, and for the assimilation of immigrants. (For details see Appendix A.)

(e)   Subjects such as music, art, and sports, for developing teamwork, self-discipline, creativity, personal depth, and self-confidence. Some students, if they do well in these subjects, may be motivated to do better in more academic subjects.

(f)   Life skills subjects, especially managing personal health and finances. Some of these subjects, such as driver education, may be electives, either because they can be handled by families or because educational resources are limited. For an outline of what the life skills of health management and money management might cover, see Appendix B.

Curriculums should be sequential: In order for the student to reach the more advanced levels of a subject, the student must have mastered the basic levels.

Finally, the scope and content of the curriculum should be clear. Therefore, if a curriculum is to include a category described as "social studies," it should clearly specify–to students, parents, and the public–exactly which subjects are included in this category.

Part 4: Who educates (parents, teachers, peers, media)?

All of these have important roles in educating the child, but the first and most important is the parents' role, which begins at birth. Talking to the child and encouraging responses, with pauses and smiles, helps develop vocabulary and the social skills of interacting positively with others. Reliable research makes clear that if the child is to get a good start on that most vital of subjects—reading—the child must see the parent often reading newspapers, books, and magazines. Also, parents must read to the child, and the child should hear parents discuss what was read.

Today many parents must leave children in child-care centers. These centers vary greatly in their ability to continue the education of the child. Their first function is to provide a safe and peaceful place for children. But they should also provide kinds of guided play that involve numbers, letters, words, and polite behavior. Some states now recognized the importance of better child-care centers in early childhood development. Parents might encourage these governmental efforts, and consider making unannounced visits to these centers. Just as weak K-12 education hurts our colleges by diverting their efforts into remedial education, so does weak early childhood readiness degrade K-12 education.

After the child enters school, the responsibility of parents is not transferred to teachers; it is shared. Reading at home with discussions should continue. Parents naturally like to believe their children are doing well in school, but they need an accurate picture when improvement is called for, through report cards that they must read and sign, and through required conferences with teachers, usually involving the student as well.

Parents are responsible for seeing that homework is done, that there are good conditions at home for developing effective study habits, and that children learn to organize their time. (Parents who cannot help with homework due to language barriers or because they work in the evening when homework is done may be able to find help from neighbors or other community resources.) Parents and teachers also have important responsibilities in the area of character education—values, ethics, and attitudes—especially in helping children develop responsible conduct and respect for others. Naturally parents have the primary responsibility for the health of their children.

The roles of parents and teachers involve the question of "home schooling." This is of two kinds—as a substitute for school, and as a supplement to school. Within each kind there is great variety, partly dependent on the quality of the school and on the capabilities of the parents. Franklin Roosevelt was home-schooled until he was 14, but his family provided tutors. Other presidents have done well with little formal schooling. When home schooling is a substitute for school, it may result in a limited or single-viewpoint education. Therefore, state education departments should provide standards and assistance to parents who home-school, particularly with curriculum outlines and tests, since society has a strong interest that education, whether at home or school, be successful.

For most families, home schooling will be of the supplemental kind, including home discussions, chores, and entertainment and travel with important educational values.

For suggestions on how schools might help in preparing parents to support education more effectively, see Appendix G.

The role of teachers in education is of course pivotal. They are in the front lines of protecting and hopefully advancing our civilization. Among other things, teachers are often expected to remedy, as best they can, the shortcomings of parents.

Successful teaching depends on teachers who love children, love learning, and are good role models. It also depends on effective recruitment and retention of teachers. Good recruitment means finding teachers who know the subjects to be taught and how to teach. Both are essential. Since teaching seldom offers great rewards of money or fame, it is important not to deter interested applicants. Unfortunately, some technical certification requirements for time-consuming courses in pedagogy are of questionable relevance to teaching effectiveness and discourage very promising applicants. These may include persons who have retired from significant careers, are a very valuable educational resource, and would enjoy teaching.

Retention of teachers depends on pay, benefits, and working conditions. The latter include class size, resources such as textbooks and other things, and whether teachers have truly professional and supportive relations with parents, principals, and headquarters staff. Even if bad working conditions do not cause a teacher to quit, they are likely to impair his or her motivation to teach. According to a recent study by the National Education Association, half of the new teachers will quit within five years; the Bureau of Labor Statistics provides similar information (*Washington Post*, May 9, 2006). This rate of attrition seems excessive.

In addition to teachers, many schools provide school nurses and school counselors. These professionals deal with a variety of health matters that can affect education, including mental, social, and emotional problems, and provide guidance to students about college and employment decisions. The value of quality services in these areas is obvious. They can improve education by giving individual attention to the problems of students, and thus should be able to reduce the nation's excessive dropout rate, recently reported to average 30 percent. However the scope and quality of counseling services vary greatly from place to place.

Others who educate include a wide variety: other students ("peer pressure"), coaches, neighbors, relatives, and friends; the entertainment media (TV, movies, the Internet, video games, popular music, etc.); organized groups such as scouts and churches; and libraries, books, and the news media. Some of these are inevitable and probably beneficial. But suggestible youths may be dangerously affected if they are exposed to entertainment heavily loaded with violence, sex, gang values and contempt for women, or to peer pressure for crime or substance abuse. Therefore parents and teachers should be aware of the "others" affecting students, and counteract harmful ones by substitutions and by encouraging the development of students' critical capacities.

Finally, those who educate must to a large extent be those who motivate. Children, like adults, are motivated by desires, fears, and interests. Subjects that are interesting, or presented in an interesting way, attract attention, study, and learning. The desire of a student for recognition for success, whether measured against peers or against one's previous performance, is a powerful motivator if recognition is skillfully applied. Similarly, fear of disapproval by peers, or failure, if the fear is real but not severe enough to cause hopelessness, is sometimes an effective motivation for increased effort. Those who educate successfully have used or relied on one or more of these motivations.

Part 5: Who controls education (administrators, politicians, others)?

Many officials and many organizations share some degree of control over education, though direct control is chiefly exercised by or through the local school systems.

From a legal standpoint, the states have basic control over education, because local governments are subject to state control, except to the extent that (a) state and local authorities must abide by the federal Constitution, and (b) they choose to accept conditions attached to grants of federal money.

Traditionally, most responsibility for education has been assigned by the states to local governments and their school systems. However, with today's ever-increasing movement of persons, trade, and information across both state and national borders, the trend is towards more exercise of both state and national powers to help assure that states, and the nation as a whole, do not fall behind other states and other nations.

As just indicated, Congress has some control by funding certain education activities and by setting conditions for obtaining federal funds, and the Department of Education has some control by administering the laws passed by Congress.

The states have overall power over local (city or county) governments and their public school systems, but are chiefly involved in helping fund them and setting standards. In many states, the State Superintendent of Education, the State Board of Education, and their staffs have important functions in education.

City and county governments approve budgets for local school systems and support them, chiefly by property taxes, but usually leave the operation of schools to the school system management, consisting of a school board, a school superintendent, and their assistants.

School boards are either elected or appointed. In most places, acting like a board of directors of a corporation, they hire a school superintendent to run the system, and they have general authority over the system's policies, operations, textbooks, and reading lists. This authority is often exercised without collaboration with teachers.

The school superintendent is the executive who runs the system, with assistance from the school system's headquarters staff or the "bureaucracy." This work includes personnel matters such as hiring, promoting, and assigning teachers, principals, and others. It also includes supervising the curriculum, instruction, and procuring of textbooks and other materials, construction and maintenance of buildings, providing the school bus service, and many other matters. In large systems, some of these functions may be delegated to area authorities.

The system headquarters staff assists the superintendent. Most school systems are small. But large systems may have a large headquarters staff, which may exercise considerable actual control over education, even though it is subject to the superintendent. Given the large number and variety of matters that can claim the attention of the superintendent, a major part of his or her function must necessarily be delegated to others. Headquarters staffs, like all the other players in education, are subject to criticism. They have been criticized on several grounds: that they are too large and costly in relation to the size of the teaching staffs; that they interfere with the work of teachers in ways that impair education; and that they serve as a place to which the system can transfer persons whose work in schools was substandard. The validity of such criticisms, and the questions of what can be done about them, may obviously vary from system to system.

School principals (and, in large schools, department heads) have a unique role in helping to control education, because they come in closer contact with teachers than to headquarters personnel. Principals should understand both the practical business of teaching, and the arts of leadership among professionals and students. While the authority of principals varies from place to place, they should have an important role in building a strong group of teachers—in recruitment, selection, motivation, retention, re-assignment, and/or departure of teachers. In addition, they can foster supportive relationships with the community—parents; students; business, labor, and professional groups; news media; and the various parts of government—which all can affect the school's success.

Charter schools are public schools that are independently managed. Thus they are largely free from control by the headquarters bureaucracy of a school system. However, they are funded by the system and are expected to meet standards set by the state. They are organized by citizens who are dissatisfied with local schools, and are chartered as non-profits by local school boards, or in some states, by colleges or other institutions. Some charter schools have worked well and some have not. Charter schools are also referred to in Part 8, in discussing various forms of school choice.

The courts exercise some control over education, particularly in interpreting legislation and applying legislation affecting education, and in resolving various issues about equal treatment in education.

Teachers unions exercise considerable control over education, since they represent teachers who, of course, are major players in education. These unions are especially concerned with school budgets; the pay, benefits, and working conditions of teachers; and any proposals that might divert education funding away from public schools. Unions are also concerned with teachers' job tenure. Generally speaking, public school teachers can be removed only for cause, as demonstrated after prescribed procedures, and "cause" in many places does not include incompetence. However, there are other possible remedies for incompetence, such as further training or reassignment. Unions may also support strict certification laws, which protect teachers by reducing the number of applicants for teaching jobs. Thus unions, although necessary to protect their members, may give less attention to the interests of other stakeholders in education, arguably including the students.

Vendors of textbooks, computers, and other items purchased by schools may have limited control of education, by the way their products are designed, and by persuading schools to purchase particular kinds of materials that they sell.

In addition, business groups such as the Business Roundtables for Education, neighborhood groups such as PTAs, and various civic, political, scientific, religious, and other groups may exercise some control, or at least influence, on education.

Finally, as is natural in a democracy, the citizenry has ultimate control of education, as over other areas of public policy, but the effective exercise of this control requires much effort.

The Problems (Parts 6 through 9)

Part 6: What are the greatest obstacles to quality in education?

The following list of obstacles to quality is not necessarily in the order of their importance. It is a checklist, and only a checklist, for use in evaluating the quality of education in a particular class, school system, or larger entity.

(a)   Insufficient competence or insufficient authority in teachers or in principals, even to maintain discipline. (Incompetence can often be alleviated by proper training. An insufficiency of authority that impedes quality work may be due to legal, administrative, political, or bureaucratic causes.)

(b)   Insufficient emphasis on student writing, especially in classes that are too large.

(c)   Cheating. (Cheating may be aggravated by "teaching to the test" in preparing for standardized tests.)

(d)   Excessive use of, or poor quality, audio-visual materials.

(e)   Automatic promotions and mainstreaming of children who disrupt classes or require that teachers divert excessive attention away from the rest of the class.

(f)   Student intimidation, including bullying, coupled with a lack of effective student government.

(g)   The need of public schools for some alternative to selective admission and retention that is available to private schools.

(h)   Bad outside influences on children, including excessive or improper TV, antisocial subcultures of "success," and gangs.

(i)   Bad textbooks; poor quality, "dumbed-down," or not enough for each student.

(j)   Inadequate funding. Salaries are the biggest part of most school budgets, followed by technology, especially computers, which increase access to information, but do little to develop critical thinking.

(k)   Misallocation of funding, especially to excessive headquarters bureaucracies and to over-emphasized spectator sports.

(l)   Substandard administration, including administration that interferes with quality teaching.

(m)   Loss or absence of a required "core" curriculum that covers all the basic parts of a quality education, including the development of critical thinking.

(n)   The educational philosophy or attitude that children should be taught only the things they like to learn.

(o)   The presence of "turf" attitudes by some of the   players in education, to the extent it may interfere with cooperation and progress toward quality education.

(p)   Failure to provide adequate analysis, service, and funding to meet the need of handicapped children for special education.

(q)   Failure to identify and correct the causes of lagging academic performance by minority children, including inadequate educational services, insufficient home support, negative peer pressure by students who discourage academic effort by their classmates, and social and cultural factors that delay effective assimilation.

(r)   Failure to recognize and to adequately prepare the increasing percentage of students who will need post-secondary education to cope with an increasingly competitive world.

(s)   Failure to adequately measure the high school dropout rate, reportedly 30 percent as a national average (*Time*, 4/17/06, pp. 30-40), and failure to determine its causes and take actions to reduce the rate.

Two warnings: This list is not necessarily complete; there are other possible obstacles to quality education— for example, community attitudes that do not sufficiently understand or support quality education. Secondly even when a particular obstacle is found to be present in a school or system, it may be wise not to overcorrect if that may cause other problems.

Part 7: What are the best ways to improve the quality of education?

(a)   Update the relationships between classroom teachers and headquarters staffs to improve teamwork and morale, and to take better account of modern conditions. Bright and motivated young women are no longer limited to careers in nursing or teaching. To attract and retain good teachers of either gender in today's competitive world requires greater efforts, including overall compensation, professional status and recognition, and job satisfaction. (See, in this connection, the high attrition rate among teachers noted in Part 4, above.) At the same time, both teachers and students are confronted with increasing complexity and volatility in society and technology. This requires many kinds of specialized efforts, which in turn call for effective headquarters staffing.

Good teamwork between frontline personnel and headquarters is important in any large organization. Thus it seems vital that headquarters staffs establish and maintain good, cooperative relations with classroom teachers—relations involving two-way discourse, two-way support, and mutual respect. Teachers should generally feel that they have sufficient freedom in their classrooms to teach effectively. Have an overall policy of what should be taught, but give the faculty the freedom and the means to carry it out. In order to do this, more money may be needed for classrooms, plus more realism and flexibility in restrictions and rules. Subject to review, teachers must be able to control student behavior and the academic demands placed on students. (See also problems with recruitment and retention of teachers discussed under Part 4, above.)

(b)   Parents must become more involved in academic and ethical education. They must set a moral tone related to that of the school. They should help their children enjoy learning for its own sake, as well as for future financial advantage. Parents should know what and why their children are learning, should be involved in school activities, and should become an influence on education. Serious attention should be given to parenting education. Disadvantaged parents need special attention starting as early as the time children are born. Hospital personnel, social workers, the clergy, and outreach agents of schools and Head Start should be mobilized to equip these parents with their importance to education as described in Part 4 above. Similar contacts should be made with providers of child-care for pre-school children, since they share the responsibilities and opportunities of parents. See also Appendix G.

(c)   The effectiveness of teachers and principals should be enhanced by the following: better compensation; improved community status; and a stronger preparation for excellence in both teachers and principals that includes (i) a solid, liberal-arts group of college courses in the sciences, history, and public and personal concerns, before these future professionals are immersed in specialized studies, and (ii) special training for principals in the skills of leading other professionals, such as the techniques of good administration and of fostering collegiality, teamwork, and esprit de corps.

(d)   Student participation and leadership are important elements in improving education. If it is made popular to study, people will study. This has been proven in a number of schools and colleges in this and other countries. Studying can be encouraged by old-fashioned or updated spelling bees and by contests that are variations on knowledge-based TV programs. If students feel some recognition for their education efforts because they see it affects their present and future, they will accept standards that improve discipline, learning, and general interest in learning.

(e)   Supporters can be found to help improve schools. Newspapers have a strong interest in better literacy. Realtors have a natural interest in communities with good schools. Businesses have a natural interest in competent employees. And public officials, especially in law enforcement, have a natural interest in encouraging responsible citizenship.

(f)   Finally, parents and other interested citizens can join together to evaluate their schools using the checklist of "obstacles" in Part 6 and then develop any necessary and appropriate response.

Part 8: What are the major issues in education policy?

(a)   Class size;

(b)   Financing (amounts, sources, and allocations);

(c)   Balancing excellence and quality;

(d)   Ideology: evolution, sex education, etc.;

(e)   Teacher certification and compensation;

(f)   Accountability, standards, and testing;

(g)   Parental and community involvement;

(h)   Administration and professionalism;

(i)   Questionable innovations;

(j)   Student empowerment;

(k)   School choice (vouchers, charter schools, etc.);

(l)   The No Child Left Behind Act; and

(m)   Regional versus local schools.

This list does not include all aspects of education that may be subject to major dispute. For example, we do not discuss current controversies about whether big city schools should be controlled by the school board or by the mayor, whether our schools should borrow certain ideas from other countries, whether middle schools should be more like elementary or more like high schools, or whether modern curriculums sometimes tend to be "a mile wide and an inch deep."

Also, this list is partly a kind of checklist. It is not an exhaustive, definitive treatment of the issues discussed below. But it is a useful introduction to most of the main issues in American education. Obviously, some of the following issues are not a problem in all schools

(a) **Class Size.** Smaller classes are a vital factor in the quality of education. (A large part of the attraction of private schools is that they often have much smaller classes.) Most of the tasks in teaching—effectively monitoring the progress of each student, giving help to those who need it, maintaining each student's sense of participating in classroom activities, and even preserving order—are much more difficult if the class is too large. These factors apply at all grade levels. Of course, reducing class size means more teachers will be required, which calls for additional, or at least re-allocated funding. Also, large classes can be improved by better teaching methods and by summer school, where teachers have smaller classes and less outside interferences. The conclusion seems clear: Smaller class size is a priority.

(b) **Financing.** Public schools are financed almost entirely by taxes although some may beg funds from PTAs or commercial concessionaries. Private schools are generally financed by tuition charges, plus endowment income or support from religious or other organizations. School taxes are chiefly on real estate, and vary among localities. Local school taxes are supplemented by state and federal grants.

A major issue about public schools funding arises from differences among counties and cities in their ability to raise money: Rich counties can raise more per student with a low tax rate than can poor counties with a high one. This leads to lawsuits and efforts to have states give more help to the poorer localities, or to have the federal government give more help to the poorer states. The pro case of these efforts is fairness and upgrading the poorer school systems. Opponents assert that each community should determine its own level of school spending, be encouraged to raise more money on its own, and expect less money in places with a lower cost of living for teachers. The outcome is often some kind of compromise, which should help to achieve more equal funding.

There are many other issues around financing schools. One is whether realty taxes should be partly replaced by sales, income, or other taxes, or by bond issues, lottery earnings, or fees. Another is the total level of spending and how the money should be divided between the headquarters staff and the schools, or between academics and sports. These complex issues are handled by school superintendents and their staffs, by school boards, and by various elected officials, after getting views from the business community, teachers' unions, PTAs, and parents and citizens generally.

(c) **Balancing Excellence and Equality.** This issue arises because children do not all learn at the same speed, and because it is more difficult to teach a class effectively when there is a big difference among the students in learning progress. In such situations teachers and schools are torn between excellence (helping all students, including the brightest, to do their best), and equality (helping the slower students keep up with the rest of the class). Both are valid goals which somehow must be balanced.

The issue has taken two forms—disputes about track systems (in which there are fast, average, and slow classes) and disputes about mainstreaming (in which students with serious learning handicaps are placed in regular classes). While, as just noted, there is a good case for some kind of track system (sometimes called "advanced placement" or an "honors program"), some track systems have been properly criticized as too rigid. For example, a student who is excellent in one subject but poor in all the rest probably should not be placed in a slow track for everything. Similarly, a student who is slow but who may later improve—so-called "late bloomers"—should be able to move to a faster track later. It is also important that any track system be conducted so as to minimize damage to self-esteem and morale of the slower students; for example, by favoring comparisons with students at the same level, or with the student's own past results, rather than with faster students; in addition, enrichment subjects can help (see under curriculum, above.) Educators should recognize that differences in student achievement are sometimes based on differences in motivation rather than ability.

Mainstreaming refers to placing in regular classes a child with mental, emotional, or physical disabilities of such a nature that the child (a) may disrupt or distract the rest of the class, or (b) present the teachers with very difficult or time-consuming problems. Such children are usually considered in need of "special education," and they require experts on what is best for the child and how to work with parents and the child to this end. Some of these children can be successfully included in regular classes if the teacher is provided with qualified specialized helpers, and all students benefit from this experience. To deny that a child needs special placement, if indeed this is the case, is unfair to the child and to other students.

About 20 percent of American school budgets is said to be devoted to special education. Part of this may be spent, at some schools, on children mistakenly classified as having mental disability, when, in fact, their real problem is ignorance, which calls for remedial education. The need for great care on this subject should be clear.

Ideology. These issues often are about teaching evolution or some form of sex education. Such disputes reflect deep-seated differences between traditional cultures and modern approaches to these subjects. In various parts of the country, educators and citizens who are familiar with the scientific and factual pros and cons support teaching these subjects. Parents or others who oppose such teaching may request curriculum changes, or request that their children be excused from such lessons, or seek alternative schooling, or seek to counterbalance such lessons by training at home or in religious settings.

Other ideological issues of a more political nature may arise in various subjects, particularly history, economics, and current affairs. Such disputes can be handled by presenting the view of expert professionals together with dissenting views. Teachers should not be discouraged from presenting their own views on these issues if this is a part of a balanced presentation. This approach can stimulate students' thinking and make them aware that some important matters are still unsettled, thus preparing them for responsible citizenship in a democracy.

(e)   **Teacher Certification and Compensation.** To recruit and retain well-qualified teachers is essential to quality education. Most states require that teachers be certified as qualified before employment in the public schools. In many places, certification requires years of study in special schools of education emphasizing the history and philosophy of education, and the techniques and problems of classroom teaching, rather than emphasis on the subject to be taught. This excludes from teaching persons with careers that gave them excellent subject knowledge and good teaching skills (based on teaching in other situations), but lacking required credits from schools of education. Shortages of qualified teachers have generated pressure to revise certification rules to admit such persons, based on their experience, tests, and perhaps a short course in school-based teaching.

To retain as well as recruit good teachers several things are critical: adequate compensation (salary, benefits, and retirement), an attractive and truly professional work environment, class sizes that are not excessive, and community support by parents and citizens who appreciate good teaching.

The compensation of teachers has long been far less than the average incomes of other professions like law and medicine. Given political realities, the teaching profession can expect only gradual improvement in compensation. Although teachers are attracted by other factors (love of learning, love of children, job security, longer than average summer vacations), it is important that compensation be adequate for a reasonable standard of living or else teachers will leave for better paying work, or not choose teaching in the first place. The compensation should also include benefits such as health insurance and pensions.

Efforts to increase compensation through "merit pay" have usually been opposed by teachers unions. They point to the risk of favoritism or political influence, and the difficulty of evaluating teaching effectiveness accurately. Perhaps a carefully crafted form of peer review or some objective form of measurement might alleviate these difficulties.

In most other professions, as well as in the career military and civil services, superior performance is stimulated because it is a significant factor in recognition, advancement, and increased compensation. A similar development in some public schools may be expected, according to Edward J. McElroy, president of the American Federation of Teachers. In a letter to *The Washington Post* of September 22, 2007, he described as a "common misconception" that teachers unions oppose performance pay for teachers. He added that some AFT local unions have helped develop local plans in which test scores are among several factors to consider on how teachers should be compensated.

(f)   **Accountability, Standards, and Testing**. This subject is clearly of great importance because it focuses on whether education is or is not producing good enough results. Yet it is very contentious, especially on (a) what results should be required (standards), (b) how to measure the results that are being produced (testing), and (c) what to do if results are inadequate.

In 2001 Congress passed legislation to improve school accountability nationwide. This federal law, the No Child Left Behind Act, discussed below as a separate issue, came on top of efforts by several states to compel improvement in substandard schools operated by county and city school systems. For example, in Maryland, statewide tests have been in use for many years, and schools with consistently bad results that do not improve are subject to being taken over by the state.

The standardized tests under the recent federal law and those used in statewide programs have been criticized by parents and teachers as too severe and harmful, in that teachers are pressured to shift efforts from good teaching to "teaching the test." These criticisms are mostly aimed at the common multiple-choice or "objective" kind of tests, which may test skill in test-taking as well as knowledge of the subject of the test. There is also criticism of essay-type tests, which may better show a student's understanding of the subject of the test, but which are time-consuming and difficult to grade accurately. The response to these criticisms is that some testing is necessary—for example, good teachers often give informal quizzes on their own— and that if standardized tests are not satisfactory, they should be revised rather than eliminated. Perhaps the worst response, from the viewpoint of education quality, would be to obtain improvements in test scores by simply making the tests easier for public relations purposes.

Even if accountability includes good standards and good testing, it may fail if testing shows standards are not being met, but that nothing effective is being done to change this. Actions to end substandard performance in schools and systems can be of two general types: the carrot and the stick. The first means providing more money and attention to upgrading the talent, facilities, and leadership in substandard schools. The second may take several forms: disciplining, transferring, or terminating personnel; turning the school over to new or outside managers, such as a for-profit education company that operates the school under contract; or possibly some form of school choice that will subject the school to competition pressures.

But it should also be borne in mind that the failure of a school to meet established standards may, in some cases, be partly due to community factors beyond the school's control: crime, drugs, gangs, poverty, slum housing, unemployment, and widespread family breakdown, all perhaps aggravated by entertainment saturated with violence and sex. In such situations, restoring quality education probably will need additional remedies from sectors outside of education.

(g)   **Parental and Community Involvement.** There is much uncertainty on this issue. On the one hand school systems want parental and community support in helping make education more effective, and also in helping obtain larger school budgets. On the other hand, parental and community involvement sometimes takes a questioning or critical turn, presenting problems for school personnel. That some involvement is unwelcome should not be too surprising—educators, like police, transportation people, etc., have a "turf" tendency to question the competence of critics who are assumed to lack experience in their fields.

There are two main pros for parental and community involvement: It is necessary to have parental action in educating children (see Part 4 above), and it is necessary to have community support for better schools. Parental cooperation should begin at the preschool level. Small children who see their parents reading newspapers, books, and magazines every day are more likely to become good readers, which is essential for success in school and later in life. Parents should also give proper attention to students' health, homework, use of TV and other mass media, grades, and conduct, and should meet with teachers and other school personnel from time to time.

Another form of community involvement is frequently to invite outside speakers in the classroom—lawyers and judges; doctors and nurses; engineers and businessmen; and others, including retirees, depending on the subject. This not only stimulates learning, it also builds community support for the schools. Therefore schools should promote establishment of speakers bureaus that will (a) present significant subjects including controversial ones, (b) hold the students' interest, and (c) present various sides of debatable subjects, including unpopular opinions.

While cooperation must come from families, pressure for school-wide or system-wide improvements usually requires some organization, perhaps through a PTA or some other group. Such groups can collect information, develop an agenda, and have representatives to deal with school authorities or, if necessary, with elected officials or the voters. The value to education of such efforts depends on the soundness of the agendas and the effectiveness with which they are pursued.

The cons of parental involvement are (a) a tendency to assume things are okay, leading to weak or absent involvement, and (b) misguided complaints. Thus, parents who are unhappy about poor grades sometimes demand more lenient grading, instead of looking for ways to help the student improve. The cons of community involvement also stem from dubious agendas; for example, overzealous support for competitive school athletics at the expense of academics, or indiscriminate objections to any and all standardized tests that are needed to find out how a school measures on established standards.

(h) **Administration and Professionalism.** In administration, one recurrent issue is the performance of the school superintendent and his/her staff, and the relation between the superintendent and the school board. Here, the pros and cons obviously depend on the facts in each case. Another common issue, especially in large systems, is the size and value of large bureaucracies at school system headquarters. Fair questions include whether the growth of these staffs is at the expense of teaching staffs, whether some headquarters activities are really worthwhile, and whether some of these activities may actually interfere with teaching. Again the pros and cons depend upon a careful review of the facts in a particular system. Perhaps some headquarters activities common to several counties could be consolidated or coordinated more efficiently at the state level. However, any such actions should allow for local conditions. Also it would be wise to have a general policy that those who directly supervise teachers usually have several years of successful teaching experience, plus some training in management.

Issues about professionalism in education invite comparison with medicine, law, and other professions, as contrasted to business and other occupations. Professions are generally defined by (a) tradition, (b) laws, (c) knowledge and skills for practicing the profession, (d) peer enforcement of standards of competence and ethics, and (e) an obligation to temper the pursuit of personal gain by serving others or serving the public at large. The teaching profession, like the clergy, rates well on most of these criteria.

Issues of teacher professionalism are chiefly related to inadequate compensation and to the weakness in peer enforcement of competence. On compensation, the pros and cons are fairly plain: More money would help support pride in teaching, even though wealth is usually not a priority for a teaching career. As for peer enforcement of standards, no profession enjoys this unpleasant task, but a profession's willingness to discipline its own members if they fall below standards is important, both in maintaining the standards and in gaining the public's respect for the profession.

(i)   **Questionable Innovations**. The teaching profession is not the only one to be afflicted with fads and fashions—there was a time when doctors routinely recommended that all children have tonsillectomies. But the list of questionable fashions in teaching is fairly long: "new math," the "whole language" method to teach reading, unstructured classrooms, team teaching, excessively or exclusively bilingual education, injurious or indiscriminate use of computers or other devices, etc. Why teaching fads come and go may be something of a mystery— perhaps someone has done a good selling job on persons in authority—but fads are seldom a good substitute for time-tested methods of teaching important subjects. The pro of innovations is that sometimes they offer real progress, and they may keep interest alive in some educational circles. The con is that they are distracting and waste precious classroom time.

In addition to fads, schools sometimes experience "pendulum swings." Examples: math and science, up after Sputnik, then neglected, now up due to global competition; character education, long rejected, then oversold, now apparently fading. The answer may be more stability, based on better perspectives, to minimize the waste of chasing "the next big thing."

None of the foregoing should be read as against changes based on research and observation. Progress often requires some innovation, and education needs progress. The best hope for changes that will be successful is to apply good judgment, fortified by experience, research, a variety of perspectives, and a realization that changing cultures, in education as in other fields, is sometimes a tricky business.

(j)   **Student Empowerment.** This issue relates to school morale, discipline, character education, and citizenship training. These largely depend on the school as an effective community—a community that enhances the maturity and confidence of students, and strengthens society at large.

While conditions vary from school to school, student participation in decision-making on non-academic matters, starting at about the sixth grade, works in many schools. It requires some form of student government, with regular elections by each class or grade, and regular meetings with defined functions. As in the case of adult governments, decisions may be either general or specific. General matters, such as some aspect of extra-curricular activities or school dress or decorum, go to a student council. Particular cases, such as bullying or other bad behavior, go to a student court or committee. School faculty or administrators will participate in, or at least monitor, these student activities, but will avoid the appearance of dominating them, even though the school will retain ultimate authority and responsibility on most matters. Of course, student government is only effective if the students perceive it to have power.

The pros of student participation have been noted above. The cons are a fear of loss of control by school authorities, or other harms. But education in democracy should provide students experience in orderly discussion and decision-making, and in the selection, practice, and evaluation of leadership. An elected and admired student government is an excellent asset against bullying, harassment, and racial or ethnic discord.

(k)   **School Choice.** The drive for some kind of school choice (vouchers, charter schools funded by taxes but independently administered, or easy transfers between schools) arises from (a) dissatisfaction with inadequate schools, (b) the right of parents to choose another school they can afford, if necessary by moving, and (c) a belief that competition among schools is good. Opposition to school choice is based on (a) the belief that inadequate schools should be improved rather than abandoned by some students, (b) the view that choice by means of vouchers will encourage attendance at religious schools and thus erode the separation of church and state, (c) the view that helping some student to leave an inadequate school is unfair to the students who remain there, (d) the belief that school choice is disruptive and (e) that it diverts needed funds from public schools. Both sides have reasonable arguments. Which side is better seems to depend largely on the specifics of a particular situation, a particular school, or a particular proposal.

(l)   **The No Child Left Behind Act.** This law, passed by Congress in 2001, has become controversial. Despite its sweeping title, its goals are limited. It is aimed at public schools whose students do poorly in major subjects. It seeks to improve these schools through various means such as tests, funding controls, and giving students the right to transfer to better schools in the same system.

The act has two important pros and several cons. It recognizes that the nation has many substandard schools, damaging students, the economy, and communities. The act also recognizes that public schools have some of the characteristics of a monopoly, thus tending to lag in quality and value unless there is outside intervention.

But experience under the act has generated several cons. First, it is asserted that the act is underfunded. Second, the act disregards the fact that educational progress does not depend solely on the quality of a school's efforts. There are great differences among schools in the socio-economic character of their students' family and community situations. Some live with poverty, broken homes, poorly educated parents, and a youth culture of gangs, drugs, and junk entertainment. Also, some schools have more students who are difficult to educate, such as those who do not speak English, and ones who need special education. Third, in order to measure progress, many states rely heavily on standardized tests (multiple-choice, true-false, matching, etc.). Many, perhaps most, teachers feel pressured to teach only the facts likely to get better scores. This can lead to rote learning and to neglecting some aspects of the subject. It also may crowd out useful essay-type tests. While the value of standardized tests is usually recognized, the objection is the overemphasis on them. Fourth, and very important from a national viewpoint, the act only tests English, math, and science. It thus omits subjects essential for responsible citizenship in a democracy, particularly history and civics. This omission is not justified by various interpretations of history; such variations can foster maturity by presenting each side. Citizens should consider whether young voters should grow up without the data bank of experience that history affords. Fifth, it is asserted that the act's transfer rights have created unforeseen problems for both the schools involved in the transfers. Sixth, it has also been asserted that the act, by concentrating school efforts on poorly performing students, causes neglect of the gifted students, and that the act may tend to create a caste system, in which poor students get drilled to improve test scores, while schools in affluent, well-educated areas provide education that qualifies students for advancement.

These criticisms of the No Child Left Behind Act do not apply to all schools. With more time, money, efforts, leadership, and a spirit of open and collegial cooperation, including a primary focus on upgrading the performance of teachers and principals, the No Child Left Behind Act can develop into an important plus in American education.

It has recently been suggested that the act be extended to cover high schools. Consideration of that idea might be combined with a review of the above pros and cons.

(m) **Regional Versus Local Schools.** In the late 70s and early 80s, regional schools became all the rage. Two or three local schools were often merged into a large school of 2000 to 4000 students. This saved money on administration, staff, the number of teachers, purchasing, sports, transportation, and maintenance. Also, larger schools can offer a greater variety of courses and course components, and a greater choice of classes to fit slow, average, and fast learners. But in time drawbacks appeared: Classes were larger, rules and regulations were imposed impersonally ("zero tolerance" and its often counterproductive results), the ability of teachers to make sensitive judgments about individual students was decreased, local pride and interest in schools diminished, parental authority and parental influence on schools weakened, and more children became isolated, disgruntled, and neglected (shootings at schools like Columbine were a symptom). Students had less personal contact with adults, bullying increased, the best teachers tended to work only with the best students, and both discipline and academics suffered.

In recent years many states have reverted to local, smaller schools because of problems with the larger, regional schools. However, many of the latter still exist and occasionally new ones are built.

To the extent that it may be possible to have some of the advantages of big schools in smaller local schools, and to have advantages of smaller ones in big ones, there are obvious challenges to school leadership and to school system leaders and management.

*Part 9: How can parents and other citizens improve edu-
cation?*

The answer to this question has two parts: Which
improvements should be chosen for priority, and how can
they be achieved?

A.   **Which improvements should be given
priority?** This depends, in turn, upon two things—the
relative merits of various improvements, and the relative
acceptability of various improvements to decision-makers
and to those parts of the public that influence them.

The merits are the comparative costs and benefits
of various improvements, and acceptability is the comparative degree of support or opposition to be expected
from the public and leaders.

Parts 6 and 7 of this primer should help directly in
identifying priority improvements for a particular school
or system, and the rest of this primer also provides important factors to consider.

B.   **How can educational improvements be
achieved?**

(a)   The concerned parent and citizen can have
some effect acting alone, for example, by letters to school
officials, newspapers, and legislators, and of course by
voting and encouraging others to vote. But it is usually
more effective to work with others—friends, other parents, PTAs, neighbors, etc. If necessary, organize a small
civic committee to work for better education.

(b)   Citizens and parents should be able to list—
clearly and with specific illustrations—the benefits of the
improvements they seek and the detriments of existing
conditions. They also should be prepared to discuss meth-

ods of meeting the costs and other problems that the desired improvements may involve.

(c)   Parents and citizens should identify and coordinate with **allies** in working for better education. These include newspapers, businesses, chambers of commerce, some political leaders, and some education professionals. But in addition, the social, economic, and quality-of-life benefits of better education might be brought to the attention of churches, civic groups, and nonprofit agencies that work to assist the disadvantaged and handicapped. Society as a whole benefits from better education.

(d)   Thought and attention should be given to possible opposition groups. Sometimes opponents can be led to recognize that the desired improvements will do more good than harm. The view of opponents should be given reasonable consideration, but their opposition should not override the interests of the general public. Taxpayers worried about the cost of improvements can be reassured by sound methods of funding and cost control, and by pointing out that the benefits of improvements will actually make them a bargain, and to oppose this would be "penny wise and pound foolish." Sometimes it helps to show that similar improvements are in effect in other schools with good results.

(e)   A careful strategic plan should be developed, one that would withstand public scrutiny. It should identify and stress the desired improvement's good features. It should, of course, include proper timing and organization so that its messages are heard, understood, and remembered. And it should be flexible enough to make adjustments as they may be needed.

(f)   Finally, parents and citizens should not overlook the value of justified passion in obtaining improvements. Human nature and human institutions being what they are, actual examples of waste, stupidity, destructive values, inadequate standards, or other negatives may not be hard to find, and can sometimes be useful and legitimate tools to stimulate action. History shows that reforms and progress in many fields occurred partly because of well-documented and well-publicized muckraking. Considering that the objectives of educational improvement could hardly be more important—the future of the child, the community, and the nation—it is both natural and necessary that advocates of improvement should tap into strong feelings, both to fortify their own efforts and to enlist support from others.

There is, however, some need for caution: Passion is strong medicine that can backfire. If it is excessive, or its target is defensible, it may stimulate opposition, or even create division among those favoring improvement. For these reasons, advocates of school improvement may be well advised to be alert to the risk that they might be identified with some ideological, political, sectarian, commercial, cultural, or other special interest group.

Appendix A—Suggested Contents of History and Civics Curriculums

I.   The three purposes of teaching history are (a) to provide a basis for personal identification with the community and the nation, (b) to introduce students to stories about events and persons of great interest, including good role models and some persons who became famous in one field and then were mistakenly assumed to be experts in another field, and (c) to provide a vital data bank for the exercise of responsible democratic citizenship by exploring the causes and circumstances of major events, plus their after-effects.

In some societies, history may be taught so as to re-ignite ancient grievances. In others, it may be taught selectively to foster national pride. But in today's complex world, including information of varying reliability on the Internet, responsible citizenship and national pride can best be formed by accurate history, including our nation's success in making major corrections so as to better approach the ideas of our founders.

II.   History should not be perceived by students as a long list of dates to be memorized. Instead, to the maximum practical extent, it should include

(a)   In-depth, factual United States history, to the present time, and regional and local history;

(b)   In-depth, factual world history, beginning with pre-history;

(c)   Chronological markers (dates) to the extent needed to make history coherent, so that relationships between various developments, and their causes and effect, can be understood;

(d)   History of knowledge and belief (philosophy, religion, science, and technology);

(e)   Major historical events, including their causes and effects, and important historical persons, including their accomplishments, failures, and the conditions that they faced;

(f)   History and functions of social organizations (families, tribes, clans, feudal arrangements, nations, empires, business firms, guilds, unions, clubs, villages, work, play, political, religious, and other groups); and

(d)   History and functions of cultural sectors (economic, military, educational, medical, recreational, spiritual).

History should also include current history, with emphasis on the past background and future significance of current issues.

There are some excellent documentaries and movies, some biographical and some event-focused, available online or on DVDs, which can stimulate interest in teaching history. Use of them might be accompanied by a well-planned, critical classroom discussion on their accuracy, context, and significance.

III.   Civics should include:

(a)   Levels of government, separation of powers, how legislation is developed, how positions are filled, and the legal basis for government (constitution, laws, court and administrative decisions, and agency and executive regulations);

(b)   Nominating, campaigning, and procedures for primary, general, and special elections, initiatives, referenda, and recall;

(c)   The United States Constitution and its amendments, including their history, structure, major concepts, and impact on American life;

(d)   Individual rights and responsibilities (paying taxes, serving on juries and in the military, assisting in law enforcement, voting after studying candidates and issues);

(e)   Organization and functions of political parties and interest groups;

(f)   Status of persons (minors, citizens, immigrants, lawful and unauthorized visitors, persons declared incompetent, and convicted persons); and

(g)   Information resources for active citizenship—libraries, academics, news media, and open records and open meetings laws.

Appendix B—Life Skills for Health Management and for Money Management—Suggested Curriculum Elements

Note: These two subjects are intended to help the student cope with two of the most serious problems of adult life. Moreover, effective education on these two subjects should prove of great help to our nation. As doctors and nurses know, patients often develop serious illnesses for lack of adequate health-related knowledge, which results in heavy financial burdens on all concerned, including taxpayers and businesses whose foreign competitors have far lower healthcare costs. And as regards to money management, lack of competence leads to excessive debt, excessive interest costs, purchases that are wasteful, defective, overpriced or unnecessary, vulnerability to con men, bad credit, personal and family unhappiness, and difficulty in paying for things that are really important or even necessary. These effects tend seriously to degrade not only the lives directly affected but also our economic system and the strength of our communities and nation.

1.   **Health Management: Suggested Curriculum Elements** (This subject might well be covered in the 5th, 6th, and 7th grades.) It should include

    (a)   basic biology, especially of vertebrates, to the extent not already covered in a science course;

    (b)   basic human anatomy, physiology, and pathology;

    (c)   hygiene, including protection from microorganisms, carbon monoxide, etc.;

    (d)   nutrition, including functions of various nutrients, and their relations to foods;

(e)   safeguards against various infections, degenerative, traumatic, and other health problems, including substance abuse and sexually transmitted conditions;

(f)   when and how to consult a doctor or other health professional, on both physical and mental health questions; and

(g)   emergency procedures.

2.   **Money Management: Suggested Curriculum Elements.** This subject is appropriate for middle and high school students. Due to the broad scope of the subject, it is important that the presentations be clear, careful, and to-the-point, and that the students realize that only the basics are covered.

Note: The arrangement and emphasis of this curriculum subject should be adjusted to the students' ages and circumstances, but students should be alerted to long-range concepts, such as how modest, regular savings can produce large results with compound interest and wise management, subject, of course, to inflation and other market conditions.

This subject should include

(a)   the difference between income and net worth;

(b)   understanding basic financial statements;

(c)   making personal or household or club budgets

(d)   types of taxes and their effects

(e)   inflation and deflation;

(f)   good and bad borrowing—college debt, credit cards, mortgages, etc.;

(g)   avoiding fraud, identity theft, and other losses;

(h)   insurance types, needs, and features;

(i)   types of securities and their features;

(j)   types of ownership and other beneficial interests, and liens;

(k)   cost/benefit analysis in buying cars, houses, etc.;

(l)   comparing prices and comparing price with value;

(m)   renting vs. buying, and handling checking accounts;

(n)   starting a business or making an investment;

(o)   sources of advice and information;

(p)   offers and contracts; and

(q)   guarantees, warrantees, endorsing checks, etc.

In developing curriculum details for both the above subjects, it would be wise to seek assistance from professionals in appropriate occupations.

There are other important life skills besides these two that might warrant curriculum attention: driver education, and the management of personal time, information, records, relationships, and reputation.

Appendix C:—Suggestions for Further Reading and Websites

There is a vast amount of reading material on education: books, magazines, newsletters, websites, and more. To locate material of interest to you, here are some suggestions:

First, decide what interests you—for example, technical research reports or more easily readable material, information about your own school district or something that pertains to many districts.

Second, seek help from librarians, education professionals, other knowledgeable persons, and various other sources, for example,

(a)   public libraries,
(b)   school system headquarters libraries,
(c)   state education agency libraries, and
(d)   Federal Department of Education publications.

The Department of Education's annual *Guide to U.S. Department of Education Programs* is available free by calling 1-877-433-7827. It contains over 300 pages of information on many aspects of education, such as academic improvement, assessments, career and technical education, civics, English language acquisition, reading, research, safe and drug-free schools, school improvement, special education, and teacher and principal quality.

Current education news may be in your local newspaper or in *Education Week*, which may be accessible locally, or you can call 1-800-346-1834 for information about subscriptions.

There are many education websites, which may be located through Google or other search tools. We can note only a few, namely

(a) *Education Week's* website, a large part of which is free is www.edweek.org

(b) *The Guide to U.S. Department of Education Programs* referred to above includes a resources list of websites on the inside back cover.

(c) Websites suggested by an experienced academic with a special interest in civics education, namely: (1) www.cep-dc.org [Center on Education Policy], (2) www.edtrust.org [The Education Trust], and (3) www.all4ed.org [Alliance for Excellent Education].

(d) Websites suggested by a federal career professional in education, namely: (1) www.ecs.org [Education Commission of the States], (2) www.CCSSO.org [Council of Chief State School Officers], and (3) www.NCES.ed.gov [National Center for Education Statistics].

(e) The websites of the three organizations named in Appendix D are www.pta.org [Parent Teacher Association], www.nea.org [National Education Association], and www.aft.com [American Federation of Teachers].

We hesitate to single out some books for listing among the many that merit mention, but here are a few:

(a) *Endangered Minds* by Jane Healy, a Ph.D. in educational psychology, Touchstone, NY,

1990. Discusses the effects of TV, video games, etc. on student learning.

(b) *Cultural Literacy* by E. D. Hirsch, Jr., a professor of English at the University of Virginia, Random House, NY, 1987. Discusses what truly educated Americans should know.

(c) *Emotional Intelligence* by Daniel Goldman, a *New York Times* writer with a Ph.D. from Harvard, Bantam Books, NY, 1995. Discusses emotions in relation to human behavior and education.

(d) *Mega Skills* by Dorothy Rich, president of the Home and School Institute, Houghton Mifflin, 1992. Discusses how to develop ten basic skills for success.

Finally, additional information on education may be available from local, state, or federal government agencies by request under state or federal open records and open meetings laws.

Appendix D—Selected Educational Organizations

There are lots of educational organizations in the United States. Some, e.g., teachers unions, are concerned only with education; some, like the American Enterprise Institute, are concerned with education along with other public policy sectors.

If you are concerned about education, such organizations may be important to you, especially because organized groups usually have more influence for or against changes than one or two persons acting alone.

Some education organizations have separate but connected parts that operate at three levels—national, state or regional, and local. This is generally true, for instance, of PTAs, with the national headquarters in Chicago (1-800-307-4782), and the two large teachers' unions—the National Education Association (202-833-4000) and the American Federation of Teachers (1-800-238-1133)—both headquartered in Washington, DC.

If your primary concern is about your local school or school system, you chief interest will probably focus on local organizations, such as

(a)   local teachers union;

(b)   local Chamber of Commerce, partly because good schools, despite their need for higher taxes, attract business and provide a better supply of potential workers and customers;

(c)   local real estate groups, because good schools increase land values,

(d)   service clubs, such as Rotary, Kiwanis, Lions, Civitan, etc., because of their general interest in community concerns;

(e)   local political parties;

(f)   local newspapers, which have an obvious concern about literacy and general education;

(g)   various local nonprofits, such as homeowners' associations and ethnic or faith oriented groups; and

(h)   local police, welfare, recreation, or other public service organizations, official or nonprofit, because of the value of good schools in reducing crime, disease, poverty, and other socioeconomic problems.

Other important education organizations, primarily national in scope, are identified in Appendix C.

This is not a complete list of education organizations. It does not, for example, include private school groups, or suppliers of school equipment, textbooks, and supplies.

Your efforts to improve education can be enhanced by working with sympathetic groups, and by being aware of other concerned groups, perhaps to arrive at satisfactory compromises.

Appendix E—About CQC and the Education Policy Primer Participants

CQC (Citizens for Quality Civilization, Inc.) is a volunteer civic organization under Section 501(c) (3) of the Internal Revenue Code. CQC's mission is to safeguard and improve the quality of life in the United States through advanced civic leadership. CQC focuses on selected public policy problem areas. It has an 18-year track record of working to improve our nation's education, health care, and transportation, and to clarify globalization. In the 1990s, we developed a classroom program to stimulate academics and character education that was praised by many educators and introduced into hundreds of classrooms. We operate informally and always check our products with outside experts.

Robert L. Saloschin is a lawyer, community leader in a Washington suburb, licensed commercial pilot, and the founder and president of CQC. He graduated from New York public schools, was a Phi Beta Kappa graduate of Columbia College with honors in economics, and a law review graduate of Columbia Law School. After WWII Navy service in the Pacific, he practiced law on Wall Street, in a federal slum clearance program, in the Civil Aeronautics Board, in the Justice Department, and in Maryland. At the Justice Department he chaired the Freedom of Information Committee and worked on civil rights, immigration, and international and constitutional matters with leaders of both parties (Attorney General Robert Kennedy and later Chief Justice William Rehnquist). He was elected president of a large elementary school PTA after arranging a settlement of community opposition to its principal. He is certified flight instructor, has been a guest lecturer in the DC public schools, and has authored various publications.

Robert Anastasi is a former school principal in Montgomery County, Maryland and for many years headed the county's Business Roundtable on Education.

Delegate Charles Barkley is a former schoolteacher and a member of the state legislature in Maryland.

Heinz Bondy has almost 50 years experience as a teacher and as an administrator, at all levels from preschool to college, in both private and public institutions. A BA at Swarthmore and a Masters at Bryn Mawr, he worked in a Montessori school, in both regular and boarding schools at the middle and high school level, and as associate vice-chancellor for student affairs for the University of Massachusetts College System.

Mary Rose Curtis has a Masters in administration and is a certified quality assurance coordinator. As a parent with two children in the county school system, she encouraged adding art and music to the curriculum, and worked to improve the schools' communication with the parents of students in the upper grades. She has supplemented the efforts of schools by home schooling her grandsons, chiefly to develop independent, critical thinking. Her main concern is the weakness in many American schools of citizenship studies—history, civics, and current issues—leading to indifference and ignorance on matters important to the future of American democracy.

Herman Richard ("Dick") Menzer has Bachelors and Masters degrees from George Washington University, and taught high school for 35 years in the Virginia and Maryland suburbs of Washington. He also taught journalism, and speech and debate, and served as faculty advisor to student newspapers and yearbooks. In Maryland he worked with School Board candidates and members on policy issues, wrote curricula for language skills, tested for English teachers to the School Board, and worked with the local teacher's federation and civic associations on school budgets.

Jane S. ("Sue") Rogich, a retired elementary school teacher, is a graduate of Barnard College at Columbia University and earned her Masters in education at George Washington University. She taught in Lebanon County, Pennsylvania and then in the Fairfax County, Virginia public schools for 24 years, where after extensive peer and supervisor review she was awarded merit pay. She has addressed various education conferences and co-authored a published report on successfully educating disabled children through an "inclusion" program that was well staffed and funded. After retiring she tutored in a multi-cultural school in Northern Virginia.

Robert Schoenberg is a former member of the elected school board in Montgomery County, Maryland, a large and rapidly growing suburb of Washington, DC. For many years, he has been a consultant to colleges throughout the country, and has monitored trends in the output of schools from which colleges obtain their entering students.

Donna Britton Smith taught science for over 30 years in junior and senior high schools in Florida, New Mexico, and Maryland. After two years of liberal arts studies she earned a B.S. in chemistry at Old Dominion University and a Masters of Education Science at Loyola College. She served as science department chair, student teacher mentor, science curricula writer, and presenter and coordinator at science workshops, conferences, and fairs. In 1995, she received the Prince George's outstanding science teacher award.

Outside experts who have served as vettors of the draft of this primer

We wish to thank the following individuals who have reviewed the draft of this primer and have given us their comments and suggestions on it. After each name we have given the person's organizational affiliation or background so that readers can see the broad range of perspectives that we have tried to take into account. These organizational references should not be taken to mean that the individual's comments or suggestions necessarily reflect the position of any organizations with which the individual is or was in some way affiliated.

Joseph Villani, deputy executive director, National School Boards Association

John P. O'Sullivan, secretary-treasurer, Texas Federation of Teachers

D. W. Johnson, principal, rural elementary school in North Dakota

Professor Michael Krist, Stanford University

Buzz Bartlett, former member Maryland State Board of Education and former corporate executive

Joy Mathews, *Washington Post* education reporter

Milton Goldberg, consultant, formerly with the Business Alliance for Education

Rebecca Wagner, executive officer of CMMC, a non-profit service organization in Montgomery County, Maryland, a large demographically diverse county

Monica Barbaris-Young, director, Friends in Action, CMMC

In addition to the nine vettors listed above, two more vettors provided helpful comments but requested anonymity. One was a professor of public policy, the other a parent with children in the public schools. We believe that the variety of backgrounds of these 20 people (nine at the drafting stage and eleven during the review by others) provided a reasonably broad spectrum of perspectives on the subject.

Appendix F—Public Schools in Other Modern Industrialized Countries

This is a short summary of schooling in about 30 advanced countries, mostly European and some Asian. Many of these countries compete or will compete with the U.S. in various ways. Of course, there are many differences among these countries, but there are also many similarities, some of which clearly contrast with American schools.

In almost all these countries, public schools are run by a central ministry of education. All school personnel including teachers are state (i.e., national) employees. The curriculum and textbooks are set by the ministry. The curriculum for "academic" courses usually includes six years of math, six years of science, eight years of national language and literature, six years of foreign languages, ancient, European, and world history, plus six years of history of the native country. This represents the core curriculum.

These subjects are taught in class every day over the course of several years. Most countries have 14 years of schooling, with a decision to follow "academic" or "vocational" curricula made through testing students, usually between the ages of 12 and 14. Most students graduate at the age of 19 or 20. In most countries it is against the law to cheat or leave school before the age of 18. There are in fact only a small number of dropouts.

The schools are strict and have far fewer discipline problems than we do. This is due in part to tradition and in part due to the power vested in teachers to administer punishments.

In most countries there are no private day schools, except for Catholic schools in countries such as France and Spain. In countries like England and Germany, there are a number of very prestigious private boarding schools, which serve mostly the elite and very rich.

There are no interscholastic sports in either high schools or universities; however, there are intramural and club teams.

After passing the "academic" curriculum, there are oral and written exams that, if passed, entitle the student to go to the university of his or her choice.

One of the biggest differences between their schools and ours is that, by tradition and salary, teaching is a well-respected profession and teachers are solidly in the middle class.

In most European countries, class size is limited to 25 or smaller.

Appendix G: Suggestions about Parenting Education

The vital role of parents in education is summarized in Part 4—Who Educates? The role of parents has three phases: in early childhood, during school years, and in "home schooling." All these depend on parental effectiveness: what actions and skills parents bring to their role.

Parenting can be good, bad, or so-so. And parenting, even with loving care, is not always easy. But effective parenting is vital for children and for the nation. It is also important for the parents themselves, since it affects their own lives and happiness.

Seeming to tell parents how to raise their children is a touchy thing, especially in a free country. Yet there is a big market for parenting education, as shown by the books, magazines, and organizations that deal with the subject, supplementing what parents may have learned from their own parents, relatives, and friends.

Here are some suggestions for schools to enhance the effectiveness of parental cooperation in education:

1.   Distribute appropriate information early. Provide maternity hospitals with literature and/or videos that will be useful to mothers and fathers. Provide child-care centers and selected clinics or other venues with similar materials. And, at or even before the beginning of kindergarten, make every effort to have parents attend carefully crafted briefings and workshops on effective parenting: what to do, how to do it, and why to do it.

2.   During the school years, enhance parental involvement in the child's academic and behavioral development with teacher conferences, report cards, and

the activities of PTAs, school boards, and other groups. Problems such as bullying, student badmouthing of academic success, or using schools to recruit for political or sectarian groups should be rectified. Parental attendance should be encouraged at sports events, school plays, and concerts, and spelling bees, debates, and the like. Difficult situations such as child neglect, child abuse, and dysfunctional families should, as necessary, be referred to law enforcement or other non-school resources, not only to protect the children directly imperiled but also for the sake of the other children and the school's mission.

Appendix
Metropolitan Transportation

D

What Every Citizen Should Know

Citizens for Quality Civilization (CQC)
6603 Lone Oak Drive
Bethesda, MD 20817
www.citizens-quality-civilization.org

EXECUTIVE SUMMARY: This civic primer is a condensed analysis of traffic congestion, its relation to other policy concerns, and its various remedies. For concise, comprehensive, and objective answers to the eight main parts of this important subject, see the Outline.

Outline

Introductory Overview

Transportation has major impacts on land use, economic activity, and the quality of life. In recent decades, transportation policy has received less civic attention than other public policy areas such as environment, foreign affairs, crime, etc. During these same decades, transportation has deteriorated in many ways, but it is now beginning to receive more attention. This Overview, together with the preceding Outline, is designed to help provide a broader perspective on transportation in large metropolitan areas.

The historic role of transportation in the progress of civilization began with the ability to walk—and was limited by the distances covered and by what could be carried. Transportation and mobility increased with the horse and carriage, and with boats that were rowed or sailed. Railroads and steamboats increased the speed of transporting people and goods.

Two hundred years ago, travel was slow, uncomfortable, costly, and sometimes dangerous. There was little travel except for that felt to be urgently necessary. Today, the average person in an advanced nation has more and better mobility than did kings at that time.

During the past century, the development of motor vehicles and aircraft, and technological improvements in electronics and telecommunications have opened fresh new horizons in mobility by land, sea, and air. These changes have consumed and will probably continue to consumer major investments In both public and private capital. As the quality of any sector of life increases dramatically—as in the case of health care and other sectors, as well as transportation—that sector will tend to attract more resources from consumers, investors, and governments.

Transportation is of basic importance to our present way of life. In the United States, the average breadwinner spends one to three hours a day in travel, and a large portion of family, business, governmental, and other budgets is spent on the transportation of persons and goods. The price of almost everything is partly based on transportation costs.

Transportation is of special importance to our major metropolitan areas. It made possible the development of these metropolitan areas, and it provides the lifeblood for the survival, growth, and improvement of these areas. Very large parts of the nation's population, wealth, and significant activities are in these areas. Yet these areas are increasingly subject to worsening traffic congestion that degrades both economic and personal activities.

Finally, transportation—freedom to travel—has been recognized as a human right. Thus, *The Universal Declaration of Human Rights,* adopted in 1948 by the United Nations, with the concurrence of the United States, declares, "Everyone has the right to freedom of movement…" (Article 13). This does not spell out the quality of transportation, and it may also have been aimed at governments that denied their citizens the freedom to travel. Yet freedom of movement is abridged when mobility is degraded. And for most Americans today, on most trips, mobility means "automobility."

Our focus is on the movement of persons within these metropolitan areas, but we recognize that this is related to the movement of goods by truck, and to intercity movements of both persons and goods by air and surface.

A lively debate is in progress about transportation problems in major metropolitan areas. This primer is designed to help illuminate that debate.

Part 1—What Are the Current Transportation Problems in Major Metropolitan Areas, and What Are Their Causes?

The problems of transportation in major metropolitan areas full under six headings: (Most of the information below on these problems is from the U.S. Department of Transportation.)

     A.   ***Congestion.*** This is the worst problem. From 1982 to 2000 delays by congestion grew by 278 percent in 78 metropolitan areas, and the delays were worse in the larger ones. Areas with over 3 million people had much worse delays than areas with under a half million. The average person in the large areas lost 27 hours stuck in traffic in 2000; in Washington in 2001, it was 58 hours, plus much wasted fuel. Since one of the dimensions of life is time, congestion results in wasting life. This occurs more starkly when congestion delays ambulances, police cars, and fire engines. The cost of wasted time and fuel to businesses and individuals is in the billions—money that could be shifted to meet other urgent public and private needs.

     B.   ***Environment.*** Despite an increase of 148 percent in vehicle miles traveled since 1970, some pollutants have fallen sharply and others have risen slightly. Carbon dioxide has risen 19 percent since 1990. (Carbon dioxide is not technically a pollutant—it is created by breathing and is removed by green plants—but it is primarily caused by burning fossil fuels, and it is implicated in global warning.) In the Washington area, one of the nation's most congested, the average number of days per year with an unhealthy Air Quality Index has dropped from 29 in 1992-1994 to 24 in 1999-2001.

C. *Cost.* Transportation as a part of household expenses is second only to housing. Transportation was under 10 percent of household budgets in 1935 but is almost 20 percent today. Most of the cost is in owning and operating cars, including gasoline, sales and tag taxes, insurance, repairs, parking, tolls, etc. For low-income Americans, transportation may take up to 40 percent of their incomes. Transportation costs also include, indirectly, various factors in government budgets such as health (emergency rooms) and police (highway patrols). Costs vary by area: around Washington, with fair public transit, it's about 15 percent of household budgets; around Tampa, with less transit, it's 25 percent.

D. *Accessibility (Financial and Physical).* Access to public transportation (transit or taxis) is a special problem for several groups: low income, persons with disabilities, travelers and commuters from rural or distant homes, some of the elderly, and visitors arriving by plane or train.

E. *Safety.* In general, transportation is safer in metropolitan areas than in rural areas, although pedestrians and bicyclists may be less safe. However, growing road congestion seems to have exacerbated such problems as aggressive driving, "road rage," and red light running.

F. *Sprawl and Other Problems.* "Sprawl" is commonly used to describe (or to criticize) building new homes, each usually on a fair-sized lot, further and further from the center of a city. By causing longer commutes this increases traffic. This may also tend to accelerate the decline of older, central-city neighborhoods, reducing their tax bases and their public services. In addition, as employment opportunities develop away from city centers, a new commuting problem arises—suburb to suburb—because most transportation facilities were built as radials (in and out of downtown). A further problem is increased density—more people per acre—which also usually means more traffic. These problems are based largely on underlying market forces. These forces may include the motivation for farmers or speculators to sell open land at higher prices, the tendency of many home buyers to favor more spacious houses and grounds, and the desire of home builders to sell many homes. Since most homebuyers are limited in what they can pay, builders must keep down their costs, either by moving out for cheaper land or by building more homes per acre, or both.

A serious potential problem can be a large-scale emergency evacuation due to a terrorist attack or the like. Such an event might overload surviving modes of transportation in and around the affected area.

A recently recognized problem is obesity, which creates serious health risks. While obesity also occurs in small towns and rural areas, the decline in walking in favor of driving, especially by suburbanites, is believed to be one of the causes of obesity.

The main causes for these problems include:

A. *Population Shifts*—the shifts of population from rural areas and small towns and from the interior of the nation to large metropolitan areas, most of which are near the coasts. This is largely a result of the movement of jobs, which in turn reflects the movement of businesses. Businesses often move away from places that suffer declining inter-city transportation. During the past half-century, most railroads ended their passenger services and some of their related freight services. Airlines also, under deregulation, understandably provide less service to smaller communities.

B. *Population Increases*—the result of increased longevity in the general population, and legal and illegal immigration.

C. *Increased Affluence*—improved standards of living that offer consumers larger houses on larger lots, more resources for travel, and general improvements in automobile durability, in greater ease of operation, and in comfort, resulting in the almost universal ownership of cars.

D. *Inefficient Use of Existing Facilities*—including, for example, traffic lights that are poorly timed and roadwork that could be shifted to off-peak traffic periods.

E. *Failure to Expand Facilities*—to keep pace with increased demands that result from the population shifts, population increases, and growing affluence of the past half-century. During that period, a large part of the planning to accommodate the increased travel demand in large metropolitan areas has remained just in the planning stage. There has generally not been enough political or financial support to bring about the development of actual facilities that would accommodate the growth in our nation's largest metropolitan areas.

F. Finally, the two kinds of land development ("sprawl" and excessive density) that are referred to above under the heading of "problems" in large metropolitan areas should also be recognized as among the "causes" of traffic congestion.

Part 2—What Are the Six Main Factors in Transportation Quality and Value?

History makes clear that when there is significant improvement in the quality of any sector of the standard of living, people will probably demand and use more of it. Transportation quality and value can be described under the following six headings:

A. *Speed*—determined as the total time from the point of origin, such as a home, to the destination—not just station-to-station time. Speed is a matter of both personal satisfaction and economic benefits: "time is money."

B. *Safety*—including both actual risk—the number of accidents per million passenger miles (or per trip or per capita) and the varying seriousness of accidents—and the perceived risk, which may be more or less than the actual risk. Perceived risk can affect the potential traveler's peace of mind as well as travel decisions. The volume of accidents is largely a function of traffic volume, and the seriousness of accidents is largely a function of road design, vehicle design and weight, and speed. Also, transportation safety involves not only hazards in vehicles but also risks, such as crime, in parking lots or transit stations.

C. *Reliability*—both ordinary and emergency. Ordinary reliability is degraded by adverse weather, the tardiness of a given mode of transportation, and the cancellation of scheduled trips. Emergency reliability (in case of terrorist attacks or other disasters) is also an element of quality in transportation. It may depend, at least in part, on the number and diffusion of routes and mobile equipment, factors where roads and cars have obvious advantages. On the other hand, numerous roads and cars present difficulties in providing security against car bombs, except at a few sensitive locations. Also, since many cities are next to navigable waters, the availability of vessels to assist in evacuations might enhance emergency reliability.

D.   *Comfort*—in seating, lighting, climate and noise control, and, in some situations, the availability of rest rooms in transit stations, on vehicles, and at bus stops. Some of the factors that go into comfort and satisfaction may be psychological rather than physical: the sense of control of power in driving; that status felt in driving an impressive car; or a taste for being alone or for choosing one's passengers, compared to a gregarious interest in the variety of passengers in other forms of travel.

E.   *Convenience*—which is many-faceted. Can the traveler bring a friend, children, or pets without added cost? Can the traveler bring along large or heavy objects easily, as on shopping trips, or when going to sport or musical practice? Can the traveler make intermediate stops for pickup and delivery, to drop a child off at school or daycare, or to attend a meeting, class, or other activity? Can the traveler read a newspaper, or listen to news, music, or books on tape—or use a cell phone en route? Can the travel avoid the need to wear rain gear or a heavy coat on walks to, or waits at, a transit stop? Can the traveler start a trip, perhaps on impulse, or in case of emergency, at any time? If the trip involved "intermodal" transportation (e.g., changes between trains and bus or some other mode), can the traveler, even if handicapped, count on a smooth, quick, and reliable transfer?

F.   ***Cost.*** While not strictly speaking an element of quality, cost is an adjunct to quality and should be considered as affecting the consumer's decision on whether and how to travel. Cost may be important, but with distinct limitations. For the affluent traveler, cost is less important. Some travel will be made regardless of cost—including trips to and from work and to fulfill critical family obligations. For a car owner, the cost of a trip is usually perceived as the added out-of-pocket expense, since the cost of ownership must be paid in any case.

Part 3—What Other Domestic and International Policy Concerns Are Related to Transportation Policies?

Transportation policy is significantly related to several other important areas of public policy, chiefly

(a) environment, including land use and air quality (air quality covers both pollution levels and greenhouse gases), and energy, including the development, conservation, reliability, and cost of various sources of energy;

(b) economic vigor and social equity; and

(c) national security and foreign relations.

Therefore, these areas of public policy must be considered in deciding to what extent—and in what ways—transportation policy should improve our roads, vehicles, and public transit.

A. ***Environment and Energy.*** These is no doubt that more and better transportation, whether by car or transit, like many other human activities, tends to place at least a potential burden on both environmental and energy policies. Methods for minimizing these burdens are well known, though not always used.

Economic and population growth leads to development, and development tends to go where transportation is available, sometimes overburdening the transportation capacity. This is true whether the development is "sprawl" (development further out) or an increase in density on land already developed, e.g., tearing down farms or homes to build big apartments or big employment or shopping structures. Proper land use policies (planning or zoning) con control and channel growth to preserve the environment and ensure adequate public facilities, including transportation. Also, congesting can be reduced if some of the traffic magnets, such as employment locations, can be placed near the residential end of commuting routes.

B.   *Economic Vigor and Social Equity*. Despite environmental and energy problems, there is no doubt that more and better transportation tends to benefit both economic vigor and social equity. The welfare parent with small children in day care who must spend over an hour on the bus getting to a job and a similar time returning home, not to mention the problems of other necessary trips, lives under a discouraging strain both as a worker and a parent. The average citizen, who can have a backyard, a garden, and a patio while building equity in his or her home, would probably not enjoy these benefits were it not for more or less adequate travel, typically by car, to work and other destinations.

Social equity is not limited to welfare parents; the needs of the disabled and some of the elderly may require costlier special attention, such as handicapped parking, vehicles that handle wheelchairs, and other assistance devices such as kneeling busses, wheelchair-accessible paths, and taxi and other volunteer services. These can be encouraged by favorable tax and insurance treatment.

C.   *National Security and Foreign Relations*. Better transportation, unless done more efficiently, increases our already excessive dependence on imported energy, much of it from the unstable Middle East. In addition, our well known indulgence in ever bigger and heavier gas guzzling vehicles probably has some adverse effects on the way our country is viewed by most other nations, both in turning people against us and providing talking points for our adversaries.

With these other policy factors influencing plans for better transportation, some experts have called attention to two concepts that may restrain plans for improved transportation—"induced traffic," and "demand management." Both warrant consideration.

A. *Induced traffic.* Improving transportation will tend to increase the demand for it. Whether a better road or better public transit service is provided, more people will use it. This is called "induced traffic." Induced traffic is sometimes used as an argument against any improvement, on the theory that increased traffic and congestion will result. This may have validity in some situations. Yet, if roads and transit had not been built and improved, people all over the world would still be using horses on unpaved roads and taking rowboats to cross bodies of water. New schools are built when the student population expands, and perhaps more transportation facilities need to be provided as the traveling population expands. Almost anything that is improved may induce more use—health care, food, clothing, shelter, entertainment—but that must not be the controlling argument against improvement.

B. *Demand Management.* This suggests a number of ways to reduce congestion by reducing the number and extent of trips that people make. These include telecommuting, staggering work hours, encouraging the use of car pools, and developing land use policies to make it easier for people to live near their jobs and near such frequent trip destinations as stores, schools, and entertainment centers. Demand can also be discouraged by various kinds of tolls, taxes, or charges: toll roads, peak-hour toll lanes, parking charges, high fuel taxes, etc. Such devices, of course, present questions of public and political acceptability. They burden socially useful travel as well as other trips, and may not fully succeed in curing congestion, which sometimes occurs even on toll bridges, toll tunnels, and toll highways.

Such measures can help restrain the growth of traffic, but they are limited by what the public, or parts of it, will accept. An imaginative campaign to encourage people to combine trips and to ask, "Is this trip necessary?" may be helpful. But such measures are also faced with powerful forces of modern life which create more traffic: increasing population; improved standards of living, technological improvements in the automobile and other transportation vehicles; the movement of our population from the interior of the country to metropolitan areas that are mainly near the coasts; the movement of population from central cities to suburbs and even further out; and local government policies and practices in zoning and related subjects.

A realistic answer to the challenge of the increasing demand for transportation in metropolitan areas should be based on two groups of factors: 1) public benefits of better transportation, and 2) public needs that may require restraint.

A.   ***Benefits.*** The benefits of better transportation are easy to summarize. These include a greater choice of places to live, work, shop, and obtain health, educational, and recreational services. The individual will have more time for family, community, recreational, or civic activities and will be able to spend more time with friends. Transportation improvement will offer greater efficiency for businesses and other productive institutions as well as greater opportunities to reduce cultural isolation.

B. **Needs.** The restraining factors for which improved transportation might prove detrimental, depending on how improvements are achieved include (a) the need to consider environmental issues such as pollution and global warming, while also considering that traffic congestion increases pollution and global warming as compared to the same amount of traffic moving smoothly; (b) the need to consider and conserve supplies of energy and to reduce dependence on unreliable sources; (c) the need for land use policies that preserve natural areas and agricultural areas; and (d) the need for a proper balance in the allocation of the nation's financial resources between transportation and other factors that affect the standard of living.

These restraining factors can be given greater weight, over time, by improving technology, population stability, and the building of a program of better citizen information to develop a stronger sense of civic responsibility and civic participation. A first step might be laws creating financial incentives to manufacture cars with greater fuel efficiency, using the savings in fuel costs to pay for needed transportation improvements. This also means promoting hybrid engines and developing vehicles powered by hydrogen that is produced by electricity made without releasing carbon dioxide.

Part 4—What Are the Options for Better Metropolitan Area Transportation?

To identify the options for better transportation, all modes of transportation should be considered, bearing in mind that some trips use more than one mode. Below we summarize the options for metropolitan area travel under six modes: walking, bicycles, cars, rail and bus transit, taxis and jitneys, and other technologically newer modes.

For what is mean by better transportation, please see Part 2 above. Also please note that better transportation may present problems relating to other important public policies (see Part 3) or relating to financing, technology, or management (see Part 7).

A. *Walking*. While a good form of exercise and free of harm to environmental or energy policies, walking involves real limitations: slow speed; poor weather; risks of traffic and, in some places; of crime; and limited capacity to bring parcels, children, etc. This capacity can be increased with baby carriages, strollers, and personal shopping carts. The usefulness of walking can also be increased by land development that puts homes within easy walking distance of stores, schools, jobs, etc., but such developments are uncommon in most suburbs. Larger shopping centers, schools, or work places offer certain advantages over small ones, such as greater variety and economies of scale, but they must be supported by larger areas, parts of which require long walks. Even in walk-oriented developments, some trips to places beyond an easy walk would be made by choice or necessity. Walking also serves to get to transit stations and parking places: possible improvements for such walks may include footbridges over major roads. There is support for sidewalks near schools or other destinations, but many suburban streets lack sidewalks, perhaps because residents see little need for them or have esthetic or financial objections, or because elderly residents or those who travel frequently are concerned about laws requiring them to remove snow and ice from sidewalks.

At busy intersections, "walk/don't walk" signs that display the remaining seconds for walking may help. In some places, better facilities for walking may also be utilized by a variety of devices that benefit the handicapped or elderly as well as other persons. Curb cuts at corners, pursuant to the Americans with Disabilities Act, can serve not only wheelchairs (some of them powered) but also other devices: electronic tricycles with two side-by-side seats, modified golf carts, and a powered, stabilized device resembling a scooter known as a Segway, referred to under "Other modes." Such devices, of course, will need space for movement and for parking.

B. *Bicycles (including motorcycles, mopeds, tricycles).* Bicycles are much faster than walking and can be adapted to carry small parcels or small children. They also offer good exercise with no harm to the environment or energy policies, but they are not well adapted to poor weather, are a subject of safety concern (a collision that is only a fender bender for a driver can be far more serious for a bicyclist), and are less useful in hilly places, or by travelers who are aged or infirm. A recent government survey shows that bike paths or bike lanes improve bicyclists' sense of personal safety. Recreational bicyclists tend to prefer bike paths (separate from roads), while bike commuters prefer lanes (part of roads). Motorcycles and mopeds offer speed advantages but have similar disadvantages as to weather, safety, and older users; also motorcycles may be noisy. Like walking, bicycles are useful to reach transit stops, especially ones with secure bicycle parking. Bicycles would benefit from safe, locked, lighted storage racks at various destinations to reduce theft.

C.   ***Cars, carpools, and car rentals.*** Cars are an increasingly dominant mode of transporting persons in advanced nations, for a variety of reasons that center generally on personal convenience and utility. As an option for transportation, cars are dependent on roads and parking places, but this is also true of busses and to a lesser extent of bicycles. As an option for better transportation, cars in major metropolitan areas need three things: (a) better roads and parking, (b) better safety as discussed in Part 3 of this primer, and (c) better fuel efficiency, for the reasons noted in Part 3 of this primer.

Carpools can reduce commuting traffic, but carpool members who are slow in the morning, or sometimes have to work late, or need to stop en route, or are simply not compatible with others, erode the viability of carpools. Carpools can be strengthened by carpool information exchanges, by helping drivers give lifts to strangers, and by preferential parking.

Car rentals (a form of car sharing) are chiefly used in conjunction with air travel, or to substitute for cars being serviced. But car rentals can serve a further role to reduce congestion in urban areas such as New York, as a substitute for car ownership by persons who need cars only occasionally, especially if rentals are offered by some convenient, per-arranged, simplified system.

For specifics on how to improve car travel, please see Part 6 of this primer.

D.   *Rail and bus transit.* These traditional forms of transit play a dominant role where land use is very dense, as in lower and mid-town Manhattan. In addition, rail transit can be a very useful supplement to cars in metropolitan areas where it has its own right-of-way, as in the subways of New York, Washington, and other cities, particularly if there is adequate parking and bus service at the suburban stations. Rail services that share right-of-way with road traffic—trolleys—have operational problems and have gradually disappeared from most American cities. However, "light rail," a kind of hybrid between trolleys and regular rail, such as New York's or Washington's, may be making a limited comeback. In general, light rail is cheaper and quicker to build; it either shares the road with cars or has its own lane which however intersects with roads; it runs as one, two, or three cars; and it tends to be a bit slower than regular rail transit.

Bus service generally shares roads with cars and trucks, and thus to improve bus services in congested areas generally means, among other things, better roads, or possibly dedicated bus lanes or HOV privileges.

For specifics on how to improve the options of bus and rail transit, please see Part 5 of this primer.

E.   *Taxicabs and jitneys.* Taxicabs combine many of the advantages of both cars and transit. Good taxi service approximates the "at any time, from any place to any other" utility and convenience of cars, plus the ability to take children or parcels at little or no extra cost, all without the burdens of car ownership and parking, and without the rigidities of fixed-route, fixed-schedule rail or bus transit. In addition, with the cooperation of taxis and their insurance companies, taxi drivers can assist the handicapped or disabled between the taxi and building entrances. On the other hand, taxis are not very cost efficient—they do not produce many passenger-miles of service per vehicle-mile of operating expense. Taxi service can be enhanced by better communications (e.g., cell phones to hail cabs), by more consumer-oriented regulation, including improved opportunities for competition, and by allowing cabs to pick up additional passengers under proper conditions.

Better taxi service will mean better transportation and may help reduce congestion. To reduce the cost of taxis, trips that serve health, education, or occupational purposes might receive some sort of favorable tax treatment.

Jitneys are a hybrid between taxis and private autos, specializing in commuting service. Car owners who are driving to work pick up commuters going the same way for a nominal charge. Jitneys can provide quality service at low cost, but jitneys are vulnerable to legal and legislative blockage by lawyers and lobbyist for transit companies, who regard jitneys as dangerous competitors. Since transit services are heavily subsidized by governments, letting jitneys divert transit revenues would tend to require additional subsidies, which may turn governments against jitneys. Yet is seems obvious that jitneys offer an efficient, if limited, potential to provide good service and reduce road congestion at low cost.

F. *Other modes (Segways, maglev trains, monorails, monobeams, helicopters, moving sidewalks, water taxis, etc.).* Exotic or experimental modes of transportation may offer exciting options for improvement. They call for open-minded but guarded consideration. On the one hand, all present modes of transportation originated as experiments, usually starting with many practical drawbacks. On the other hand, some that were in regular service disappeared for various reasons; e.g., dirigibles, electric interurban railways, railroads and trolleys, and early automobiles that were propelled by steam or electric batteries.

A Segway is a one-person powered and stabilized two-wheel scooter with wheels at the side only, and with speeds up to twelve miles an hour, initially priced at about $5,000. Segways are being introduced in some cities for rental to tourists who receive 30 minutes of training in their use. Monorails are often thought of as a Disney World attraction, but actually are used for public transit in several cities in Europe, Asia, and even in the United States: Seattle has a monorail system which may be extended. A monobeam is type of monorail which requires even less space on the ground for its supporting structures. A 19-mile maglev train (magnetic levitation, i.e., magnetically propelled and supported) has opened for commercial service in Shanghai, China using German technology, and it has a top speed of 267 miles per hour; reportedly it may be extended 775 miles to Beijing. Other possibilities, such as helicopters, moving sidewalks, water taxis, etc. may warrant consideration in particular situations.

The best chance for improvement in transportation through innovative modes probably depends on creativity, fortified by rigorous research and testing that considers user-friendliness and public acceptance. A combination of public and private funding, which would include studying progress in other nations, is a likely path to progress. And care must be taken to help insure that existing transportation interests do not stifle progress from fear of competition.

Part 5—How Can Transit Be Made More Attractive?

The answer to this question must be found largely in the reaction to transit services of potential passengers of various ages, preferences, attitudes, and needs.

A. ***Make transit faster***—not just between station and station, but between the passenger's actual points of origin and destination. This means bus and rail stations that are a short walk from homes, or a short drive away with good, quick, cheap, and reliable parking. It also means frequent and reliable bus or train service with minimal waiting time at the stations. Busses and trains should have enough doors to permit easy entrance and exit for the passengers.

B. ***Make transit more comfortable***—with shelters at bus stops that have adequate seats, or at least benches, and vehicles that are properly heated, cooled, ventilated, and illuminated, and are reasonably quiet. All passengers should have comfortable seats, preferably with an outside view. Clean, safe restrooms at transit stations are also desirable.

C. ***Make transit more affordable.*** Many passengers will have their own cars and will judge the cost of a car trip as fuel, and perhaps parking and tolls—not including the total cost of ownership. Transit costs often involve the cost of driving to and parking at a transit station. Free transit and/or free parking would be an added attraction, though this might not outweigh the convenience of a car for some trips, such as those with several passengers, several packages, or en route stops.

D.   ***Make transit more hassle-free.*** The fare structure should be simple to remember and simple to pay. Fare and parking fee machines should be reliable and user-friendly, even for infrequent users and strangers. Insure that bus drivers will make change, so far as practicable, or develop change-making machines. Provide good, clear route maps that plainly relate routes to local streets, plus schedules that are easily read and up-to-date. The maps and schedules should be available at bus or rail stations and other convenient places. Insure that phone calls from the public are promptly, clearly, correctly, and politely answered at all hours, that the phone numbers are well-publicized, and that maps and schedules will be mailed free upon a telephone request. Provide good protection against rowdy youths or other threatening persons—not only in transit vehicles, but also in parking lots, especially after dark. Respect the right of passengers to complain, however heatedly, about broken escalators or other problems. Make sure transit police are well trained, friendly, and exercise common sense. Provide free transfers and weekly and monthly passes that can easily be purchased by phone and online, and are good for all bus and rail services in the metro area. Minimize service disruptions and delays due to breakdowns, labor disputes, or other causes. Provide prompt emergency guidance and assistance to passengers in case of service disruptions.

E.   ***Make transit more accessible.*** Transit is more attractive for users who live, work, shop, or play near transit stations. The number of such users can be increased by high density, mixed-use development near transit stations.

F. *Publicize the availability of transit more effectively.*

The above kinds of improvements may require considerable effort and subsidy, but they could go far towards counterbalancing the generally greater convenience of cars. They could also help counterbalance the inherent detriments of transit, such as the rigidity of fixed routes, fixed schedule service, and the occasional proximity of coughing, sneezing, contagious, or otherwise fear-inspiring passengers.

Part 6—What Realistic Changes in Automobile Travel Would Make It More Desirable?

Changes that would make automobile travel more desirable are based on the transportation goals of speed, safety, and convenience. These are shaped by three transportation elements—drivers, cars, and roads (including parking).

A.   *Speed.* Speed is an ambiguous term. We use it to mean reduced travel time, not the highest miles per hour. In congested metropolitan areas, the goal of reduced travel time has little to do with faster cars or drivers. Speed in traveling depend chiefly on more and better roads, more lanes (by new roads or widening existing roads), center turning lanes for left turners, and relief of bottleneck intersections through a variety of improvements, such as an overpass, underpass, or traffic circle. Speed also depends on better road use: for example, (a) better timing of traffic lights to include more frequent and consistent switching to red and yellow flashing lights during off-peak periods; (b) improved off-peak road maintenance, (c) repaid deployment of assistance vehicles to help and clear roads at accidents and breakdowns; (d) continuous, well-publicized radio traffic and delay reports by zones; and (e) the availability of better, more attractive public transit, including the construction of pull-off bays at bus stops to the extent practical. Recent attention has also been given to the idea of providing toll lanes on major highways. Attention should also be given to providing bypasses for long-haul, intercity traffic that now mixes with and aggravates local metropolitan traffic, to the detriment of both.

B. *Safety.* In contrast to speed, better safety depends on three transportation elements: drivers, cars, and roads, with unsafe driving the chief safety problem. Obvious priorities include better, more comprehensive, and more universal training and testing for teenage drivers, who are four times as likely as other drivers to be involved in a crash and three times as likely to die in one. Teen crashes often involve speeding and alcohol, subjects that demand more and better attention, as does the effectiveness of driving schools. Other priorities are more effective monitoring and enforcement of laws against all drivers who may be drunk, drugged, distracted, fatigued, or experiencing health difficulties. Some elderly drivers need to be regularly reminded about the risks to themselves and others that could result from such conditions.

In addition, the general public needs to be encouraged to become more safety-conscious. Insurance companies can help by counseling more on the dangers of such distractions as the use of cell phones while driving. Training for drivers should include the ability to read road signs in English. The greatest potential for safety improvement, however, rests with law enforcement. The driving public should be reeducated to consider traffic police as a source for protection rather than punishment. Major changes in both the day-to-day operation and public relations attitude of traffic enforcement personnel could bring most drivers to regard them as friendly and protective factors, rather than only sources of punishment to be avoided because they seem more prone to write tickets for technical violations than for truly dangerous driving.

Discourteous driving creates road rage, which is a real hazard. This should be taught, and learned, in driver education and, if necessary, in re-training. It is best taught by constant, tactful, and imaginative methods, hopefully with media support, and with legal coercion as a fallback. Training should emphasize that traffic congestion aggravates stresses which tent to overcome courtesy, but also that even under stress courtesy is possible, and perhaps is even more important: combat pilots gave friendly waves to enemy pilots in WWI but still did their stressful jobs.

Law enforcement personnel could issue more warnings and fewer tickets; develop traffic conferences and training courses for drivers as an attraction or a requirement rather than as a punishment; and by example encourage courtesy in driving as a part of respectable, responsible citizenship. They should be trained to sympathize when a driver is justifiably angered at wasted time or poor facilities, and to avoid such comments as "calm down" when they encounter a driver that is upset. The traffic officer and the driver should be reminded that driving is not a "privilege" but a regulated right.

On the other hand, stronger enforcement should be aimed at the truly aggressive, irresponsible driver—including the one who tailgates or weaves in and out excessively on expressways. Such visible enforcement would be welcomed by most drivers. Road signs that say "enforcement by aircraft" would receive more serious attention if small aircraft were actually used, in conjunction with police cars, to apprehend the dangerous driver. They would prove even more valuable if camcorders were employed to photograph these drivers, and if the films were shown in court and on local television screens. The great human and financial cost of traffic accidents merits consistent and urgent attention.

There is also room for safety improvements in cars and roads. For example, cars with a high center of gravity, such as some SUVs, are more rollover-prone. Cars with too many gadgets may distract drivers. Road signs and street signs are frequently inadequate—too small, hidden by foliage or even by other signs, or of insufficient contrast under certain light conditions—thus confusing drivers or diverting their attention from collision avoidance to navigation. Signs and signals should conform to uniform standards and be reasonable. Red light running and other intersection problems might be reduced by lights designed to show graphically the remaining time before a change in color. Navigational signs on major roads should allow for the less-than-perfect attention of many drivers. Therefore signs should give advanced warning of decision points and other signs should label them clearly. For example, "Exit" tells little beyond the obvious; "Exit 17" is better; and "Exit 17, Main Street" is better yet. Shoulders and barriers are often inadequate or absent, resulting in collisions and the possible dropping of heavy trucks from an overpass onto the traffic lanes below. Reflective white and yellow stripes at the edges of lanes and pavements are also valuable, especially on rainy nights.

C.   *Cost.* While keeping cost is desirable in principle, cost savings that come at the expense of quality may actually prove to be "penny wise and pound foolish." Individuals can personally control costs by their choice of a vehicle. Such costs as tolls and parking fees may be burdensome, but customers, businesses, workers, and residents will tend to move away from places where costs are excessive. This, in effect, helps to explain the great modern shift from cities to suburban areas. The cost of better roads to relieve congestion, traditionally funded by some type local, state, or federal tax, can be more than counterbalanced over time by the benefits of choice, a better quality of life, time and lives saved, and other significant efficiencies.

The paradox of cost, however, is striking where road building in major metropolitan areas is concerned. The same person who will spend many thousands of dollars for a fine new car may often be stuck in traffic behind the wheel of that car and yet be unwilling to support an extra nickel or dime in gas taxes to provide the better roads that are needed. This attitude endangers the quality of life for that driver and for the many of her drivers who could be using those new, better roads.

A broader view of costs would also include costs that relate to environmental and energy factors. Here, the trend for two, three, or even more cars per household may offer a good opportunity, namely the ownership and use of small, fuel-efficient cars for commuting and short trips, and of larger cars for family travel, longer trips, or larger loads. Over time, educational or other measures may help encourage an affluent society to use the car that is best adapted for the particular kind of use.

D.   ***Convenience.*** Improvements in convenience will depend largely on the features of the vehicle being used. For most people, cars are already the most convenient mode of travel. Yet, some improvement is still possible. In some places parking is inconvenient, which also may affect the speed and cost of travel. In addition, if commuters who park in the central urban area all day could obtain such routine services as oil changes, tune-ups, and car washes at competitive prices where they park, time would be saved for the commuter, and urban facilities would find an additional source of revenue.

Part 7—How Can the Financing, Technology, and Management for Better Transportation Be More Efficiently Obtained?

The answer to this question must be based on the clear understanding that people and governments will probably get no more effectiveness in transportation than they are willing to pay for.

    A.   *Financing.* As people allocate resources, they are willing to spend quite a lot on vehicles—securing a very high standard of performance and comfort—but not nearly as willing to pay, in taxes, for the roadways and other facilities needed to carry these vehicles at a comparable level of quality and safety.

    Many citizens are also quite willing to pay the taxes needed to provide other community services at the same levels of quality that characterize the privately produced goods and services on which they spend most of their money. Thus, inadequate highways, bridges, and rail facilities are just one part of a more general phenomenon that people tolerate—with or without complaint. Yet historically, the construction, maintenance, and even operation of transportation facilities have generally required some form of government subsidy.

    Adequate funding of transportation must be based on alerting citizens and government officials to the need for allocating funds at local, state, and federal levels. This means sustained, adequate funding for construction of additional facilities, maintenance, services, and especially forward-looking planning for future transportation needs.

It is generally cheaper to provide transportation in anticipation of population growth than to catch up with needs after traffic congestion has worsened. A small increase in the gas tax or tolls will support large improvements funded by bonds.

B.   *Technology.* New transportation technology is hard to predict, but it seems likely that communication technology will have significant effects on future metropolitan area transportation. Recent communication developments are already reducing the importance of place in human interactions, and thereby substantially cutting back on the need for people to travel from place to place, especially for some kinds of work, education, and entertainment. Nevertheless, humans are mobile by nature, and both travel itself and the face-to-face exchanges it facilitates seem to be not only necessary or useful, but even enjoyable or psychologically beneficial.

The gradual exhaustion of petroleum, and the uncertainty of foreign sources, suggests more fuel-efficient cars, such as hybrids, with hydrogen power as a possible ultimate answer. This will reduce air pollution but also reduce gas tax revenues.

Traffic engineering technology in the form of informational road signs and devices and systems for automatic collection of tolls, offers some potential. Other technology, such as the movable footpaths in some airports, or the Segway (a powered scooter) may also be helpful in providing more efficient "people movers" for dense urban centers. Additional attention should also be given to monorails, monobeams, and light rail.

C.   *Management.* Interpreted narrowly, the management of most transportation systems seems to be in pretty good shape. There may be some loss of efficiency in highway construction and maintenance because of preferential treatment of politically connected contractors, but this is not as common as it used to be.

As to transit systems, the management of the rail system in the Washington, D.C. area, for example, has been criticized for repeated failures of escalators, trains, rails, and other equipment; for arresting women, children, and disabled passengers for minor violations or uncouth language; and for shortages of services and parking spaces. Such problems may be partly due to defects of design or funding, or due to increased demand, and it is not known to what extent these problems are common in other areas.

Coordination of planned highways crossing city, county, or state boundary lines can be difficult, but federal and state governments usually have the power to resolve such problems. Citizens who live in one jurisdiction but work in another must depend on cooperation among these levels of government. Management of the flow of traffic to assure safety is a growing problem, as ever-worsening congestion—and perhaps cultural change—brings an increase in the running of red lights, "road rage," and aggressive behavior on the highway. (See the discussion of highway safety in Part 6.)

If management is interpreted more broadly—to include the management of traffic flows to maximize throughput—a whole new field of inquiry is opened up. Devices such as by-passes, tolls, center lanes for left turns, better signs and signals, and better intersections (such as traffic circles, overpasses, or underpasses, like that at Dupont Circle in Washington), together with more attention to the view of travelers, offer prospects for improvement. Management should also plan for responses to terrorism or other emergencies, including effective communications with the public.

In the case of major projects that will cause serious impacts on nearby communities or on the traveling public, particularly during construction, it seems essential that management devise and carry out timely and extensive programs of effective liaison with all the affected or concerned groups. For example, the Virginia Department of Transportation, in embarking on the Woodrow Wilson Bridge replacement and the Springfield Interchange (both near Washington, D.C.), organized a Community Resources Board. This board involved local civic, business, women's, minority, and other sectors in exchanging information on all aspects of the projects, and in mitigating problems, such as congestion, safety, noise control, relocation, and alternate travel options. A related activity was Bridge Bucks, which gave commuters $50 a month for one year for the cost of alternate transportation.

Part 8—What Can the Citizen Do to Improve Transportation?

The answer to this question has two parts: (1) which improvements should be chosen for priority and (2) how can these improvements be achieved?

A.   *Which improvements should be given priority?* This depends, in turn, upon two things: the relative merits of various improvements, and the relative acceptability of various improvements to decision-makers and to those parts of the public that influence them.

The merits are based on the comparative costs and benefits of various improvements. Acceptability is based on the comparative degree of support or opposition to be expected from the public and from leaders.

In major metropolitan areas suffering from congestion, citizens seeking better transportation would usually be well advised to support "balance" between better road for autos and better transit. These goals can be harmonized if transit is by bus, which like autos benefit from better roads. Yet rail transit, though more costly in construction time and money, has definite advantages, especially if ample, safe, and free or low cost parking for cars and bicycles is provided at stations, particularly in medium or low-density residential areas. (Light rail should be less costly than heavy rail.)

Deciding between bus and rail transit, or some mix of both, should depend on the costs and benefits, both short and long range, of particular plans for bus or rail projects. Improvements for walking, bicycles, and handicapped travel, as well as emerging technologies, should also be considered, to the extent practicable, and with an open mind. But realism strongly indicates that, in view of established trends of long-term growth and affluence, the auto with its intrinsic conveniences and other attractions, will continue to be the dominant mode of travel for most trips, even including most commuting to work.

Decisions on which road and transit improvements to support should, of course, take into account the views of qualified and disinterested experts, including professional people in engineering, behavioral sciences, and other specialties. Transportation plans should be made before problems occur, and if possible carried out before problems become acute.

B. *How can transportation improvements be achieved?*

1. The concerned citizen can have some effect acting alone, for example by writing letters to newspapers and contacting legislatures. But it is usually more effective to work with others: friends, work colleagues, and neighbors. If necessary, the individual could organize a small civic committee to work for better transportation and persuade local governments to provide a Citizens' Transportation Policy Report Task Force.

2. Citizens should be able to list—clearly and with specific illustrations—the many benefits of transportation and the many detriments of congestion. Citizens should also be prepared to discuss methods of meeting the costs and other problems that transportation improvements may involve. These matters are summarized in this primer.

3.   Citizens should identify and coordinate with allies in working for better transportation. These include businesses, chambers of commerce, some political leaders, some news media, and various transportation professionals. But in addition, the social, economic, and quality-of-life benefits of better transportation should be brought to the attention of members of churches, civic groups, and nonprofit agencies that work to assist the disadvantaged and handicapped. Society as a whole benefits from better transportation.

4.   Thought and attention should also be given to possible opposition groups. Environmentalists can be educated to see that traffic congestion is a major cause of pollution, which could be reduced by carefully developing better roads, better transit, and better technology. Not in my backyard individuals (NIMBYs) often add environmental reasons for their opposition. They should, of course, be given reasonable consideration, including appropriate modification of planned improvements, or possibly compensation. However, public officials should not let NIMBY opposition override the interests of the general public. Rival advocates for roads and transit can be brought together on major projects by reserving space for transit in a highway median strip. Advocates and opponents of large projects can sometimes be induced to support a compromise on smaller improvements. Taxpayers worried about the cost of improvements can be reassured by sound methods of funding and cost control, and by pointing out that the ongoing ben-

efits of improvements will make them a bargain, to oppose which would be "penny wise and pound foolish." And if there are persons or interests that fear economic injury from improvements, they should be reassured, or given compensation where appropriate, or be subordinated to the greater public interest.

5. A careful strategic plan should be developed, one that will withstand the light of day. It should include obviously good features, such as greater safety and better fuel efficiency for auto travel, and the alleviation of notorious local or regional bottlenecks that have bedeviled the public. It should, of course, include proper timing and organization so that its messages are heard, understood, and remembered. Effective organization should include liaison with the various jurisdictions and the interest groups in or near the affected area, to facilitate communication and agreement. Concerned citizens might check out how other metropolitan areas achieve such coordination; see the discussion above, at the end of Part 7C. And the plan should include preparation to counter the not uncommon fear that improvements will chiefly benefit developers and land speculators, by providing and publicizing good planning and zone controls, and by clearly showing the specific benefits to the general public from improvements that will relieve present congestion. Also, citizens should bear in mind that opponents of improvements (NIMBYs or others) will typically be much more vocal at public hearings or in the media than those who express

the interests of the general public. This strongly suggests the importance of presenting careful surveys of all affected persons. Finally, citizens must recognize that some political leaders my feel insecure and thus hesitate to act in the public interest if they fear serious opposition. In such cases, citizens can either support these leaders if they act in the public interest, or find other leaders with more backbone.

Appendix A—About CQC and the Transportation Primer Participants

CQC (Citizens for Quality Civilization, Inc.) is a volunteer organization under Section 501 c) (3) of the Internal Revenue Code. CQC's mission is to improve the quality of life through responsible civic leadership. CQC focuses on major public policy problem areas, with due regard for related areas. CQC has a 14-year track record of working to improve our nation's education, health care policy, and transportation, and to clarify globalization. We operate informally, and always check our products with outside experts.

Robert L. Saloschin, chairman, is a lawyer, and has practiced law with the Civil Aeronautics Board (a transportation regulatory agency); the United States Justice Department; a housing and real estate agency; and on Wall Street. At the Justice Department he chaired the Freedom of Information Committee and worked directly with the leaders from both political parties (Attorney General Robert Kennedy and Nicholas Katzenbach, and later Supreme Court Justices Rehnquist and Scalia. He is a commercial pilot and flight instructor, and has made 14 boat trips on the Intracoastal Waterway and to offshore islands. He has driven approximately 500,000 miles in and outside the United States, is a retired naval officer, and a longtime civic and community leader in a Maryland suburb of Washington, D.C. He is the founder and president of Citizens for Quality Civilization (CQC).

Marlon G. ("Lon") Anderson is the staff director of public and government relations for the American

Automobile Association (AAA) Potomac. He directs government and public media efforts for AAA Mid-Atlantic, serving over 3.5 million members from New Jersey to Virginia. On the national level, he has served as press secretary to two U.S. secretaries of education and vice president of public affairs for a Washington trade association. He has also served as chairman of the board of the Washington Regional Alcohol Program (WRAP), a nationally recognized business/government coalition to fight drunk driving and underage drinking, and on the Pedestrian Blue Ribbon Panel and the Transportation Policy Review Task Force in Maryland. He has a wealth of experience in local and national public affairs, was recently honored as Montgomery College's Outstanding Alumnus of the Year, and serves as chairman of the college's alumni association. He is a graduate of Montgomery College, the University of Maryland, and American University—where he earned a Master's degree in public administration.

Harry Bain is a nationally known transportation specialist, and has worked as a consultant, researcher, university instructor, and a government employee. He helped plan the Washington area's regional transportation system and worked on the legislation that initially authorized it. He served on the planning staff of San Francisco's Bay Area Rapid Transit (BART) program and was the technical manager of a large, federally funded study of the impact of BART on the region it serves. He has taught at the University of California, Los Angeles (UCLA); George Washington University; and the University of Maryland, Baltimore County.

John H. Bruce, a U.S. Coast Guard captain, retired after 33 years of active duty as a surface operations and law specialist, and as a commander of oceanographic survey, buoy tender, search and rescue, and icebreaker vessels. He also served in various legal, intelligence, law enforcement, and legislative positions. He operated a fishing troller in Alaska. Since retirement, he has served as counsel to a congressional committee and as director of a university adult education program. He has also been active over the years in various civic and military associations.

Emanuel Karbeling, an editor and information consultant, has developed and edited military, historical, and technical features for the Army and Army Materiel Command; the Naval Electronics Supply Office; Stewart-Warner Corporation; National Provisioner; Digital Equipment Corporation; and TRACOR. He has also worked with the Freedom of Information Program for the Department of the Army and the Army Materiel Command, and served as a volunteer entertainment coordinator at the White House Social Office.

Philip L. Melville, PhD, a registered civil engineer, supervised worldwide construction with the Army Corps of Engineers, and was chief of the international and technical staff of the Airport Directorate of the Federal Aviation Administration. He was also employed by the Virginia Department of Transportation and the Virginia Transportation Research Council. He has published professional papers and lectured at the University of Virginia. Dr. Melville currently serves as a transportation consultant and carries out pro bono activities on transportation-related matters.

Herbert Stone, a civilian engineer retired from the Department of the Navy and a retired lieutenant commander in the Naval Reserve, has traveled frequently by auto up and down the East Coast. He has also flown to and driven around cities that he visited in connection with his work. He recently traveled across the country by train and is acutely aware of the traffic challenges he hopes to see remedied. He is a volunteer computer instructor with SeniorNet, introducing seniors to the digital age, and a volunteer with Maryland's Bethesda Regional Library and with his area citizens association. He is also a member of his district's Police Citizens Advisory Board. Special interests include staying current on modern technology and finding ways to employ it in solving people's problems.

John V. ("Jack") Wells, Chief Economist at the Bureau of Transportation Statistics (BTS) in the U.S. Department of Transportation, is also editor-in-chief of the *Journal of Transportation Statistics*. He has served as deputy administrator of the Federal Railroad Administration; Democratic staff director of the House subcommittee on railroads; and staff director of the subcommittee on investigations and oversight of the House public works and transportation committee. From 1979 to 1993, he was an economist at the U.S. General Accounting Office, working on a wide range of transportation, regulation, and science and technology issues. He also served as an assistant professor of economics at George Mason University. He holds a Bachelor of Arts from Harvard University and a Doctor of Philosophy degree from Yale University—both in economics.

CQC also wishes to express its gratitude to the outside experts on various aspects of transportation who reviewed and commented on the draft of this primer.

Appendix B—Sources of More Information and Assistance

To obtain good sources of information and assistance on transportation problems in your metropolitan area, you must first decide two questions:

First, what are the problems you are interested in solving? Do you want to relieve traffic congestion in your area or your neighborhood? Do you want to limit the traffic congestion by zoning laws that will cut down on excessive building that overtaxes the roads in your area? Do you want improved travel between your home and your work? Do you travel during your workday in ways that need improvement?

Second, how deeply are you prepared to get involved in relieving the traffic and transportation problems that concern you?

Transportation improvements start at the local, state, and national transportation planning levels. Planners search for the best ways to get you to where you live, where you work, where you shop, where your children go to school and to play, and where you go on vacation.

The next step is transportation decision making—looking for ways to solve today's problems while avoiding future transportation and environmental problems.

Transportation professionals seek the help of many different public and private groups that provide employment, housing, schools, services, and parks. You can get involved with some of the following: Metropolitan Planning Organizations (MPOs) covering areas with a population of 50,000 people or more; local governments, which schedule planned improvements and maintain local streets and roads; transit agencies—which includes public and private organizations that provide transportation for the public; and the federal government, which oversees the transportation planning and project activities of state and local agencies. The key federal government role is to provide funds and establish standards for state and local transportation improvement decisions.

To get involved in the transportation planning, decision making, and implementation process, you can

A. Attend meetings of local transportation boards and offer your input;

B. Volunteer to serve on a citizen focus group or citizen advisory committee;

C. Put your name on the mailing list to get newsletters, updates, and other information from Metropolitan Planning Organizations (MPOs), state Departments of Transportation (DOTs), and other transportation and environmental agencies;

D. Invite transportation officials to attend your Rotary, Kiwanis, and other service clubs—as well as meetings of community organizations, schools, and other civic organizations—and discuss transportation matters and how you and your organization can help them;

E. Find out what other public involvement opportunities are available by contacting your MPOs, state DOTs, and officials in transportation agencies, local governments, and federal transportation offices; and

F. Work with other friends, neighbors, business associates, church groups, local chambers of commerce, agencies working to improve the lot of the disabled, the news media, and political leaders to identify transportation problems and develop recommendations to avoid, minimize, alleviate, or solve them.

A very helpful, 32-page booklet entitled *A Citizen's Guide to Transportation Decision Making* is published by the U.S. Department of Transportation. Copies of this booklet, as well as other helpful materials, can be obtained without charge by phoning the USDOT Office of Planning, (202) 366-0106 or 0150, or by writing to DOT/ FHWA, 400 7th Street, S.W., Washington, D.C. 20590.

There are, of course, many other sources of reference materials on transportation and related subjects: libraries; the Internet; and academic, governmental, and other concerned organizations.

We also strongly suggest that citizens working for better transportation should, from time to time, refer back to Part 8 and other parts of this primer.

Endnotes

Introduction

[1]Rosemary Williams (ed), *Gibbon's Decline and Fall of the Roman Empire - Volume 1* (Rand McNally and Company 1979), p. 9

[2] President Ronald Reagan is often quoted out of context in talking about government being the problem and not the solution. In actuality, the assertion was made in the 1981 Inaugural Address while focusing on the nation's economic ills. The entire quote is as follows: "In this present crisis, government is not the solution to our problem; government is the problem. From time to time we've been tempted to believe that society has become too complex to be managed by self-rule, that government by an elite group is superior to government for, by, and of the people. Well, if no one among us is capable of governing himself, then who among us has the capacity to govern someone else? All of us together, in and out of government, must bear the burden. The solutions we seek must be equitable, with no one group singled out to pay a higher price." [Ronald Reagan Inaugural Address, January 20, 1981] Reagan's works were therefore aimed at the economic problems he inherited from President Jimmy Carter including the very high rate of inflation. Unfortunately, in terms of historical accuracy, the part most quoted by both liberals and conservatives is "government is the problem."

Chapter 5

[1] Luis Fleischman, *Latin America in the Post-Chavez Era* (Potomac Books, 2013), p. 1

[2] "10 foreign policy priorities for Obama", November 8, 2012

[3] *Education Week*, June 10, 2010

Chapter 12

[1] A charter school is a school receiving public funding but operating independently. New Orleans' initiative with charter schools is likely the most radical experimentation with the model in the nation. After Hurricane Katrina, the New Orleans Public Schools system engaged in reforms aimed at decentralizing power away from the pre-Katrina school board central bureaucracy to individual school principals and charter school boards, monitoring charter school performance by granting renewable, five-year operating contracts permitting the closure of those not succeeding, and vesting choice in parents of public-school students, allowing them to enroll their children in almost any school in the district.

Chapter 13

[1] http://redistricting.lls.edu/why.php

Chapter 15

[1] *JAMA Pediatrics*, Vol. 167 (No 6), June 2013

Author Biographies

Robert L. Saloschin was born in 1920 in New York City and passed away at the age of 95 at his home in Bethesda, Maryland.

Valedictorian of his high school class, he graduated Phi Beta Kappa from Columbia University with honors in economics, and entered Columbia Law School, where he was elected to the Law Review at the end of his first year.

Interrupting his legal education to enter the Navy, Saloschin served during WWII, earning a pilot's license, and then becoming a flying boat navigator in the Pacific Theater. He returned to the United States as a lieutenant-commander in the Naval Reserve.

After completing law school, and two years in a Wall Street law firm, Saloschin married Neita Smith, a Navy flight nurse, in 1949 and moved to Washington, D.C. where he began his federal legal career. He served for two years in the Urban Redevelopment Program before transferring to the Civil Aeronautics Board, handling airline economic and safety cases. In 1958, he joined the Justice Department's Office of Legal Counsel. His varied assignments included civil rights, the Olympic Games, immigration, communications satellites, oil importation, racketeering, conscientious objectors, and airline high-jacking. He was a member of a U.S. diplomatic delegation to a conference of 72 nations in the Hague to develop a treaty to extradite hijackers. The United States delegation cooperated closely with the Soviet delegation, despite the Cold War, because both nations had suffered from hijackings.

In 1970 Bob Saloschin became the Chairman of the newly formed Freedom of Information Committee, and in 1978, the Director of the Office of Information Law and Policy, advising all federal agencies on openness and secrecy issues under the Freedom of Information Act (FOIA).

During his more than 20 years at Justice, Saloschin worked directly with Attorneys General Bobby Kennedy, Nicholas Katzenbach, and Ramsey Clark, in addition to William Rehnquist (later Supreme Court Chief Justice). Katzenbach, author of *Some of It Was Fun: Working with RFK and LBJ*, openly credited Saloschin with stopping violence against the Freedom Riders by suggesting use of the existing statutory powers of the Interstate Commerce Commission, which prohibited discrimination in inter-state bus transportation.

After retiring from government, Saloschin consulted on law and national security for a committee of the American Bar Association. He also worked for the law firm of Lerch, Early and Brewer, and founded Citizens for Quality Civilization, a nonprofit that published civic handbooks to improve education, healthcare, trans-portation, and globalization policies. Saloschin was also a community leader, organizing recreational and library facilities and taking a lead role in land use disputes for homeowners.

Bob Saloschin was a licensed commercial pilot and flight instructor. Until his death, he provided commentary on current events and history through programs such as NPR's *Here and Now*.

Maryann Karinch is the author of 31 published works of non-fiction and a 20-year veteran of lobbying and work on behalf of non-profit organizations.

She holds BA and MA degrees from The Catholic University of America in Washington, DC. in speech and drama and has been certified as a personal trainer by The American Council on Exercise since 1998. The Explorers Club elected her to membership in 2010; she is also a long-time member of The Authors Guild.

In 2004, she founded The Rudy Agency, a literary agency specializing in non-fiction. Earlier in her career, she served as the Director of Communications for a prominent lobbying organization in Washington, DC. Before that, she managed a professional theater and raised funds for arts and education programs in the Nation's Capital.

Index

www.ingramcontent.com/pod-product-compliance
Lightning Source LLC
Chambersburg PA
CBHW020522270326
41927CB00006B/413